Surviving After High School

Overcoming Life's Hurdles

By Arthur J. Heine

First Edition

J-MART PRESS, Virginia Beach, Virginia

Surviving After High School

Overcoming Life's Hurdles

By Arthur J. Heine

Published by:

J-MART PRESS
Post Office Box 8884
Virginia Beach, VA 23450-8884 U.S.A.

Copyright © 1991 by Arthur J. Heine
First Printing 1991
Printed in the United States of America

Publisher's Cataloging in Publication Data

Heine, Arthur J.
Surviving After High School: Overcoming Life's Hurdles/1st ed.

Bibliography.
Includes Index.
1.   Life Skills, Guides, Handbooks, Manuals.
2.   Job Hunting. 3. Health Education. 4. Budgets, Personal.
5.   Housing   I. Title   II. Heine, Arthur J.

Library of Congess Catalog Card Number 90-91976
ISBN   0-9628376-0-1 $22.95 Hardcover
          0-9628376-1-X $14.95 Softcover

ATTENTION: SCHOOL SYSTEMS, TEACHERS, PTA ORGAN-IZATIONS, COLLEGES AND UNIVERSITIES, BUSINESSES AND FUND RAISING ORGANIZATIONS: J-MART PRESS offers quantity discounts on all bulk purchases of this book when offered as sales promotional, educational, premiums or fund raising purposes. Book excerpts or specified imprinting can be accomodated to meet the needs of your organization. For more information, write to **J-MART PRESS** at the above address or call our Sales Division at **(804) 498-4060** in the Virginia Beach area or **1-800-487-4060** if outside.

DEDICATION

This book is dedicated to
Timothy M. Sedberry
and the thousands of other young adults
who never had the chance to try.

ACKNOWLEDGEMENTS

Many, many thanks to:

My wife, Jean, without who's love, shoulder, continous daily support, patience, and hard work this book would never have been completed.

My children, Kim, Cindy, Karen, Christopher and Jeffery, their spouses and friends, for identifying the problem and supplying the stories that bring life to my words.

Jane McNaught, for her patience, support and editorial criticism, but even more for her friendship. I never realized why authors always thanked their editiors; I do now.

Diane Miller, for the typesetting. It is the work of a true professional.

Louis Cafiero, M.D., for insisting I tell it like it is.

The service counter personnel and staff at the Virginia Beach Main Library. Your friendly and patient assistance, when I was being a pest, was warmly appreciated and did not go without notice.

The many friends and even strangers who after listening to me describe my project, boosted my spirits and ego with their very favorable comments.

Cover picture by Ken Storey

Inside artwork by Todd M. McGovern

Perfectus liber est. Approbatus sit.

*** WARNING *** DISCLAIMER ***

This book has been written as a guide for independent living and as such provides much thought provoking information on a number of areas. **This information is not construed or represented as financial, legal, medical or other professional advice**. Should, after reading this book, you determine that you require this advice, you should seek it from a qualified professional.

A book covering day-to-day living and life could not be written without including financial, legal, medical and other professional information. It is not the purpose of this guide to reprint all of the material available on each of these topics but to package the information in a manner that is enjoyable and easy to read. (See the Appendix for a list of additional readings.)

As with any other book, the material contained herein was carefully researched, verified and edited. However, as with any work of this size, **there is the possibility that typographical and content errors exist**.

The whole purpose of this book is to inform, educate, and entertain. The author and J-MART PRESS do not accept any liability or responsibility for loss or damage, real or implied, which may be represented as a result of reading this book.

The author personally finds it appalling that this statement is required in today's society. However, **if you cannot accept and be bound by the above stipulations, return this book to the publisher for a full refund.**

TABLE OF CONTENTS

INTRODUCTION

Every Spring, baby birds all over this earth are gently nudged from the warmth and safety of their nest by their mothers. As they find themselves falling towards the rapidly approaching ground, nature takes over, and, by instinct, they flap their wings. Slowly at first, then in panic, very rapidly, and to their surprise, they first slow their descent, and then, as if by a miracle, they actually defy gravity and fly.

Every May or June, all over the United States, large buildings open their doors, and 2.5 million young adults, our children, are dumped out of their nests. Some are dumped a little more gently and more prepared than others, but, for the most part, they are dumped. We call this High School Graduation! These young adults do not have nature to tell them to flap their wings before they hit the ground.

Unfortunately, during their school years, we as parents were busy devoting our energies to guiding them away from drugs, alcohol, and delinquency. At the same time being sure these young adults were fed, clothed and housed in the best manner possible. These most necessary efforts, though commendable, also distracted us from always teaching the skills needed to cope with this jungle called "real life."

This book is designed to fill this gap in their training. It doesn't take the place of nature, nor does it take the place of parental guidance in establishing a value system. It does, provide a wealth of information, emphasize the need to develop one's resourcefulness and identify many of the pitfalls that will be faced as the young adult begins his or her independent flight through life.

The idea for the book and the writing style are mine. However, the book contains editing and contributions from my most loving critics, whom I have listed under Acknowledgments. After all, they closely lived the experiences and were faced with identifying and solving the problems, sometimes more than once, more recently than I. It was their experiences that motivated this book, and if you can extract one helpful piece of material or avoid one pitfall, all the energy devoted to its writing will have been rewarded.

Containing 36 chapters, organized into nine sections, *Surviving After High School* starts with the Job Search and proceeds through each of the major hurdles faced daily by independent adults in our society. Each of the chapters can stand alone, and, because of the detailed index provided, the reader always has available a ready resource when problems or challenges arise.

THE JOB SEARCH

Why hasn't someone offered me a job?

I

The first step in living independently is finding a job. Unless you are already wealthy, you will not be able to provide for your basic needs, much less your wants without a job. This section uses a three step approach to tackle the challenge of finding a job: developing a resumé, getting an interview, and maintaining confidence and control.

Chapter 1 covers writing your resumé. The chapter guides the reader from the identification of objective through the meaning and classification of education, experience and personal traits. Chapter 1 concludes by having you develop your ever important resumé.

Chapter 2 explores the steps for obtaining and preparing for the job or college-entrance interview. The marketing of your most important product -- yourself -- is discussed in detail.

Chapter 3 focuses on maintaining confidence and control during the interview. The interview is analyzed from the applicant's and interviewer's perspective. Rejection and some suggestions for dealing with it are presented. A method for performing post-interview evaluations as a learning tool is introduced.

Meet Jo Ann T. Graduate, Jo Ann is a fictitious 18-year-old high school senior. She has had a couple of part-time jobs and has even been in business forherself. She presently lives with her parents in a fictitious place called Soft Life, OK. Throughout the book we will follow Jo Ann as she makes *"the big break"* and becomes a surviving, independent-living, young adult.

THE RESUMÉ
Emphasizing the positive.

1

You're out of school! So, what's next? Summer you say...or college...or maybe even work ... I would like to confirm that you can have a lifetime of summer vacations, but you know that isn't true.

However, you are entitled to vacations and to have fun. In fact, as discussed in Section VIII, it is accepted that if you are going to maintain your mental and physical health, really relaxing vacations are very important.

If you are going out on your own for the first time, whether starting college or entering the work force, do not despair. According to the Department of Commerce, you are only one of approximately 2,653,000 young adults doing the same thing this year.

Job or College

This chapter covers a number of items associated with finding employment or getting accepted into college. It has a dual purpose because applying to college or for a new job are basically the same. You have to sell yourself. This chapter is focused toward finding employment. To use it for applying to college, simply substitute "college" for "employer" and "school" for "job."

Preparation

There are as many ways to get interviewed as there are to get a job. But before we look at these, it is important to discuss the very first step: getting prepared. The most important thing you will do to get prepared is to set an objective.

THE OBJECTIVE

You must set an objective before seeking employment. The objective will not only guide you in applying for a job but will give you a strong feeling of accomplishment when you are employed. Everyone knows the end result -- money. But you must ask yourself the following questions: What do I want to do? What am I qualified to do? Where and when do I want to do it?

Suppose your answer is: "I want to do Landscaping, I know how to cut grass and I don't mind starting work after noon on weekdays." You have a problem. No, you have a number of problems.

First, though you have an objective, you may not possess the required skills and your expectations may not be realistic. Landscaping requires more than just cutting grass. And, you are not likely to get a job landscaping where you can start work after noon.

Be Creative

When working on your employment objective, list anything that comes to mind. Make your first list with "no holds barred." Your initial list may look like this:

Objective

Make money
Work outside
Work five days a week, no Saturdays or Sundays
Work days, no nights
Do landscaping work
Design yards
Learn the nursery business
Meet people but, no sales
Stay in local area
Work in hospital

Go through your list and weed out the "nice but not practical," and take a good long look at what you have left. This is your target list. By the way, keep the list of items you really like but are lacking the required training or skills for right now. We will take another look at these in Chapter 33.

Now take the time to make your own list. Get a large piece of paper and start writing. I will help you get started by providing the first item -- make money.

Your Resumé

From the list you have just made select one or two objectives that state the kind of work you would like to be hired to do. These become your targets that you are going to match with employment opportunities. Wait! Don't go to the newspapers just yet. There is still more preparation to be done. You need a "Resumé."

What It Is

Simply stated the resumé is a profile of what you want in employment and what you will bring to the job. What you want is your objective. What you bring are skills, education, and a willingness to work. Don't panic! Writing a resumé is not difficult. It just takes a little work, and the results are the fulfillment of your objective. There are many, many books explaining, with examples, how to write the job-winning resumé. See the Appendix, at the back of the book, for some recommendations.

What It Does

For all practical purposes, the resumé only provides your prospective employer a quick glimpse of who you are and what you have to offer. It is a most important starting point and does require very special consideration.

Parts of the Resumé

The resumé should have the following parts:
Your Name, Address, and Phone Number
Objective:
Education:
Experience - Abilities - Capabilities:
Awards:
Activities:
Personal:

Sequence

Except for name and objectives, the sequence should be guided by the strength of your background and the target position. For example: the resumé applying for a position requiring and stressing education would list education before experience. However, if experience is your strength, you would place it before education.

These are tricks that you will learn as you gain experience, but for your first resumé, list your strongest point first. Sequence the other sections based on their relevancy to the job you are seeking. The awards, activities, and personal sections are optional. If you do not wish to use any of these sections, just leave them off the resumé. However, if you use the personal section, it should be last.

Type, Type, Type

Before we look at the details of each section, there is one more rule you must follow: *The resumé must be typed!* At this time you don't have to worry about having a printer do it for you. Also, the type of paper you use should not be a concern. But, you definitely need it typed. Surely you know someone you can sweet-talk, bribe, or otherwise coerce into typing it for you.

Oh, and you will want to make several copies. Post offices, libraries and other public buildings have copy machines for public use. Copies cost between 10 and 25 cents each.

Be Positive

All resumé statements must be *positive*. Ideally they start with action verbs i.e., graduated, constructed, received, wrote, competed, supervised, etc. This means that, if you haven't begun to yet, now is the time to start thinking positively. If the information can't be put into positive terms, leave it off the resumé.

Be Truthful

Do not lie. Employers take the time to check resumés and applications. Even the smallest of lies will mean no opportunity for an interview or job.

Put It On Paper

Center your name, address and phone number on the paper. The word "resumé" is not needed if you follow the suggested format. Against the left-hand margin of your paper put the word **OBJECTIVE** in capital letters followed by a colon (:). State your objective in a sentence that starts with:

Find employment as…
or
Work (with…or as…).

Using the landscaping example mentioned previously, the resumé for our fictitious character will look like this:

JO ANN T. GRADUATE
2246 HOME STREET
SOFT LIFE, OK 12389
(405) 324-8971

OBJECTIVE: Find employment as assistant to a Landscape Architect.

EDUCATION OR EXPERIENCE

The education section of your resumé contains a list of all formal or informal courses of instruction you have attended that are relative to the job you are seeking. Don't just list High School Diploma, expand on it by listing any vocational education or other work-in-school programs you have completed. These can also be repeated in the experience section of your resumé. This is also true of any shop type classes where apprenticeship certification is achieved. Experience needs a little more explanation and clarification.

Experience

Every day of your life you gain experience. This experience, no matter how you gained it, may be applicable to your job resumé. Any experience that is applicable to the job you are looking for should be listed on your resumé.

The experience section of a resumé is not limited to paid experience.

Hobbies

A large number of people have started careers based on experience gained from hobbies or volunteer work. For example, one of my sons, Chris, made good summer money by doing exactly that. Chris was not interested in the normal summer beach related jobs. Nor was he interested in working in a fast food restaurant.

"I want to work in construction" he said one May evening, "but I don't want to be a gofer." A gofer is a helper. The nickname comes from being told to "go for" this or "go for" that. With his objective stated, his next step was to put together his list of experiences.

When Chris was seven years old, he helped his mother and I build a house. Since that time he had assisted me in a number of construction projects. They included home improvements, building several storage sheds, and building a barn.

Chris sat down and began listing the times he worked with me and the kind of work he had done. After that, he made a list of the tools he was experienced in using. By the time he was finished, he had an impressive resumé. However, he never got to use his resumé.

The Contradiction to the Rule

Chris's job hunting experiences have contradicted all the rules. He was hired through a telephone call.

What actually happened was that after he had identified his experience and the tools he could use, he started calling for interviews. The owner of one of the companies Chris called answered the phone. He asked Chris some questions, was impressed with his understanding of the building trade terminology, and requested he start work the next day.

I recount this story for two reasons. First, though my son did not get paid while he was gaining experience, he was able to document it. Second, to show that even though the "telephone interview" is not the normal way to get employed, it does happen.

The next year he got a job as a painter almost the same way. He did have to go to an interview that time. But, he did not have to start as a painter's helper. Experience, even unpaid, resulted in a job at least one level above amateur which also meant higher pay.

Only Experienced Applicants Accepted

There is another story I will relate that demonstrates how experience can be acquired. This is a story of a heavy equipment operator One day he was on the job and a helper approached him. The helper seemed to want to talk but was embarrassed. The older worker asked him what he wanted, and after a few pleasantries, the helper asked this question: "How did you get your experience?"

The older worker explained that he had always wanted to be a heavy equipment operator, but every time he applied for a job the employer wanted only experienced personnel. He put his arm over the helper's shoulder and related the following:

"I needed work. Times were hard and there was very little money to be had. I went to a construction site. The foreman asked me if I knew anything about a front-end loader. I looked around and saw this big yellow machine. Taking a chance, I said 'sure' and pointing to the machine, said 'there is one over there.' The foreman told me I had the job and he directed me to fill a truck from a large pile of trash.

"After about 20 minutes, the foreman knew I didn't know how to operate a front-end loader. Even though I did manage to get it started and moved it a few feet. He fired me. So, I still didn't have a job and still needed money. I knew I wanted to work in construction so I answered another ad for a machinery operator.

"At this site the foreman was a little sharper. After I had completed the standard application and we had talked for a little while, he asked me what I did on my last job. I was only too happy to tell him I had operated a front-end loader. This time it took me two hours to get fired. I was back on the street but I had gained more experience. The same thing happened at another site, but I actually lasted two days.

"Then I applied with this construction company. That was 18 years ago. I was a shoo-in for the job. After all, I had worked as a front-end operator for the previous three companies. Experience doesn't fall from the sky like rain. You must work for it and you must recognize it when you have it."

Experience Comes With Everything You Do

I don't know if the above method of gaining experience will work today. I would not be surprised if it did. Even applying for a job and not being selected provides you with experience: the experience of looking for work and of interacting with professionals.

This experience must not be ignored. With each interview you will become wiser and smarter. Your delivery will get smoother and the nervousness should lessen. I will discuss this more in Chapter 3 under the topic "Dealing With Rejection."

Open Eyes, Open Mind

Open your eyes and your mind. Sit down and try to recap what you have done in the past. Make a list of the clubs you have belonged to Junior Achievement and the National 4-H clubs are only two of the clubs that provide valuable, possible job-related experience. You can either list your membership under experience, activities, or both.

Add to the list any volunteer work you have done. Even baby sitting for a younger brother or sister will provide experience. It may not all be pleasant, not even all job related, but experience just the same.

The key is to have a list. This list will be expanded to include tools which you are skilled in using. Then, when you need to write a resumé, you will not have to start from scratch.

Let's go back to Jo Ann's resumé.

JO ANN T. GRADUATE
2246 HOME STREET
SOFT LIFE, OK 12389
(405) 324-8971

OBJECTIVE: Find employment as assistant to a Landscape Architect.

For our example, Jo Ann can either list her education or experience next. For this type of job, she decides experience is more important than education. She leaves a couple of spaces and then, remembering to be positive and starting at the left margin, adds:

EXPERIENCE: 1987-1990 -- Self employed as neighborhood lawn specialist. Responsible for the maintenance of 16 Lawns. Increased revenue over 220% in three years.

1986 - 1987 -- Responsible for "front counter" and cash register at Didley's Deli.

Now Education

Your education section can range from simple to very lengthy. The length should be determined by the amount of job-related education you have. Remember to be positive. The prospective employer is looking for action not failure.

Add any courses you have taken, even if they were taught outside of school. By listing additional courses, you demonstrate a commitment to further your education.

Any of the following will be acceptable:

EDUCATION: Graduated from I. M. Smart High School, Soft Life, OK in May 1990.
or
EDUCATION: Will Graduate from I. M. Smart High School, Soft Life, OK in May 1990.
or
EDUCATION: Working on my GED. I am scheduled to take the exam in May 1990.

Each of the these examples present an equally positive image to your prospective employer. The last two indicate that you have not yet completed high school but that you are still determined to complete that phase of your education. Since, in the example, Jo Ann is ready to graduate from high school she uses the second statement.

AWARDS AND ACTIVITIES

Do not go overboard when listing awards and activities. List those that are job-related and have meaning. I have read some resumés where the individuals listed every award possible except the Oscar. They should have been given that one for creating a literary masterpiece. What is important is to keep all entries on your resumé both positive and relevant.

PERSONAL

The use of the personal section is an individual choice. You have already given your name, address and phone number. If you feel providing other personal information will have positive impact, you should include this section. There are some jobs where personal information is a must. When applying for a job as a model, your resumé should not only include your measurements, but at least one photo. For the sample resumé which is for a position requiring some strength, a statement about physical ability is desirable. Jo Ann uses the following:

PERSONAL: Five foot eight inches tall, 145 pounds.
Member of school track and field team, 1987-1990.

WHY?

Always keep in mind the reasons for the resumé. You will mail them to prospective employers to create interest, and gain an interview. You will also attach it to your application to provide additional information. When you go an interview with a prospective employer who has not been supplied a copy of your resumé, carry one with you.

Jo Ann's Completed Resumé

JO ANN T. GRADUATE
2246 HOME STREET
SOFT LIFE, OK 12389

OBJECTIVE: Find employment as assistant to a Landscape Architect.

EXPERIENCE: 1987 - 1990 -- Self employed as neighborhood lawn specialist. Responsible for the maintenance of 16 Lawns. Increased revenue over 220% in three years.
1986 - 1987 -- Responsible for "front counter" and cash register at Didley's Deli.

EDUCATION: Will graduate from I.M. Smart High School, Soft Like, OK in May 1990.

ACTIVITIES: Member of Junior Achievement 1989 - 1990.

PERSONAL: Five foot eight inches tall, 145 pounds. Member of school track and field team, 1987 - 1990.

RESUMÉ DOS AND DON'TS

Do identify an objective.
Do keep everything positive.
Do keep everything relevant.
Do have it typed without errors.

Don't lie.
Don't be wordy.
Don't be negative.
Don't provide more information than necessary.
Don't use the same resumé for different types of jobs.

Update

The most successfully employed people still update their resumés at least every six months. This is not done because they are afraid of losing their job. This is done so they can take immediate action when the opportunity for advancement is presented.

Before entering your experience on your resumé, state it in positive terms. Only include the job-relevant experience unless you are trying to create the impression of having many and varied interests. This is appropriate if you are applying to work as an aid in a home for the elderly or a recreational facility.

YOUR TURN

Using the heading and objective statement you wrote earlier, fill in the rest of the sections. This is just a draft, don't worry about punctuation and sentence structure. You can smooth the resumé before you have it typed. What is important is to carefully review your objective, education, and experience. As you review, begin to formalize the resumé by placing your information in the proper format and sequence.

Once you have a rough draft of your resumé, read it again to correct spelling, punctuation, and sentence structure. Double check for positive statements and verify that everything is job-related.

SELF-TEST

You are finished your resumé when the answers to the following questions are all yes:

Is the resumé accurate?
Do you feel comfortable with your objective?
Does it contain all relative experiences and education?
Is it easy to read and understand?
Is it you?
As an employer, would the resumé interest you enough to want to talk to the person?

With resumé in hand, you are *almost* ready to start your search.

GETTING AN INTERVIEW
The foot in the door

Now, you are *finally* ready to actively seek employment.

HOW TO FIND INTERVIEWS

There are three basic ways to find that job you are searching for. They are:

1. The ever popular "classified ads"
2. The "good old boy" system
3. Employment agencies

They will be discussed in sequence.

CLASSIFIED ADS

Classified ads, as you are aware, make up the largest part of many major city's Sunday newspaper. However, this is not the only place that these ads appear. You can find them in trade papers, magazines, church and other local papers. Ads posted on the front window of businesses also fall into this category. When you are looking for a job always carry a pencil and a piece of paper.

Big Piece of Paper

Be sure the paper is large enough not to fit in your wallet. It is surprising how easy it is to forget that you copied down a lead, while shopping, if you can tuck it away in your wallet. This is not a predominately male trait! The purse can and will contain items that will sometimes shock and dismay their owners.

Success!

You look and find one or more leads. It's Sunday and those ads with phone numbers say only call between 8 a.m. and 5 p.m., Monday - Friday. Don't head for the beach just yet. Read over the ads. Do you understand what the employer is looking for? It's no problem if you are not sure. Often employers are not sure what kind of person, or even what skill, is required for a given position.

Categorize

Separate the ads into two or more stacks. The ones that you understand and are interested in, but require a call tomorrow, go into one stack. The ads that you might want to call can be placed on the bottom of this stack. The second stack can contain the ones that have addresses but no phone numbers.

Cover Letter

Take care of the second stack now! This is one of the reasons you wrote your resumé. Write or type a cover letter identifying the ad you are answering. If necessary, use your cover letter to expand on the resume but only a little. Be sure to include the phone number where you can receive messages during the normal work day -- 8:30 a.m. to 5:00 p.m. Address the letter and put it in the mail today.

Questions?

Go back to the other stack and write down specific questions you want to ask when you call your future employer. Once this is done you can take a break. Seriously, looking for employment is not a five, ten or even 20 hour-a-week effort. If you need and want to work, you must devote whatever time it takes to land that job. Remember, through it all you are gaining a vast amount of experience.

GOOD OLD BOY -- NETWORKING

Let's look at the next way of finding a job: the "good old boy" system. Recently, the professional community has picked up on this method and given it a name: networking. A simple definition of networking is: "the use of all contacts, personal and professional, to find a job."

You Even Tell Aunt Kate

This means that you tell everyone you know that you are looking for work. When you do this, be specific as to your objectives and your willingness to work. Respond to any leads you receive. It is a good idea to carry a few copies of your resumé for others to pass along for you. A better idea is to receive the contacts' names, addresses and, if possible, phone numbers. Then, you follow up on them yourself.

More people are hired where the process started with a personal recommendation, than from any other method of contact. Don't forget family and friends. This is not begging; it is positive job hunting.

EMPLOYMENT AGENCIES

Last, but maybe not least, is the employment agency. There is an interesting thing about most employment agencies. Except for the people working directly for the agency, they do not employ. They screen and place applicants. They remove the administrative burden of initial screening from a company's personnel office. They try to match the job hunter with the job vacancy.

Private Agencies

For this effort, private agencies get paid. The amount of payment ranges from a percentage of the first year's salary to an amount stated as one or even two months' gross pay. This can create a real burden for you if the vacancy you are interested in is a "fee" position.

A "fee" position requires the employee to pay the fee. You are the employee. A "fee paid" vacancy usually does not cost the employee any fees. The agency receives their payment from the employer. The employer will require you to sign an agreement stating that you will work for the company for a given period of time -- usually one year.

Membership Agencies

Another type of private employment agency is the "membership" agency. At this agency both you and any interested employers pay a membership fee. Job vacancy lists are then made available to you. When you find a vacancy that interests you, you will make an appointment to be interviewed by a "job counselor." Your membership is for a fixed period (six to 12 months) depending on the agency and the fee.

Free Agencies

In addition to the agencies described above, there are state and other government funded employment agencies. These agencies are paid for from tax receipts and are free to the individual seeking employment.

One of these agencies may be very helpful. You must treat the use of an agency as part of your overall job hunting strategy. However, what an agency can do for you is still limited. It does not get you employed. You will be interviewed by the agency and your resumé will be reviewed. If you pass the initial screening, an interview with a prospective employer may be made. Whether or not you get a job offer still depends on your qualifications and the employer's needs.

Hunting for a job will be very frustrating if you ignore everything else and go straight to an agency. The first question you will be asked is: "May I see a copy of your resumé?"

Only Free or Fee Paid

Early in your career look at only "fee paid" vacancies or use the government supported agencies. You will find that if you have to pay an agency's fees in addition to all your living expenses, which are discussed later, you only create additional stress for yourself.

BE AGGRESSIVE

Alexander Graham Bell to the Rescue

Monday morning. Time to get busy and find that job, or at least get an appointment for an interview. You have your stacks of ads. Included in them may be agency ads and contacts you received from your networking efforts. Review the stacks again to see if specific times are given for phone calls.

Why Call?

Your objective in calling an employer about a job is either to get additional information or schedule an interview. It is not to conduct a telephone interview. Though my son did get a job this way, it is the exception. Most employers or hiring officials want to see the applicant face-to-face. When you get an interview, either through phone calls or as a result of mailing your resumés, be prepared by knowing when you will be available.

Now is not the time to be indecisive or uncompromising. If the employer asks: "Will 2 o'clock Wednesday be a good time?" you should not have to think about it. Your response does not have to be yes, but you do have to respond.

Offering an alternate time and date is acceptable if presented correctly. When asked the question about 2 o'clock Wednesday, you may reply with "I am busy at that time but I am available Wednesday morning or all day Friday."

Don't Blow It

If the ad says call between 2 and 4 p.m., you can destroy your chances for an interview by calling at 9 a.m. Remember, in the phrase, "the early bird gets the worm," there are two players.

Timing

Timing is important in all phases of job hunting. It is acceptable to be a little early. "Little" is the key part of this statement. Five minutes early is acceptable, 35 minutes early is not acceptable. Being late, even five minutes, is never acceptable. Keep this in mind as you make appointments for interviews.

Give yourself sufficient time between interviews to complete an interview and get to the next one. Unfortunately, interviews can last as little as 15 minutes or as long as two hours. You will get a feel for timing as you gain experience.

Is It Luck?

Everyone is not always as lucky -- if it is luck -- as my son, Chris. As in the earlier example,

jobs seem to fall out of the sky for him. He recently received a job offer by drinking coffee in a coffee shop. He happened to be discussing how much he liked the coffee and the quaintness of the shop to a stranger sitting at his table. The stranger was the shop owner. Before Chris left the shop he was asked if he could report to work the next evening.

Follow Up

Remember the resumés you mailed out earlier. If you do not hear anything from a local company in a week, it is time to mail a follow-up letter. The letter should state the ad you answered, the date of your original letter and your concern that it was not received.

Sending a follow-up letter demonstrates a strong interest in the job. Without being over dramatic or too wordy, write the letter so the person receiving it will want to reply. This will get attention and, nine times out of ten, you will get a response. The response may not be positive, but it will confirm receipt of your first letter and, at the very worst, you get to scratch them off your list.

References

You need references. No, your parents do not count. You need professional, responsible people who know you. They can be friends of the family, school personnel or others who are able to attest to your reliability, skills, and character. If possible, the references should be from the local area. You must ask their permission before listing them as your reference so they are prepared for the queries from your potential employer.

When you approach them, explain the kind of work you are looking for, and that only with their permission will you use their names. You will also need their addresses and phone numbers.

The Pay Off

However, this is your lucky day. A secretary at one of the companies you call makes an appointment with you for Thursday at 9 a.m. You now have an interview scheduled. Don't stop, continue to go through the stack of ads and make more calls. You cannot afford to wait two weeks to find out if the interview on Thursday is going to result in a job.

You need to maximize your exposure by making as many appointments as possible. Once the phoning is done, you need to prepare for the interview. Yes, you read correctly, the next step is to prepare.

Some job applicants say that when you reach this point the hardest part of getting a job is behind you. You have an objective, a resumé and you have scheduled one or more interviews. For others, the hardest part is still to come.

Detective Work

Once you have been granted an interview, take a strong interest in the company that is doing the interview. Find out as much as you can about them. Check the yellow pages to see what they advertise as their strongest points. Ask your friends and relatives. If your interview is with a large company or corporation, check your local library.

You will be asked about acceptable salary. If you do not know the salary range of the position you are seeking, a call to your local State Employment agency will provide the answer. You want to appear at the interview with as much knowledge about your new employer and the job as possible.

APPEARANCE AND GROOMING

Being a Salesperson

Now, you must be a salesperson. You respond, "I am not interested in sales." That is an unfortunate response. You can't begin a career, any career, if you are not successful as a salesperson. The effort devoted to getting an interview was to give you an opportunity to sell yourself. Your goal in job-hunting is to convince the buyer (your prospective employer) to buy (hire) your product (you).

Packaging the Product

You have already made a list of the strongest features of your product, the resumé. The next item to discuss is the packaging and presentation

of this product, you.

Some of the books listed under resources in the Appendix devote lengthy sections to "dressing for the interview." Be careful not to overdo this, you want to dress well but you don't need to buy a new wardrobe. There is no such thing as a "dress code" anymore except in certain professions. In these professions, what is being called a "dress code" is really a uniform.

Rules

There are a few simple rules to follow when going for an interview. You want to be clean, neatly dressed, and show that a little attention was devoted to presenting a good impression.

Hair and Nails

Long hair is legally acceptable for both male and female applicants. However, some prejudices die hard. You will still find interviewers who react negatively to long hair on males. Use your best judgement.

In any case, your hair should be clean and under control. Facial hair (beard and/or mustache) must be trimmed. Fingernails on both male and female should be clean and well shaped. Even if the job you are applying for is in construction.

Shoes and Accessories

Shoes should be clean and if intended to be shiny, they should be polished. For female applicants, make-up should be subtle. For male and female alike, cologne, shaving lotion, and any other scents worn must not be overbearing.

Any purse you use should be small. At least smaller than the smallest suitcase you can buy. Interviewers have spent the valuable first few minutes of an interview trying to find a suitable place for a female job applicant to put her purse.

Wrapping

The clothing selected should, at a minimum, match the normally accepted attire for the given work place. You want the employer to hire the person, not buy the packaging. You want to impress the prospective employer with your skills and abilities. For example, you do not need to wear a suit to apply for a job as a welder. Nor, do you show up for the interview in shorts, tank top and sandals.

Exceptions

Since there are exceptions to all rules, there are exceptions to the ones I have just discussed. If you are applying for a job in clothing design, by all means show your artistic talent. This includes how you dress for the interview. The same would apply if you want to market makeup or clothing at the retail level. In these cases you are demonstrating your professional skill by how you package yourself.

Follow these simple rules and the interview will be directed to focus on your abilities, not on your appearance.

ARE YOU READY?

Thursday morning has arrived and you have an interview at 9 a.m. Time to take stock. Do you have the name and address for the interview? Do you have your Social Security card? Most companies will ask to see it at your interview. Regardless, you will need your number. Best to bring the card.

Do you have your resumé and the names and addresses of your references? Take one last look in the mirror. Would you hire the person you see reflected? If so, you are ready to face the interviewer.

NOTES

_____

_____

_____

_____

_____

_____

_____

_____

_____

_____

_____

_____

_____

_____

CONFIDENCE AND CONTROL
On the hot seat!

3

THE BIG DAY

Remember you want to be on time. Maybe a little early, but never late. Give yourself sufficient time to get to the interview. Never take a friend with you to a job interview. It is not appropriate to even have a friend wait for you in the reception area of the office. If because of other plans, you happen to be with someone else, request that they wait for you outside. Reception areas are not social gathering places, they are extensions of the company's professional image.

Never Late

Allow yourself time to look for a parking place in an area you are not familiar with. If you are too early -- more than ten minutes -- do something to relax and use time. You can walk around the neighborhood, or if the company is located in a shopping district, window shop. Take this, or some other book with you and read while you wait. This is also a good time to go through the current classified ads. Use up this extra time before going into the company office.

Don't plan on chewing gum, smoking or having a soda while you are waiting for the interview. Many companies and their office areas are non-smoking, and it is embarrassing if when you are called, you have to search frantically for a place to put your gum or soda can.

It's Now or Never

You made it. It is 8:51 and the receptionist asks you to have a seat. She informs you that Mr. D'Bos will be with you in a few minutes. If you haven't previously completed an application, she will give you one to complete. In addition to requesting personal and previous employment information, you will probably be asked to provide at least two references. If you have any questions while filling out the application, ask the receptionist. When you return the application it must be complete and readable. If you haven't already provided a resumé, it is appropriate to include one with the completed application.

Polygraph

If interested in you, the company may request that you take a Polygraph -- Lie Detector -- Test. This is a legal request and more employers are requiring the test. It is most frequently used for positions of trust where the employee will handle or have access to cash. The results of the test can only be used for employment screening. An individual cannot be charged with any crime based on a pre-employment polygraph test. You have the right to refuse the test, but don't be surprised if you are not hired.

Relax. You are prepared. Let's take a few minutes to look at the participants in the interview.

THE PLAYERS

There will usually be two participants involved in the interview. In rare cases you may be subjected to a board interview. This method is used to fill professional and technical positions. At this time we can work with the premise that we are discussing a two party interview.

Four Persons?

The two people are the interviewer and yourself. Unfortunately, whenever we have two people interacting we end up with four persons. They are:

1. The interviewer
2. The person you think he/she is
3. You
4. The person the interviewer thinks you are

Some psychologists will say there are two other persons. The person you are trying to project and the same for the interviewer. This gets far too deep for this discussion. Let's stick with the four person approach and look at your overall objective for the interview.

Your Interview Objectives

In simple terms, you want the interviewer to recognize that you and his perception of you are the same and give you an offer of employment. If you do not get a job offer, you want the interviewer to be interested enough to call you back for an additional interview.

You have other goals. They are to:

1. Amplify the information contained on the resumé and application.
2. Present, in person, your best image.
3. Receive any clarifying information about the job and company that you need.

The interviewer's goals are to:

1. Find out more about you.
2. Match your skills, personality, and character against the company's needs.
3. Establish both your willingness and availability for the job.
4. Fill the vacancy with the optimum applicant.

What is Optimum?

The use of optimum is not accidental in the previous sentence. It is very hard to use either "perfect" or "best" in that sentence. Seldom is the "perfect" selection made, because no one can define what is perfect. "Best" is not a good word because of the number of variables. The most skilled applicant may expect more pay than the company can afford. The best selection in terms of money may be deficient in either skills or personality. The list can go on, and on. An interviewer can only hope the selection of the optimum applicant will prove acceptable.

So, as you can see, you both have your work to do. In a way, you are both "on the hot seat." Don't expect any firm decision from a first interview.

Questions and Answers

With all of your answers, be positive, truthful and don't ramble. Include only what is needed to answer the questions and don't get carried away with your own importance. Be assertive but not aggressive. It is possible to overwhelm the interviewer. This will be a mistake. Think before you answer a question and if you do not understand the question ask for clarification.

Some not so good (bad) and good responses:

Q: Tell me a little about yourself.
A: I've been married four times. I don't seem to be able to find the right woman. I have two children by my ...
A: I am single. I like sports, especially football. I am taking an extension course in landscape design ...

Q: What are your hobbies?
A: I go out with the friends and "Jam" every weekend. Sometimes I don't go to bed until ...
A: I like to socialize. I like music and dancing. I go to the movies.

You should have the idea now.

An interviewer does not want to hear a list of don'ts or can'ts. For example:

I don't work on Saturday.
I don't work after 5 p.m.
I don't do windows.
I can't get to work by 7:30 a.m.
I can't eat in 30 minutes.

The above statements may be true for certain job applicants. Truth is not the issue. The method of presentation is the destructive factor.

Remember you are there to get a job, but you have the final say. Hear what the interviewer has to say and respond positively to direct questions. For example, should you be asked if you can be to work by 7:30, it is better to say you need to check out the travel time than to use the statement above or just "No."

Be Smart!

Not knowing how long you lived at an address is unacceptable. Your answers are very important. Even the ones you may think are insignificant. Stay positive and answer with confidence. This is the way to be in control.

Still a little nervous? Take a deep breath, The receptionist has just told you that Mr. D'Bos is ready for your interview. Good Luck.

Time passes.

Force The Issue

One of the ways you can take the initiative is to ask when you can expect to hear from the interviewer. If you are lucky, or catch the interviewer off guard, you will actually get a response. The response may be, "We may make a selection by next Friday." This response allows you to follow up on the interview without appearing to be over eager. On Friday, if you haven't heard anything, you can use the "I have been out of the house ..." excuse to verify that you haven't missed their call.

IT'S OVER

The interview wasn't as bad as you thought. The interviewer was a nice enough person. You didn't do anything to embarrass yourself. The interviewer was interested and promised to call you by next Wednesday.

Post Interview Notes

What now? Well, the interview isn't over until you have replayed it in your head. Make notes of any questions you were not prepared for and any answers you did not feel comfortable with. You will want to work on these before your next interview.

Make another list of what you did or did not like about the company and the responses you got to your questions. You will use this list to aid you in making a decision should you have to pick from two or more job offers.

Make a note of when you are supposed to be called. If you don't get called on the date specified, you can call the next day. If you feel you need a reason to make the call, use "I was

out all day yesterday and thought I may have missed your call." It works!

There's More Hunting To Do

While you are waiting for the call back, you should still be actively seeking a job. You still have an objective to meet. Now where is the next interview?

DEALING WITH REJECTION

You have two types of rejection to deal with. First, is the rejection you feel when you are not selected for a job. Second, is the rejection that you generate when you turn down a job offer. These are equally stressful and equally important.

You Did Not Get Selected

Most interviews end with the statement, "We'll give you a call." Don't get the impression this means that the interviewer will call you if you are not selected. Reality is, that unless they need additional information or you are selected, chances are you will not be called.

It's Not Personal

Do not be disappointed or frustrated if you do not get selected the first time you apply. There are many reasons for non-selection. The majority of these are beyond your control. Therefore, you should not be hard on yourself. As discussed earlier, only the interviewer knows exactly what he or she is looking for. In fact, quite often, even the interviewer is not sure when the selection process starts. This sounds funny and unprofessional, but it is true.

The thing to remember is, even when the job market is tough and unemployment is high, thousands of people are being hired each day. In fact, if everything is working right, you have already followed up on other vacancies and have additional interviews scheduled.

Did you say FREE trips?

My youngest daughter, Karen, wanted to be a flight attendant. She took a job in a retail store while she pursued her true objective. Karen was interviewed by four of the major airlines, but she was never hired as a flight attendant. When she received her first rejection letter she was devastated. Then she treated it like a game.

Now she looks back fondly on those 15 months. The companies each provided her with an expense-paid trip to their home office. The home offices are in different major cities in the East. As an added benefit, she also met many interesting people. Because she was living at home, the increase in her confidence was very noticeable.

That's Really Rejection!

Many more examples of rejection and success can be found in the book publishing business. For example; *M*A*S*H** was rejected 21 times, *Lust for Life* -- 17 times, and *Peyton Place* -- more than 24 times. When finally published, each of these books became "Best Sellers." Having a positive attitude, preliminary planning -- as outlined in this section -- and not taking rejection personally, are all ways to make job hunting easier. It is still hard work, but the results are very rewarding.

Gaining Confidence With Experience

The title says it all. At least one of the vacancies out there is yours. Each time you work, and this includes working on getting a job, you are gaining experience. As you gain experience you will gain confidence and with increased confidence comes a stronger ability to deal with rejection.

THE OTHER KIND

More Than One Offer?

One of the unexplained phenomena in job hunting is that after seemingly endless rejections you finally get a valid offer. This offer is immediately followed by one or more other positive responses. You find yourself faced with another decision. How to select from multiple job offers.

Total The Score

When this happens, ask yourself the following questions for each of the offers and set up a personal score card.

1. Does this offer meet my objective?
2. How far from home is the job?
3. What is the traffic like?
4. Will I have to own a car?
5. What are the company's good points?
6. What concerns did I have after the interview?
7. What is the salary range?
8. What are the fringe benefits -- paid hospitalization, savings plan, overtime, schooling, etc.?

For more information turn to Section II, "The Job." Score the offers fairly. Then select the offer that scores highest, this is your optimum selection. This method sounds very scientific. It is, but it works.

The Interviewer Was Nice.

When all is said and done, you, like the rest of us, will probably choose the job where you liked the interviewer most or the one with the highest hourly salary. No problem. The better you feel about your selection, the happier you will be with your choice. Just remember, you do not have the job until the papers are signed. So, no matter how you make the decision, do it. If you don't you will be old and gray before you take home your first pay check.

Don't Burn Bridges

The job offer or offers you are not going to accept will not just go away. You have a responsibility to notify the interviewer or company representative that you will not accept the offer. For some, this is very difficult. Guilt, embarrassment, and even fear are emotions that must be dealt with.

The easiest way to reduce all of the above emotions is to try to treat the person you are talking to as you would like to be treated. Though a simple "no" will work and sometimes that is the best you can do, try to be positive in your response.

Try: "I appreciate your company's offer, but I have already accepted a job with ..." Don't be brutal. The reply, "Joe's lawn service is paying me $1.00 more per hour," will only result in you being unfavorably remembered.

Just as you should not personalize the rejection when you are not selected for a given job, so do employers not personalize your rejection. That is, unless you make it personal. Be fair, remember the people you are talking to have feelings just like yours. If you are asked why you can't accept the offer put your answer in positive terms. Should it happen, and it rarely does, that a perspective employer insists on the blunt truth, then answer them bluntly and with total honesty. Whatever you do, you should not feel guilty because you do not accept every job offer.

JO ANN GOT A JOB

She received a call! She accepted an offer and has been asked to report at 8 a.m. on Monday to the personnel office of The Green Toe Nursery whose company motto is, "Even our feet make plants grow."

If this were your job offer, would you know what to expect?

NOTES

_____

_____

_____

_____

_____

_____

_____

_____

_____

_____

_____

_____

_____

THE JOB

Now the money comes pouring in.

II

There is a lot more to starting a new job than just showing up on the first day. This section examines the entire job evolution from what to expect the first day to looking for the next job.

Chapter 4 begins by discussing salary, benefits and taxes. This discussion is followed by a look at what to expect during check in. Emphasis is placed on the factors that affect your take home pay.

Chapter 5 continues the check in discussion by presenting the various forms and immediate decisions that a new employee will face the first day on the job. The instructions for completing the I-9 and W-4 forms are presented, with special emphasis on the documentation required for verification and certification by the employer.

Chapter 6 is devoted to employee rights. The chapter contains a practical explanation including examples of each of the seven rights discussed. At the end of the discussion, the three options available to the employee whose rights have been violated are presented.

Chapter 7 matches the rights discussed in Chapter 6 with the employee's responsibilities. The chapter focuses on the employee as an important resource in the profit structure of the employer's business. The ultimate "theft" caused by the most common forms of behavior resulting in disciplinary action is used to emphasize the employee's responsibilities.

Chapter 8 addresses the need for and techniques to use when looking for a new job while still employed. Included in this chapter is a discussion of unemployment compensation, as well as the employee's and employer's views on giving termination notice.

SALARY ... BENEFITS ... TAXES ...
You don't get to take it all home.

4

Each company has different rules and procedures for new employee check in. The consistent factor is that sometime during your first day, you will receive the company indoctrination and fill out a number of forms. The forms are discussed in the next chapter. Let's look at what you receive from the company -- salary and benefits -- and what is taken away -- taxes.

SALARY

Before you accepted your new job, you were told how much per hour or week the company is going to pay you. This figure is your starting salary. In most cases it is expressed as an hourly rate, i.e. $5, $6.25, $8, ... To compute your weekly earnings, multiply this figure by the number of hours a week that you will be working. For example, $5 per hour for a 40 hour week will result in weekly earnings of $200. At $8 per hour you will be earning $320 per week. However, your base salary may not be all the company is offering.

BENEFITS

Benefits are company supported extras. These extras may result in additional pay, better working conditions, or a better life style. As you make advancements in your career you will find that the benefits take on ever increasing importance. There are basically two types of benefits: those that are taxed and those that are not taxed. Non-taxed benefits are preferable in that you receive 100% of their value.

Taxed Benefits

Overtime

Receiving time-and-a-half for all hours worked over 40 in a given week is a benefit. If

you receive a salary of $5 per hour and you work 50 hours in a week, the extra 10 hours would earn you $75 ($5 x 1.5 x 10), before taxes. It should be noted that all companies do not pay time-and-a-half for overtime. Some pay straight-time and some give compensatory time off.

Compensatory time off or "Comp" time is time off, with pay, for each hour you work over the 40 hour week. This means that even though you do not get more pay, you do get equal free time for whatever extra time you put in. If you are allowed to accrue -- save-up -- this time, it will be like getting an extra vacation. If overtime or comp time is one of your benefits, be sure you understand the rules.

Bonuses and Awards

Bonuses, including profit sharing, are taxable benefits provided by some companies. They are treated as salary and, when paid in the form of bonuses, are taxed as salary. If a profit sharing plan is part of a retirement program, the taxes may be deferred -- put off -- until such time as the employee withdraws the money. Whether taxed now or later, this benefit is taxed and should be considered salary in disguise. Also included in this category of benefits are all performance-related cash awards such as sales bonuses, incentive awards, and cash awards for cost saving ideas.

Savings Plans

The same rules apply for savings plans where the company matches what you save. This match can be dollar-for-dollar, one dollar for each two you save, or any other formula used as an incentive for your savings. Each company that offers this benefit has its own formula including a ceiling on the company contribution. The variations on this plan are many, but in all cases you will pay taxes on the company's contributions at some time. It is important that you check for penalties and other restrictions against withdrawing your money.

Pay When Not Working

Enjoy these benefits while you can. They are the last of the really good deals. This category includes paid time off for any of the following: vacation, holidays, sickness, dental or doctor visits, and any other paid free time your employer authorizes. You have to pay tax on the income you receive. But you would have to pay the tax even if you were at work. The benefit is not having to work to earn the pay.

Non-taxed Benefits

Hospitalization

With the rising cost of medical care, everyone needs some form of hospitalization insurance. However, according to the United States Census Bureau, in 1987, 18.5 million adults working full time were not covered by any form of hospitalization or medical insurance.

If you are now providing your sole support, you cannot afford to lose the pay when you are sick and at the same time have to pay for expensive medical care. By far, the least expensive coverage for medical insurance is company sponsored group coverage.

For complete details on the various forms of coverage, including value check lists, be sure to read one or more of the books listed for this section in the Appendix. A group sponsored medical plan, whatever the type, is a valuable non-taxed benefit. The benefit is the savings that you receive by being part of a "group" over what the same insurance would cost if you purchased it alone.

An even greater benefit is received if your employer provides part of the payment. The employer's contribution is not considered as income to you and therefore is not taxed. This is a very important item to consider when evaluating job offers since medical insurance is almost a must and its cost is always increasing.

Life Insurance

The need for and value of life insurance is a very difficult topic to address for young adults without dependents. The original intent of life insurance was to allow an individual the opportunity to purchase protection for his/her dependents in case of the individual's death.

If you are single and do not have dependents or large financial obligations, the need for life insurance is not nearly as important, at this time, as medical insurance. However, if you have plans for the near future that will make life insurance an important factor, there are two types of benefits that may be offered by your employer.

First, some companies offer free life insurance to their employees. And second, in addition to what the company pays for, you may also be able to purchase additional insurance at a reduced group rate. The amount paid by the company and the savings you gain by belonging to a group plan are both non-taxed.

The Appendix contains some excellent books on life insurance.

Unemployment Compensation

Another type of insurance that your employer will provide is unemployment compensation. This insurance provides a basic income for the employee that is laid off from the job through no personal fault. The amount you receive is set by your state of residence. In addition, each state has a number of requirements that the employee must meet before receiving payment. This benefit is discussed in more detail in Chapter 8.

Prepaid Education Expenses

Take full advantage of this one. Frequently an employer will offer a number of opportunities for employees to further their education. These offers are usually work related and result in acquiring new or improved skills. Not only may the company pay for the training, but, if the classes are scheduled during the work day, you are usually provided with paid time off to attend the authorized courses.

Obviously you have the responsibility to get as much as you can from the training. Companies also look with favor on requests from the employees desiring to improve his or her educational level. If not addressed during check in, you may want to ask about this benefit.

Merchandise Discounts

Retail stores and other companies in the sales business often allow their employees to purchase merchandise at a discount. This benefit is not considered salary and does not require the payment of income tax. However, the company has the right to prevent this benefit from being abused by setting a limit on the amount available to each employee.

The value of merchandise discounts varies depending on the type of merchandise available and your specific needs. The value increases very rapidly if the discounts are on food, clothing or other general merchandise used daily.

Subsidized Cafeterias

Some large companies own and operate the eating facilities that service their employees. These cafeterias offer quality meals at a subsidized or lower cost than you will pay elsewhere. The lower cost may even make you change your eating habits. Eating your main meal at work may be more desirable and less expensive than cooking after work.

Tools and Uniforms

When the company provides tools and/or uniforms, the employee automatically receives a benefit. Uniforms provided by the employer eliminate the need for the employee to purchase work clothes. Company provided tools immediately relieves the new employee of the initial expense of purchasing his/her own. Since the company owns the uniforms and tools, it will hold the employee responsible for their loss or abuse.

If the employer also cleans the uniforms, this is an additional benefit. However, if the company reimburses you for the cleaning and the uniform is wearable off the job, the reimbursement may be considered taxable income by the IRS. Ask about this now so you don't create tax problems for yourself later.

Services

In addition to the above benefits, there are a few that fall in the gray area. Some of these are: membership in credit unions, co-op markets, health clubs and recreation programs. Also included in this group of benefits is company provided child care facilities. The real value of these benefits must be measured by each employee. The value will be based on the use the employee makes of each of the services offered.

TAXES

There are a number of taxes that are deducted from your salary before you take any money home.

Federal Income Tax

The major one of these is the Federal Income Tax. You are no longer a full time student and have lost your "exempt" status and will be taxed in accordance with the current income tax laws. The monies collected from this tax are used to provide the Federal Government, including the military, with operating dollars. The statement, "The price of freedom," fits nicely.

Federal Insurance Contribution Act

In addition to the Federal Income Tax, there is another federal tax called FICA (Federal Insurance Contribution Act) commonly known as social security tax. This tax is mandatory and is levied on both employees and self-employed individuals. It is designed to provide a minimum retirement income. If you are not self-employed, you and your employer equally share this tax expense.

The company you work for matches your contribution with a like amount. It is important that your employer withhold this tax. If it is not withheld and you are considered to be self-employed, the amount of tax you will owe will be almost double the normal amount withdrawn from your salary.

State or Local Income Tax

If you live and work in a state or city that has an income tax, it will also be withdrawn from your pay. Just as in the case of the Federal Income Tax, the State and Local Income Tax supports your state and local government. It is this tax, as well as sales and property tax that provides your police and fire protection, roads, schools, garbage collection and other services. The amount of the tax and services provided depends on your state and local government.

WHAT'S LEFT?

As you can see from the discussion, the amount of money you get to take home is equally dependent on your employer's salary and benefits program and the taxes you are required to pay. The computation of these amounts resulting in an estimate of what you can plan to take home is presented in Chapter 9.

NOTES

_____

_____

_____

_____

_____

_____

_____

_____

_____

_____

_____

_____

_____

_____

_____

_____

FORMS, FORMS, FORMS
Sign this, sign that, slow up.

5

The previous chapter discussed a number of benefit options that you may be presented with on your first day at work. Sometime during this first day, you will be asked to complete a number of forms. These forms are required to provide the employer with the necessary information for authorizing the benefits you will receive and the taxes that will be withheld from your salary.

FORM I-9

There is one form that is not for either benefits or taxes. This form is the Employment Eligibility Verification (Form I-9). Form I-9 is a mandatory form required by the U.S. Department of Justice, Immigration, and Naturalization Service. Any person hired after November 6, 1986 must complete this form, which documents their legal right to be employed in the United States.

The idea behind this form is that its use will limit the hiring of illegal aliens. All employers are required to have on file a completed I-9 for anyone hired after the above date and if, during a check, the forms are not available the employer is in violation of civil law and may be fined.

The Data

The Form I-9, which is presented on the following page, is not difficult to complete. In Section I, you enter your name, address, date of birth, and social security number. If the name you were given at birth is different than the one you use now, be sure to also give your birthname. Next you check the appropriate box indicating the legal status under which you are claiming the right to work. After reading the statement that both the information and documents you are using for verification are valid and do belong to you, sign and date the form in the blocks provided.

Verification

For the employer to verify that you are an eligible employee requires that you have, in your possession, certain documents. One document that is accepted without question is a current United States passport. Unfortunately, not too many people carry their passports to work on their first day of employment. So, if you are a citizen of the United States, you will need some form of picture I.D.-- drivers license, U.S. Military Card, Student -- and either your birth certificate or your Social Security Number Card.

Take a look at Section 2 of the Form I-9 and be sure to have the required documentation with you when you initially report to work. Your employer is required by law to request these documents before signing the certification statement on the bottom of the form.

BENEFITS

The number of forms that are required for the certification of eligibility of benefits are as varied as the benefits offered. The best way to put yourself into a good frame of mind for this task is to remember, the more forms you have to fill out the more benefits you will probably receive.

Company I.D.

For many employers, the only form you may be required to fill out to receive most benefits is an employee identification form. To complete the form you only need to know personal identification data: height, weight, color of eyes, hair color, identifying scars or marks, and social security number. Depending on the rules of your employer, you may have a photo made and be required to sign and wear the identification card at all times while on the job.

EMPLOYMENT ELIGIBILITY VERIFICATION (Form I-9)

1 **EMPLOYEE INFORMATION AND VERIFICATION:** (To be completed and signed by employee.)

Name: (Print or Type) Last	First	Middle	Birth Name

Address: Street Name and Number	City	State	ZIP Code

Date of Birth (Month/Day/Year)	Social Security Number

I attest, under penalty of perjury, that I am (check a box):

☐ 1. A citizen or national of the United States.

☐ 2. An alien lawfully admitted for permanent residence (Alien Number A _____).

☐ 3. An alien authorized by the Immigration and Naturalization Service to work in the United States (Alien Number A _____ .
or Admission Number _____ , expiration of employment authorization, if any _____).

I attest, under penalty of perjury, the documents that I have presented as evidence of identity and employment eligibility are genuine and relate to me. I am aware that federal law provides for imprisonment and/or fine for any false statements or use of false documents in connection with this certificate.

Signature	Date (Month/Day/Year)

PREPARER/TRANSLATOR CERTIFICATION (To be completed if prepared by person other than the employee). I attest, under penalty of perjury, that the above was prepared by me at the request of the named individual and is based on all information of which I have any knowledge.

Signature	Name (Print or Type)		
Address (Street Name and Number)	City	State	Zip Code

2 **EMPLOYER REVIEW AND VERIFICATION:** (To be completed and signed by employer.)

Instructions:

Examine one document from List A and check the appropriate box, **OR** examine one document from List B **and** one from List C and check the appropriate boxes. Provide the *Document Identification Number* and *Expiration Date* for the document checked.

List A Documents that Establish Identity and Employment Eligibility	List B Documents that Establish Identity	and	List C Documents that Establish Employment Eligibility
☐ 1. United States Passport	☐ 1. A State-issued driver's license or a State-issued I.D. card with a photograph, or information, including name, sex, date of birth, height, weight, and color of eyes. (Specify State)_____)		☐ 1. Original Social Security Number Card (other than a card stating it is not valid for employment)
☐ 2. Certificate of United States Citizenship	☐ 2. U.S. Military Card		☐ 2. A birth certificate issued by State, county, or municipal authority bearing a seal or other certification
☐ 3. Certificate of Naturalization	☐ 3. Other (Specify document and issuing authority)		
☐ 4. Unexpired foreign passport with attached Employment Authorization			☐ 3. Unexpired INS Employment Authorization Specify form #_____
☐ 5. Alien Registration Card with photograph			
Document Identification # _____	*Document Identification* # _____		*Document Identification* # _____
Expiration Date (if any) _____	*Expiration Date (if any)* _____		*Expiration Date (if any)* _____

CERTIFICATION: I attest, under penalty of perjury, that I have examined the documents presented by the above individual, that they appear to be genuine and to relate to the individual named, and that the individual, to the best of my knowledge, is eligible to work in the United States.

Signature	Name (Print or Type)	Title
Employer Name	Address	Date

Form I-9 (05/07/87)
OMB No. 1115-0136

U.S. Department of Justice
Immigration and Naturalization Service

This I.D. card plus the data you provided on your application may be the only requirements the employer has for the following benefits:

(1) Bonuses and Awards -- excluding profit sharing plans
(2) Educational expense refunds
(3) Merchandise discounts
(4) Service Benefits -- In some cases, such as when you open a checking or savings account at the credit union, you may be required to provide additional data.
(5) Subsidized cafeterias
(6) Tool allotment
(7) Unemployment compensation coverage

Savings Plan

Savings plans and profit sharing plans will require the completion of a form very similar to the one for opening a checking account discussed in Chapter 11. In addition to completing the form, you will have to decide how much you want to put into the program. Some companies may give you three to five days to make up your mind, but in other cases the decision needs to be made immediately. This is an important decision because normally the amount you save can only be increased on your anniversary date -- the month and day you were employed.

To be prepared to make this decision, you should read Chapter 10 on budgeting. The self analysis form explained in that chapter will help you decide what you can afford to save.

Hospitalization

If your employer offers medical insurance, chances are the only decision you will be asked to make is whether you want low option or high option. The differences between the two options are cost and coverage. The high option normally has less of a deductible and covers a larger percentage of covered expenses. The high option can be substantially more expensive. You will have to consider your past health, financial ability, the company's contribution, and the difference in coverages to arrive at this decision.

If you are in good health and have no recurring illness, the low option may be your best choice. This is especially true if the difference in the coverage between the two options is small, both in deductible amount and percentage

of payment. Be sure to verify that your choice of options contains major medical coverage. Major medical coverage limits the total amount you will pay for any single illness or hospital stay. For instance, a plan may advertise that it pays 75% of all covered items after a $200 deductible, and, with major medical, 100% of everything over $2,000. To find the real cost to you for a one week hospital stay, for an appendix operation, the computation would be:

Hospital, doctor and lab charges	$7,000
Subtract major medical limit	2,000
Major medical pays	5,000

Since major medical pays everything over the first $2,000 this is the only amount you are concerned with. Of the $2,000, you first have to pay the $200 deductible. In addition, you are responsible for 25% of the difference between your deductible and $2,000. If you subtract your deductible of $200 from $2,000 you get a balance of $1,800. You are responsible for 25% of this balance which is $450--$2,000-$200=$1,800 X 25% = $450.

Your total for this hospital stay would be $650, which is the sum of your $200 deductible and the $450 which represents your 25%. Of the $2,000 not covered by major medical, you owe $650 and your regular hospitalization will pay the remaining $1,350.

Summing it all up:	
Total bill	$7,000
Major Medical	$5,000
sub-total	$2,000
Hospitalization	$1,350
You Pay	$650

The above example, where a $7,000 medical bill would result in you paying $650, demonstrates the importance of protecting yourself with some form of medical insurance. It may not be easy to pay the $650, but it is a lot easier than paying $7,000.

Health Maintenance Organization

Health Maintenance Organization (HMO) membership is another form of medical insurance that your employer may offer. This type of plan is made up of member doctors and hospitals. As long as you use the member doctors and hospitals, your cost per visit is fixed, no matter what costs were incurred.

For example, a complete physical examination can easily cost in excess of $150 but, if you are enrolled in a HMO plan and go to your member doctor, the cost could be as low as $5. The actual charge for each visit will be determined by your plan.

Another important factor to consider is that under this kind of plan you must use a member doctor and hospital. The only complaint I have heard about these plans is that some of the member doctors appear to be reluctant to authorize visits to non-member doctors and hospitals. Another problem you may encounter is that if you are enrolled in a local plan and are traveling, you may have difficulty getting a non-local doctor or hospital to accept your coverage.

Information Required

Regardless of the plan offered or the option chosen, if you are going to sign up for medical insurance, you will need to provide information. Your age, date of birth, medical history, a statement of your existing medical conditions, and your parents medical histories are some of the types of information requested by most medical insurance companies.

The amount of medical history detail you are asked to provide will differ by company and plan. However, the request for a statement that you are free from a known medical condition is universal. Medical plans will only cover existing conditions if the whole group is changing insurance companies or you were insured by the same group at your previous job. It is very important that you do not falsify this data. If you do and the insurance company can prove it, not only will they drop your insurance but you will not be entitled to a refund of premiums.

Life Insurance

If your employer provides life insurance as part of the benefits package, you will need to provide personal information. Much of the information you provided for the medical insurance coverage will be required to be stated again for the life insurance. In addition, you will be asked to name a beneficiary. Your beneficiary is the person or persons you name to receive the insurance amount when you die.

In most states you can name your "estate" as the beneficiary. When you die, the money from the insurance will be lumped with your other possessions. This total -- your estate -- is then distributed in accordance with the instructions of your will or the laws of the state where you live. A valid will takes precedence over the state laws. The problem with identifying your estate as the beneficiary is that money from life insurance, which is usually not subject to taxation, could, as part of your estate, be taxable.

When you do not have a specified person as beneficiary, you can still get around the taxes by having the beneficiary be "the line of decent and succession." In plain English, this means that if you are not married and die while your parents are alive, the payment will be made to them. If they are not living, the payment will be made to any living brothers and/or sisters. The process continues until a living heir is named as the recipient of the insurance.

If you were legally married when you died and had used the "line of decent..." option on your life insurance, the payment would be different. First, if your spouse is alive, he or she would receive the payment. If the spouse is not living but you have living children, they are your heirs. When there is neither a spouse nor children, the line of decent is exactly as stated in the preceding paragraph.

Be prepared. In the event your company offers this benefit, it is best to have with you the names and addresses of the persons you want to name as heirs.

TAX FORMS

There is at least one additional form you will have to fill out and sign. This is the Form W-4, Employee's Withholding Allowance Certificate. This is a mandatory federal government form and is used to determine the amount of federal income tax withheld from your paycheck.

When the first revision of this form was issued in 1987, a large number of taxpayers claimed to have great difficulty reading and understanding the instructions. I believe that by sticking to a simple example, the form will be easier to understand and you will not have a problem.

The Taxpayer

As an example, Jo Ann T. Graduate, the newly employed landscape assistant starting work at the Green Toe Nursery, will complete the form. Because of her outstanding resumé and interview results, she has a starting salary of $6 per hour. She is single, has no dependents and even if she had a second job, would not expect to earn over $25,000 this year. For the last three years, Jo Ann was a full time student living at home and did not earn enough to pay taxes. For the part-time jobs she has had, she has always been able to claim exemption from withholding tax.

Dissecting the Form

Page 1 -- the only page included in this discussion -- of the W-4 is divided into three parts: (1) purpose and definitions, (2) the Personal Allowance Work-sheet, and (3) the actual W-4 Form. Take time right now to read each of the definitions in the first part of the form found on the next page.

Jo Ann is interested in the first three paragraphs. The first paragraph applies to everyone and explains the purpose of the form.

She is interested in the second paragraph because, for the last three years, she was a full time student living at home and did not earn enough to pay taxes. In the past, she could claim the exemption and have no taxes removed from her salary.

The third paragraph interests her because it introduces the authorization that gives every taxpayer the option and full support of the government to claim less deductions or allowances then he/she is entitled to. Exercising this option causes additional funds to be withheld from each paycheck. These funds are deposited with the federal government. At the end of the year, when the tax return is processed, all money collected in excess of the individual's tax bill is returned as a tax refund.

No Interest

This forced savings plan may sound appealing until you realize that this excess money does not earn interest. Unless you can't save money any other way, or you expect your tax situation to change, this is not a financially sound idea. You need your money, either for living expenses or to be working for you by earning interest.

The Worksheet

Jo Ann is ready to fill out the second part -- the worksheet. She follows the instructions and puts a "1" in line A. Reading the instructions for line B, she finds that a "1" should be entered in line B because she is single and only has one job. Jo Ann is not married so line C does not apply.

Reading on she determines that lines D through F apply to dependents and since she has no dependents, these lines do not apply to her. She adds the numbers in the lines she has filled (A and B) and puts a "2" in line G.

Jo Ann takes an additional moment to read the suggestions on the bottom of the worksheet. After reading them, she decides they are not applicable to her situation and proceeds to part 3 which is the W-4 Form.

Form W-4

Blocks (1), (2), (3), and (4) are easy for Jo Ann to complete. She enters her name and address, social security number and checks the block for single. Then she copies the "2" from line G on the worksheet.

Block (5) asks if she wants to have extra money deducted from her pay. She remembers the short discussion from earlier and decides she needs all her money each payday. She puts a zero in Block (5).

Block (6) is for exemption from withholding. Jo Ann reads over this section carefully and decides she meets the first and third requirements, but this year she does not expect to get all of her federal income tax refunded. She expects to earn more than the amount authorized as tax free income for single taxpayers having no dependents. She leaves Block (6) empty and goes on to Block (7).

Jo Ann's answer to Block (7) is no. She signs and dates the W-4 and returns it to the personnel administrator. Take a moment to go back over the form on the previous page, substituting your own responses for the ones that Jo Ann used.

1989 Form W-4

**Department of the Treasury
Internal Revenue Service**

Purpose. Complete Form W-4 so that your employer can withhold the correct amount of Federal income tax from your pay.

Exemption From Withholding. Read line 6 of the certificate below to see if you can claim exempt status. If exempt, only complete the certificate; but do not complete lines 4 and 5. No Federal income tax will be withheld from your pay.

Basic Instructions. Employees who are not exempt should complete the Personal Allowances Worksheet. Additional worksheets are provided on page 2 for employees to adjust their withholding allowances based on itemized deductions, adjustments to income, or two-earner/two-job situations. Complete all worksheets that apply to your situation. The worksheets will help you figure the number of withholding allowances you are

entitled to claim. However, you may claim fewer allowances than this.

Head of Household. Generally, you may claim head of household filing status on your tax return only if you are unmarried and pay more than 50% of the costs of keeping up a home for yourself and your dependent(s) or other qualifying individuals.

Nonwage Income. If you have a large amount of nonwage income, such as interest or dividends, you should consider making estimated tax payments using Form 1040-ES. Otherwise, you may find that you owe additional tax at the end of the year.

Two-Earner/Two-Jobs. If you have a working spouse or more than one job, figure the total number of allowances you are entitled to claim on all jobs using worksheets from only one Form

W-4. This total should be divided among all jobs. Your withholding will usually be most accurate when all allowances are claimed on the W-4 filed for the highest paying job and zero allowances are claimed for the others.

Advance Earned Income Credit. If you are eligible for this credit, you can receive it added to your paycheck throughout the year. For details, obtain Form W-5 from your employer.

Check Your Withholding. After your W-4 takes effect, you can use **Publication 919,** Is My Withholding Correct for 1989?, to see how the dollar amount you are having withheld compares to your estimated total annual tax. Call 1-800-424-3676 (in Hawaii and Alaska, check your local telephone directory) to obtain this publication.

Personal Allowances Worksheet

A Enter "1" for **yourself** if no one else can claim you as a dependent . . . . **A** _1_

B Enter "1" if:
  1. You are single and have only one job; or
  2. You are married, have only one job, and your spouse does not work; or
  3. Your wages from a second job or your spouse's wages (or the total of both) are $2,500 or less. . . . . **B** _1_

C Enter "1" for your **spouse.** But, you may choose to enter "0" if you are married and have either a working spouse or more than one job (this may help you avoid having too little tax withheld) . . . . **C** _____

D Enter number of **dependents** (other than your spouse or yourself) whom you will claim on your tax return . . . . . . **D** _____

E Enter "1" if you will file as a **head of household** on your tax return (see conditions under "Head of Household," above) . . **E** _____

F Enter "1" if you have at least $1,500 of **child or dependent care expenses** for which you plan to claim a credit . . . . **F** _____

G Add lines A through F and enter total here . . . . ▶ **G** _2_

For accuracy, do all worksheets that apply.
- If you plan to **itemize or claim adjustments to income** and want to reduce your withholding, turn to the Deductions and Adjustments Worksheet on page 2.
- If you are **single** and have **more than one job** and your combined earnings from all jobs exceed $25,000 OR if you are **married** and have a **working spouse or more than one job,** and the combined earnings from all jobs exceed $40,000, then turn to the Two-Earner/Two-Job Worksheet on page 2 if you want to avoid having too little tax withheld.
- If **neither** of the above situations applies to you, **stop here** and enter the number from line G on line 4 of Form W-4 below.

- - - - - - - - - - - - - - - - Cut here and give the certificate to your employer. Keep the top portion for your records. - - - - - - - - - - - - - - -

---

Form W-4
Department of the Treasury
Internal Revenue Service

Employee's Withholding Allowance Certificate
▶ For Privacy Act and Paperwork Reduction Act Notice, see reverse.

OMB No. 1545-0010
1989

1 Type or print your first name and middle initial Last name	2 Your social security number
Jo Ann T. Graduate	254 - 71 - 2856

Home address (number and street or rural route)
2246 Home St.

City or town, state, and ZIP code
Soft Life, OK 12389

3 Marital Status
☒ Single ☐ Married
☐ Married, but withhold at higher Single rate.
Note: If married, but legally separated, or spouse is a nonresident alien, check the Single box.

4 Total number of allowances you are claiming (from line G above or from the Worksheets on back if they apply) . . . **4** _2_

5 Additional amount, if any, you want deducted from each pay . . . . **5** $ _0_

6 I claim exemption from withholding and I certify that I meet **ALL** of the following conditions for exemption:
- Last year I had a right to a refund of **ALL** Federal income tax withheld because I had **NO** tax liability; **AND**
- This year I expect a refund of **ALL** Federal income tax withheld because I expect to have **NO** tax liability; **AND**
- This year if my income exceeds $500 and includes nonwage income, another person cannot claim me as a dependent.
If you meet all of the above conditions, enter the year effective and "EXEMPT" here . . . . . ▶ **6** 19

7 Are you a full-time student? (Note: Full-time students are not automatically exempt.) . . . . **7** ☐ Yes ☒ No

Under penalties of perjury, I certify that I am entitled to the number of withholding allowances claimed on this certificate or entitled to claim exempt status.

Employee's signature ▶ Jo Ann T. Graduate   Date ▶ April 16 , 1989

8 Employer's name and address (**Employer:** Complete 8 and 10 **only if sending to IRS**) | **9** Office code (optional) | **10** Employer identification number

MORE FORMS

If you are employed in a locale where state and/or local income tax is collected, you will be instructed to complete the required forms. They will be similar but, in most cases, easier than the W-4.

RECAP

The data you must be prepared to have with you on the first day is:

(1)   Social Security Card

(2)   Name and address of closest relative
(3)   Name, address and phone number of person to notify in case of emergency
(4)   Previous addresses and dates of residency
(5)   Complete medical history of yourself and your parents
(6)   Beneficiary information
(7)   Birth Certificate to prove citizenship
(8)   Alien registration form, if applicable
(9)   Driver's license or other form of picture I.D.

If you must make a mistake in this area, make it by having more information with you then is needed.

NOTES

_____

_____

_____

_____

_____

_____

_____

_____

_____

_____

_____

_____

_____

EMPLOYEE RIGHTS
Why can't I dress like I want?

6

At the time of this book's publication, there is no Employee Bill of Rights. Such a plan has been discussed in both houses of congress, but positive action to pass such a bill has not been successful. This does not mean that you, as an employee, do not have any rights. Just the opposite is true. You are guaranteed certain rights as a citizen and resident of this country.

YOUR RIGHTS

The rights that will be discussed in this chapter are those that guarantee you:

(1)   a safe work place
(2)   privacy
(3)   equal treatment
(4)   clear direction
(5)   freedom of expression
(6)   freedom from discrimination
(7)   freedom from sexual harassment

Safe Work Place

The Occupational Safety and Health Administration (OSHA), a government agency, has the responsibility for inspecting and ensuring that businesses follow government standards for safety on the job. Your employer is required, by law, to provide you with all safety measures and equipment that will protect you from industrial accidents which may result in injury or loss of life.

This does not mean that the company must provide you with suntan lotion because you work outside, or provide you with gloves because you might get blisters. What it does mean is that hard hats are required on construction sites, ventilating fans and respirators are required if working with toxic chemicals, and heavy equipment must be equipped with back-up alarms. Even the requirement for safety goggles, steel toed boots, and fire extinguishers is covered by OSHA.

A fine is the normal penalty for a company's disregard of the warnings. Continued refusal to comply with the standards will result in the loss of government contracts and ultimately suspension of the company's business license -- closure.

As a dedicated employee, interested in your own safety, you have a responsibility to notify your supervisor if you notice a potentially dangerous situation.

Privacy

This is one of those gray areas. There is no law on the books that guarantees non-government workers privacy. For government workers, the Privacy Act of 1974 specifically identifies what can and cannot be made public about an employee. However, there is a law -- The Freedom of Information Act of 1966 -- that states specifically what is public information. If one looks at the exceptions to this act, a case can be made for what is considered private.

All of an individual's personal information, supplied to obtain a job, is private. Your home address, phone number, age, marital status, social security number, number of dependents, and pay are all included. Verification of employment -- the fact that you work for the company -- and your office phone number can be made public by your employer. When you get paid, if presented as company policy, can be distributed as public information. For example, if someone from a bank calls your company office and asks if employees are paid weekly, it is not a violation of your privacy for the company to answer the question.

You should be aware that you can voluntarily give up some of these rights to privacy. The most common way you do this is by applying for a loan and authorizing the lending agency to verify your employment status, including the amount of your pay.

You have other rights under the heading of privacy. What you do off the job, as long as it does not interfere with your job performance, is not legal grounds for discipline unless it affects your work. For example, your employer would have difficulty finding a work relationship between you partying after work and your job. However, you do have a problem if your actions are illegal. If you were to get arrested and could not report to work, your employer would have reason to consider your actions, whatever they were, work-related and you could be either suspended or even fired. It is important to understand that you would be disciplined, not for being arrested, but for not being able to perform your job.

Equal Treatment

This right can be tough to understand. The reason is that most people immediately think "fair" when they see or hear the word "equal." To date, there has not been any legislation that has tried to measure fairness. This right -- equal treatment -- goes hand-in-glove with the right to freedom from discrimination.

While the law on discrimination addresses specific characteristics that must be present, the right to equal treatment is universal. For example, a group from your office have been going out to eat lunch. They have been taking about 45 minutes a day even though they are only authorized 30 minutes. No one has said anything and you finally decide to join them.

You guessed it. Your boss decides she is fed up with this lax behavior and when you all return, you are told that you will all be docked 15 minutes pay for your extended lunch. It's tough, and you may think it is unfair since this was your first time, but it is equal treatment and it is legal.

Another example, a number of employees frequently take extended lunch periods to have their hair done. Your hair is getting shaggy and coming back from lunch you pass the hair dresser and decide to get a quick trim. Who do you think sees you coming back from lunch 30 minutes late?

Yes, you're right again. There he is just waiting to reprimand you for taking a long lunch hour. The next day two other employees do the same thing and nothing is said. You have not been treated equally and your right to equal treat-

ment has been violated.

Equal treatment covers the entire spectrum of employment: raises, bonuses, promotions, educational benefits, special assignments and discipline. At the close of this chapter is a discussion of your options when treated unequally.

Clear Direction

Most employees and employers do not even give this right any thought or consideration. Yet, both employees and employers are always complaining about poor or mediocre performance. When an employee performs poorly the cause is usually one of the following:

(1)   the employee **did not know what** was expected,
(2)   the employee **did not know how** to do what was expected, or
(3)   the employee **did not have time** to do what was expected.

As a dedicated employee, this right can only be exercised if you make known to your supervisor that you do not understand the instructions or do not know how to carry them out. It is far better for the supervisor and the employee to spend a little time clarifying the instructions or participating in a little training than to have to redo an unsatisfactory job.

Freedom of Expression

You have the right to express your views on just about any subject. You even have the right to offer suggestions and observations to your supervisor or boss. Be aware that there is as much skill required in knowing when to shut up as there is in making tactful observations. Learn to judge when the discussion is over. Once one of the members in a discussion -- usually your boss -- has made a decision, the discussion is over. To continue to make observations or to insist on additional discussion is both annoying and pointless.

Your right to free expression is also limited. Everything is fine as long as your views do not interfere with the production of your fellow workers, or fall into the area of defamation of character or industrial theft. This is a big statement. As we are going to see in the next chapter, your actions and words can result in theft from your employer.

This form of behavior is considered justification for dismissal. If criminal intent can be proven, you may be criminally charged and face a legal trial. For example, you are a little upset because the promotion you were counting on went to another employee. You decide to pass on to your boss's chief competitor the formula used for making job bids. The competitor rewards your efforts by passing you $500. You are on your way to jail.

This is called industrial spying and theft. You will probably be dismissed from your job, charged, tried by law, and found guilty. Trying to use the right of freedom of expression will not work as a defense and, needless to say, you will undoubtedly find your next promotion hard to come by.

Freedom From Discrimination

This is the big one. Of all your rights as an employee this has the most visibility, interest, and resource backing. The Civil Rights Act of 1964 as amended, guarantees you freedom from discrimination because of:

(1)   age
(2)   sex
(3)   race
(4)   religion
(5)   national origin
(6)   color
(7)   physical or mental handicap, and
(8)   retaliation because of making a complaint.

Although much progress has been made since 1964, the problem has not been removed and will be around for many years to come. The important thing to remember is that a start has been made.

The degree of attention to this law will depend on a number of factors. Where you live, the size of the company you work for, the feelings of upper management, and the reliance on interstate commerce and government contracts are some of the key elements affecting individual company compliance.

Simply stated, the law guarantees you freedom from discrimination as an employee based on any of the listed classifications. As stated earlier, it guarantees you equal treatment, not fair treatment. There is no law in this country or any other that will make up for the incom-

petent or uncaring supervisor.

Discrimination based on all of these classifications still exists. You will see it, and may even feel the result of it. If you are a member of the work force for any extended period of time and are never exposed to discrimination, you are either living in a vacuum or totally unaware of reality. The options available to you, if you feel you have been discriminated against, are discussed at the closing of this chapter.

Freedom From Sexual Harassment

When sex discrimination or stereotyping, as the result of a supervisor/employee relationship, results in unequal treatment in a job related action, it is punishable as sex discrimination. There is another form of sex related behavior, called Sexual Harassment, that is barred from the workplace and is considered a violation of rights. Though sexual harassment is not treated as severely as sex discrimination, it is possibly one of the most prevalent forms of rights violations that exist in today's workplace and affects thousands of workers both male and female.

Unfortunately, the wording of the law is somewhat cloudy and open to individual interpretation. The generally accepted interpretation is: any verbal or physical action, of a sexual nature, that is unwanted and repeated, is prohibited in the work force. In looking at this definition, it is important to identify the key words. They are: action, sexual, unwanted, and repeated. By understanding these key words, the rights and responsibilities of the employee become obvious.

The law is specifically written this way so that normal adult behavior between members of different sexes will not be banned.

Action

Starting at the top, you do not have to be assaulted for the action to be considered harassment. Words, gestures, notes, jokes, even facial expressions have been judged to be violations. As long as all the rest of the requirements are present, these actions do not even have to be directed to a specific individual, for the behavior to be considered harassment.

For example, the posting of nude pictures -- male or female -- on the walls of an office, after the observation that someone found them offensive, is a violation of the law. In the opinion of the author, it is also in very poor taste and not acceptable work place behavior. The continued use of sexually vulgar language, after someone stated they found it offensive, has also been ruled to be harassment.

Sexual

Uncomplimentary references to race, age, national origin, and other forms of stereotyping may be harassment, but are not sex related. To be considered sexual harassment, the words or actions must be sexual in nature. Touching, in any form, and leaning closely over a member of the opposite sex, must be considered carefully. This can be very difficult for some people. My wife, Jean, is a toucher. During a normal conversation with someone, she may touch the person's arm or shoulder to make a point. If someone finds this behavior unpleasant, Jean will have to change her behavior. This may be difficult for you to accept, but it is the responsibility of the offending person to make the behavior adjustment.

Another example is the story of the personnel administrator who was called to the boss's office one Monday morning. As he stood in front of the boss's desk growing uncomfortable, the boss looked up and said: "Are you aware that a sexual harassment charge has been made against you?" The administrator's response was: "No sir." The boss lifted a letter from his desk and said: "Mrs. Klipson indicates in her letter that every time she enters your office, you address her as 'honey.' She further states that she told you she finds it offensive because in her family honey is a name implying intimacy and endearment. She charges that you still continue to use the term when addressing her. Do you have an explanation?"

The administrator hesitated for a moment and replied: "Sir, I don't only call her honey, that is how I address everyone."

The boss thoughtfully considered this response before saying: "I don't remember you ever addressing me as honey. See that this behavior stops now."

It did.

Unwanted

It is possible that behavior you find offensive, others may not. Therefore, it is important that the offending party be made aware of your feelings. You do not have to justify them, simply state them clearly. Depending on how you feel, you may want to state them in front of a witness. Earlier, I discussed touching. Not everyone gets offended when they talk with my wife, so if you found her unconscious touching offensive, you would have to inform her before you could claim sexual harassment.

Repeated

This key word goes along with unwanted. Once the individual has been told of the offending behavior, if the behavior continues it qualifies as harassment because it is now repeated. All individuals are responsible for ceasing offending behavior as soon as notification that it offends is received.

Unfortunately ...

Case after case has supported that discrimination complaints and complaints arising from alleged sexual harassment are "no win" situations. As an Equal Employment Opportunity (EEO) counselor, I have been personally involved in some of these situations and have read about many, many more. In all cases, though the winners were usually happy that they received justice, there was an underlying feeling of loss. Whether one is the accused or accuser, the original environment and relationships can never be restored. In my opinion, the only true way to win is for everyone to be accountable for his or her own behavior. If everyone really tried, all work environments could be made free of the stereotyping and behavior that leads to the violation of other's rights. Only then will we all be winners.

ONE MORE RIGHT

You, I, and everyone, has the right to refuse to do something we feel is in violation of moral or civil law. In other words, our employer cannot direct us to rob a bank, reduce safety limits, or take any other actions that will result in death or injury to other individuals.

It is possible that if you refuse to carry out a direction based on these grounds, you may be dismissed. If you are dismissed for this reason, you are eligible to receive unemployment compensation and may generate an investigation by local, state, or federal agencies into your former employer's action. There has even been a bill introduced in congress, the "Whistleblower's Protection Act," designed to keep employers from taking disciplinary action against an employee that reports illegal acts.

As with all other violations of your rights, your first step is to talk to your supervisor. If you cannot talk to your supervisor or someone in management, you may have to report the unacceptable behavior to an outside authority.

WHAT TO DO WHEN YOUR RIGHTS ARE VIOLATED!

Should you feel that one of the above or even another of your rights have been violated, you must take action. Even doing nothing is taking action. It most probably will not result in getting compensation for your loss of rights, but by not taking an active stand you are accepting the loss of the right.

You have only three possible options or actions:

(1) You can decide to live with the situation either temporarily, while you look for other employment, or permanently.

(2) You can file a formal complaint. Initially with your supervisor and ultimately, if not resolved, in court.

(3) You can immediately quit.

There are no other choices. Sulking, complaining, and/or spreading general unrest are not acceptable actions. You are the one wronged. If possible, you want immediate corrective action on the part of your employer. Usually this is accomplished by just going to your supervisor. When going to your supervisor doesn't work, there are a number of agencies that will be more than happy to help you fight for your rights. The Equal Employment Opportunity Commission (EEOC), the Civil Liberties Union, your State Labor Board and Legal Aid Society are some of these agencies and they will direct you to others. When you seek the aid of outside help, be prepared to deal with increased stress and the possible loss of your present job. As unfair as this sounds, it is reality.

WRAPPING IT UP

This country's basic premise is one of freedom and human rights. The workplace is no exception. You, as an employee, even if starting out at the bottom, have a number of rights. It is your responsibility to know those rights and to insist that they be honored.

If you think your rights have been violated, you are the only one who can initiate corrective action. You must let someone, usually your supervisor, know that your rights have either been denied or violated. Disrupting the workplace by sulking, whining or chronic complaining to other employees will not solve the problem and may make you open for disciplinary action.

Since as the saying goes "Nothing is free!", and this includes your rights, there are a set of employee responsibilities that every employee is obligated to honor.

These responsibilities are discussed next.

RESPONSIBILITIES
Oh, I didn't know you meant 8 o'clock every day. 7

WHY WERE YOU HIRED?

With all of the rights discussed in the previous chapter go a corresponding set of responsibilities. You have as many, if not more, responsibilities as you have rights. Before discussing your responsibilities, it is necessary to first look at why the employer hired you. You are saying: "Because I was the optimum choice for the job." That, you hope, is at least partially true. However, you are not looking at the situation from the employer's point of view. You were hired because the employer feels that you will increase his/her profit.

It may be true that by selecting you the employer gained some special traits, knowledge, or skills that the other applicants did not have. But the reason the employer was even looking for someone is because there was a need to either maintain or increase the company's profits. That is why the employer is in business, and herein lies the key to your responsibilities.

Your overriding responsibility is to earn your pay by helping to meet your employer's goals. Anything less than that results in theft. Not necessarily the theft of physically removing something belonging to your employer, which everyone knows is illegal, but still theft. Once you understand this, understanding your responsibilities, and the resulting discipline for lack of responsibility, becomes easy.

TWO LISTS

The responsibilities chosen to emphasize this point are:

(1) Attendance
(2) Performance

(3) Order
(4) Honesty
(5) Loyalty

For each of these responsibilities, there are one or more behaviors that frequently warrant discipline. The disregard for the responsibilities listed is the cause of the majority of disciplinary actions in today's work force.

These behaviors are:

(1) Absence from duty or job
(2) Non-performance or poor quality performance
(3) Disruptive, negligent behavior
(4) Lying
(5) Physical theft
(6) Industrial sabotage or conflict of interest

Each of these behaviors will be addressed with an explanation of the resultant theft.

Attendance/Absence

You have been hired to do a job. You can only do the job if you report for work. Only by reporting for work at the prescribed time can you do the job completely and as planned. If you are part of a work crew, your absence, even for a few minutes, robs the employer of the productivity of the entire crew. Continually being late, either in the morning, or when returning from a break or lunch, quickly adds up to an offense that is unacceptable to the employer. When a prospective employer is checking a reference, one of the first questions asked is: "Is the person reliable?" A "No" response to this question usually means that someone else will be hired to fill the vacancy.

Performance / Non-Performance

Your job, no matter what the actual duties include, requires an expected performance level. Your responsibility to your employer is not only to work, but to perform up to the level for which you are being paid. Anything less is unsatisfactory behavior. The reason it is unsatisfactory is that it results in a theft of your employer's potential earnings.

Example

You are working on a landscaping job. The job is scheduled for completion this afternoon and everything is going great. One of the owner's children comes out in the yard and starts a conversation. You are flattered by the attention shown in your work and you get distracted by the attractive, personable, individual.

Time flies. The rest of the crew are finished and ready to leave. The work you were supposed to have done is not completed. The owner refuses to pay your employer and insists that the work be completed tomorrow. Tomorrow is Saturday and another job is scheduled to begin. Your employer, and yes, you too, have a problem. Unintentionally, you have stolen from your employer. One customer is upset that their job did not get completed on time. Another is going to be disturbed when the crew does not show up on time.

Even if you make arrangements to go back on your own, the owner must still make another trip to verify the work is complete and collect the money owed. In addition, if you are part of the crew that is supposed to start the new job tomorrow, your absence will be felt.

Your employer could even experience additional losses in goodwill. The goodwill that would have prompted both property owners to recommend your employer's landscaping services to others.

Poor Quality

Poor quality performance has the same results. In many cases the results are even worse because the poor quality may be hidden and not show up until much later. No one is happy when they think they have been cheated.

It Happens

My brother-in-law took his car in to have the windshield sealed because it had a small leak. He picked the car up on his way home from work and left the next morning to drive 740 miles to my house. On the way to my house it started raining. The good news was the windshield did not leak. Unfortunately, his problems were much more serious: he did not have any windshield wipers.

He was forced to pull over repeatedly to try to keep the windshield clear. When he arrived at my house, we found the missing windshield wipers, arms and all, still on top of his engine. It took us less than 15 minutes to attach them to the appropriate motors. He was not very happy. He and his wife could have been killed because someone did not complete their job. He will not do business with that company again.

Always think and perform quality. It is why you were employed. The amount of pay does not determine the quality.

Order / Disorder

Maximum production and performance can only be accomplished in an orderly atmosphere. Your responsibility in this area is to do nothing that disrupts the order of your work environment. Fighting, loud and abusive verbal outbursts, drinking, or taking drugs on the job are just some of the behaviors that are unacceptable in this area. Reporting to work intoxicated or high is also unacceptable. Distracting fellow employees by stopping them from working to talk, make plans for later, or gossip are all forms of disruptive behavior. These actions may seem innocent enough, but in some cases they can be harmful.

Think

Think about how many common, everyday automobile or household accidents are caused by being distracted. Imagine what could happen if on a landscaping job someone distracts the backhoe operator. Stop for a minute and consider that you are in the hole when the operator is distracted.

The example doesn't have to be this gory, consider climbing a twenty foot ladder while either intoxicated or high on drugs. Picture yourself working under a ladder when someone else in that state is climbing. When you take the time, it is easy to see the connection between this type of behavior and the resulting theft to the employer.

Honesty/Lying

As was mentioned in Chapter 1, lying on the resumé is not acceptable. Lying is not an acceptable behavior at any time on the job. Your employer and your fellow workers must be able to build a trust around your honesty. That honesty starts when you list your qualifications on your job application and must be present throughout your career. When you answer yes to the question: "Did you check the water connection?", your boss and fellow workers must be able to rely on your answer. If you don't understand the question, request clarification. If you are not sure of your answer, add a qualifying statement. The answer "Yes" has a completely different meaning from "Yes, I checked it yesterday."

Physical Theft

Included in the responsibility of honesty is physical theft or stealing. Unlike the theft of earnings or profit discussed in the preceding paragraphs, physical theft is the use or removal of something belonging to the employer. This book is not long enough to list the innovative ways that people have successfully stolen from their employers. The unfortunate thing is that in a lot of cases, honest, church-going, upstanding, moral, individuals routinely steal from their bosses. The act is always rationalized -- made right in the mind of the individual -- by one or more of the following thought processes:

It's only a couple of pencils.
They throw more than this much paper away each day.
A little gasoline will never be missed.
They owe me this much fence material for the overtime I did not receive.
I'll bring the pens back next week.
What's one more long distance phone call with all the calls that are made from here daily?
These scraps will only be thrown away.
It's Sunday, the boss isn't using the truck anyway.
I am just borrowing or taking the computer

program so I can do company work at home .
and
The most popular rationalization of all:
Everyone else does it!

Everyone does not steal. And stealing it is, just as if you put a gun to your employer's head and took the payroll. If you cannot see this fact, you are missing part of the big picture. You are still living in a world of make believe and do not understand the basic premise of right and wrong. You will eventually end your career in jail. This form of stealing, unlike those discussed earlier, is not only punishable by loss of your job, it is punishable by spending time in jail.

Loyalty/Sabotage

Loyalty to an individual's home is usually the result of claiming it as home. Loyalty to another person, like respect, is usually earned. Loyalty to an employer is the result of accepting pay. You were hired because of what you brought with you to assist the employer. For those skills and/or knowledge, you are being paid. As long as you accept the pay from the employer, you owe your employer loyalty. In no way does this mean that you always have to agree with everything your employer says or does. It does mean that when your disagreement gets to the point where you can no longer remain loyal, it is time to quit or resign.

The violation of this responsibility comes in two basic forms: (1) industrial sabotage and (2) conflict of interest. Unfortunately both are rather common in today's work force.

Industrial Sabotage

Industrial sabotage does not have to be the intentional destruction of the plant or its equipment to be considered serious. Slowing down production by violating one of the other responsibilities is a form of sabotage when intentionally performed to reduce the employer's image or profit. The difference between an employee who is always coming in late and one that is involved in sabotage is the intent. When a group of employees decide to remain off the job because they want something more than was agreed to when they were hired, they are participating in industrial sabotage.

Other examples of actions that can be sabotage are:

The intentional destruction of property.
A computer "virus" that destroys the company's programs.
Intentional slowdown of production.
Sale of design specifications to a competitor.
Rumors.
Intentional concealment of poor quality.

All of the above are examples of company sabotage. They all have one outcome. That outcome is the destruction of the employer's profit or image. It may be rationalized initially that it is "no big thing," but it can result in the destruction of the employer. Not only is this behavior a violation of trust, it is also illegal and is punishable by a jail sentence.

Conflict of Interest

Conflict of interest, as discussed here, is "the earning of money by being in direct competition with your employer." The fact that you are working on your own time does not alter the seriousness of the behavior. It is still a form of theft. Like minor physical theft, this violation of responsibility is practiced daily. In fact, if a complete analysis of the founding of most businesses was accomplished, the results would be astounding. The free enterprise system is built on this violation of responsibility. It might be something as innocent as the unintentional passing of a small piece of information to a com-petitor's employee over drinks. Or, it may be as serious as starting your own business and taking with you the contacts you made while previously employed.

Example

You are working on a landscaping job when you hear the property owner mention that he wished he would have included the clearing of the area behind the pool fence in the contract. Instead of mentioning it to your boss, you wait until there is a break and approach the property owner with an offer to do it on your own time.

The property owner seems interested and to clinch the job you mention that the price will be cheaper than what your boss will charge. The property owner agrees. You are guilty of conflict of interest and of theft from your employer.

Sit back and analyze the facts:

(1)   If you were not working for your employer, you would not have heard the comment.
(2)   This is exactly the kind of work your employer hired you to do.
(3)   To get the job you emphasized that you would undercut your employer's fees.
(4)   You are now in business for yourself and if you use your employer's tools you have compounded your offense with physical theft.
(5)   Start looking for another job now, because when you are caught you will be dismissed.

If the owner had commented that since the grounds looked so good, he would like to find someone to clean his windows. And, if cleaning windows is not a service performed by your employer, you could offer to take on that job, on your own time, using your own tools, without being guilty of conflict of interest. Be careful how aggressively you look for this kind of work. Employers usually do not like their employees soliciting for personal work on company time.

Another Example

Unfortunately, many businesses got their start using this form of conflict of interest. It is a combination of moonlighting and account transferring. It is still a violation of responsibility and a form of theft.

Imagine you are employed as a plumber for "Keep It Dry Plumbing and Heating." You started as an apprentice and have learned your trade and the business very well. You recently mar-ried and are soon to be a parent. Recognizing a need for more money you decide to "moonlight."

Being careful not to solicit personal work while on the job, you put the following small ad in the local paper:

```
EXPERT  PLUMBING
All Work Guarenteed!

Call  226-7201
Nights and Weekends
```

You use your cousin's phone number because you don't think it is a good idea for your employer to read the ad and know you have branched out on your own. This is the free enterprise system. This is an example of drive and ambition. This is also a very good example of both conflict of interest and theft. You have just become your employer's competitor.

It will not stop here. You are embarked on the American Dream. Your night and weekend business will grow and prosper. Then you will have a hard time keeping awake and alert on your regular job. Initially your employer may not know what you are doing, but it will not be long before word gets around. You may even be asked if the rumors are true. You will be forced to make the big break, either because you are fired or simply because you are unable to keep up with all the work -- days, nights and weekends.

So, you quit. If you follow in the footsteps of some who have gone before, you may even take your account book from your previous employer and mail an advertisement to each and every person listed in it. It happens every day but it is still conflict of interest. It is also a violation of loyalty and if not strictly illegal at the very least unethical.

SUMMARY

To sum it all up, you only have one responsibility which is to fulfil the commitment of your employment. You were hired to fill a need of the employer. Because you fill this need, you are receiving a salary and maybe even benefits. In addition, as was discussed in Chapter 6, you are entitled to certain rights. Any action on your part that reduces the potential for your employer to pursue his goal -- owning a profit producing business -- is theft. This theft may not be punishable by law, but it is the justification used in most disciplinary actions. Many of these end with the dismissal of the offending employee. Dismissal, under these circumstances, will affect your ability to quickly find another job and may even forfeit your right to collect unemployment compensation.

NOTES

_____

_____

_____

_____

_____

_____

_____

_____

_____

_____

THE NEXT JOB
Pros and cons

For some strange reason it is far easier to find a job while employed than when you are not. There are probably many reasons for this fact:

(1) Less pressure.
(2) People out of work are often stereo-typed as losers.
(3) More relaxed approach to the job search.

Whatever the reason, the fact is that finding other employment while still working is easier and by far the best way to do it from a money standpoint.

WHY ANOTHER JOB?

There are a number of reasons to look for employment while you are still employed. The most common are:

(1) Job dissatisfaction.
(2) Advancement or increased responsibilities.
(3) Anticipated change of location.
(4) Better salary.

After reading the list, you will probably agree they could all be summed up under the first reason. However, there are slight differences as to the pros and cons of each of the reasons. Let's examine each of these reasons in sequence.

Job Dissatisfaction

The job is not what you expected. It is what you applied for and your employer is nice, but you do not like the work. You are giving it your best shot and your work is satisfactory. You just cannot see doing this for the rest of your life, not

even for the rest of the year.

You must look for other work. If you do not seek another job, you will destroy yourself with stress or frustration. Go back to the front of the book and start with your list of objectives. You may want to even consider adding objectives to the list based on your recent experience. If you need the paycheck to continue, do not let your present work suffer while you look for another job. At the same time, you want to actively seek a job you will be happy with.

If you like the employer and your work has been satisfactory, you may even consider approaching your supervisor with a request for a transfer within the company. Look carefully before you request a change to be sure you are not changing jobs because the "grass looks greener on the other side of the fence." Job dissatisfaction is one of the most common reasons that job applicants give as the reason for leaving current or previous positions.

Advancement or Increased Responsibility

Wouldn't it be great if our jobs grew as we did? This would be the ideal job, but seldom is this the case. Through school, experience, and maturity, we grow in our abilities and attitudes. Jobs rarely keep up with our changes. This leads to a form of job dissatisfaction but it is a little different from the one discussed previously.

In this case, the job was what you wanted, you could not have been happier, everything was great, but now you think you can be a supervisor. In fact, so does your employer. You even get assigned small work leader types of duties when available. The problem is that, at your present company, all the supervisor posi-

positions are filled with good, qualified people.

It's time to look elsewhere. You need to upgrade your objectives and also update your resumé. Add any new experience or training you received on this job, especially the assignments as work leader. It would be nice if you could count on your employer's support, but experience shows that the opposite is usually true. When an employer knows of the impending loss of an employee, even a very good one, the employer usually starts looking for a replacement.

Proceed with care. If you are very confident that your case is the exception, talk with your employer. The reference and support that your present employer can provide is priceless. A new employer will look very favorably on an applicant who has a positive recommendation from a present employer.

Change of Location

A pending change of location, either your own or the employer's can often restart the job search process. When this happens and you have been happy with your job, look for identical or similar work. On the other hand, if you are not really sure your present job is what you wanted, start the job search process by re-examining your objectives. Generally this type of job change is not the result of job related factors and there should be no reason for you not to talk with your employer. Your employers support and good reference will provide valuable assistance in your new job search.

If the relocation is based on personal reasons, the process can be slightly different. You may wait until you have one or more interviews scheduled before talking to your present employer. If you handle the situation tactfully and give your employer sufficient time to find a replacement, you will be assured of a good reference. You also avoid the possibility of being unemployed before you are ready to actually relocate.

Better Salary

All employers have limits on what they can pay for each type of skill and still maintain their profit. If you are happy with your work, except for the salary, before looking for another job, ask for a raise. The worst your supervisor can do is refuse. This refusal at least lets you know where

you stand with your present company. You may find that you are being considered for a raise or even that one has already been approved. No matter what the reason, when you find that your present job does not pay the salary you need, you must seek employment elsewhere. Fortunately, because of differences in management, overhead, and other factors, all companies do not have the same salary limits for the same skills.

Your approach in performing the job search should follow the processes discussed in the previous two situations. It should be professional, without malice -- after all it is not the employer's fault that you now require a higher salary than they can afford -- and should not damage your chances of receiving a positive recommendation from your employer.

There are right and wrong ways to ask for a raise. The right way is to request a meeting to discuss your performance, and during the discussion -- assuming it is positive -- ask about the possibilities of a raise. The wrong way to approach your supervisor is to threaten to leave if you don't get a salary increase by next month. Threatening or appearing to threaten seldom results in good feelings and, if for some reason a raise is not possible, the supervisor will begin to look for your replacement.

FREQUENT JOB CHANGES

Making frequent job changes presents a number of negative factors you may want to consider. Most people perform best when some form of order is present in their daily lives. Job hopping or changing does not allow this order to settle in. This can be looked at as challenging but also can result in additional stress.

There is also another factor to consider -- credit. Frequent job changing, even for the best of reasons, does not present an image of stability. Loan companies and banks are impressed by an individual's stability. Therefore, changing jobs frequently can affect your ease of obtaining credit. Credit and the requirements to obtain it are discussed in detail in Chapters 12 and 16.

UNEMPLOYMENT COMPENSATION

There are times when, through no fault of the employee or employer, employees are dismissed or laid off. Some of the reasons for this are:

(1) A changing economy,
(2) Seasonal fluctuation of demand,
(3) Company wide reorganizations, and
(4) Acts of nature (fire, hurricane, flood, even the death of the owner).

When this happens the employee may be eligible to receive from $95 to $260 a week in unemployment compensation. The amount of money received and the length of the eligibility depends upon the state of residence, length of employment, amount of salary, and a number of other factors. This entitlement is the result of Title 5, Chapter 85, of the United States Code which sets responsibility for the law with the Secretary of Labor. However, the compensation is made by the state employment security agencies, and each state establishes the requirements, including payment schedule, for its residents.

Eligibility Requirements

All states require that you have had a sufficient qualifying period. This is usually a requirement that you were fully employed 12 of the preceding 18 months. To collect benefits, you must be unemployed and must file a claim at your nearest state unemployment office. Also, you must be able to work and be available to accept full-time employment. All states provide for disqualification if you: voluntarily leave your job without good cause, are dismissed for misconduct connected with your work, or refuse suitable work without good cause.

Filing a Claim

Unemployment compensation is not charity, it is an insurance designed to help you survive while you have to search for a new job through no fault of your own. If you find yourself in this situation, immediately file your claim. This establishes your entitlement and starts the clock if your state has a waiting period. If, during the waiting period, you find another job, you have lost nothing. The filing for unemployment can reduce the stress and allow you to proceed with an organized job search. For that you will want to go back to Chapter 1 and start with your objectives and resumé.

Any time you are laid off from work, other than for poor work performance or misconduct,

and you meet the eligibility requirements, you are entitled to unemployment compensation. To file your claim, you need to go to the closest state unemployment office with your social security card and any documentation that supports your qualifying period and earnings level -- pay stubs.

You will be directed to complete a claim form and may have a short interview with an unemployment counselor.

Hearing

Your claim is forwarded from the state labor board to your previous employer. If your employer claims that you voluntarily quit or were dismissed for misconduct, your claim will be rejected. When this happens, you have the right to a hearing. You will be notified that your claim has been rejected and the date and time of your hearing. At the hearing will be a person from the state labor board, someone representing your employer and you. You are entitled to have representation but it is at your own expense. The state representative will give both you and your former employer an opportunity to make justifying statements. Yours will be as to why you think you are entitled to the unemployment compensation, and your employer will state why you don't have a valid claim. Based on these statements and the laws governing eligibility, the state representative will make a judgement. This judgement is not final, either party -- you or your employer -- may request a higher level appeal. However, only in the most complex of cases is this necessary.

If you file a claim and think you are entitled to compensation, by all means attend the hearing when one is scheduled. Unemployment compensation insurance costs your employer money. So, some employers reject all claims hoping that the employees will not show up for the hearings and thereby jeopardize their right to compensation.

The details of all the state laws fill volumes of text and are far too extensive for this discussion. This preceding discussion is just an overview of the general requirements to inform you of this right. For more information, contact your closest state labor office.

GIVING NOTICE

For a long time it has been an accepted tradition in the work force for both employer and employee to give the other notice of impending separation. Everyone has seen a cartoon or TV sitcom where the employee opens his/her pay envelope to find the dreaded "pink slip." The "pink slip" was the employer's way of notifying the terminated employee that notice was served and in one or two weeks the employee would receive his last pay check.

Why?

This custom of giving notice was intended to allow a good employee the opportunity to find employment upon separation from the current employer. Employers still provided notice when, for one of the many reasons discussed earlier, the company must cut back the work force. An employer is not required or expected to provide notice when the employee has been guilty of misconduct.

As a result of the good faith of the employers, employees started giving notice when they had found a new job. This was done as a courtesy to the employer, to provide time for hiring a replacement, and even to assist in training the replacement.

Now

For a number of reasons, a certain amount of mistrust has entered the employer/employee relationship. This mistrust has resulted in employees being laid-off without notice. Employees have also been immediately terminated when they give notice to the employer.

As a manager, I fail to see the logic of this practice. The employer needs this time to start the search to fill the vacancy. It is as if the employer is saying, "If you are not going to be here two weeks from now, I will start getting along without you now!" This does not make sense. It only turns what could be a smooth transition into a crisis situation. It does happen. My wife, Jean, and at least two of our children have had this happen to them.

The situation has become so serious that a number of states, including Virginia, allow an employee to collect unemployment compensation when an employer does not honor an employee's two week notice.

SUGGESTION

Be aware of the personnel practices of your employer. Talk to other employees, be observant, don't rely on rumors. Get a feel of not only the "why" when a person leaves but also the "how."

Continue to give adequate notice. This is the professional way to end a satisfactory work relationship. Giving notice allows you to determine when you can start the new job, and the prospective employer will be impressed that you want to honor the notice period with your present employer.

If your employer terminates you on the spot, contact your state labor office to check on your eligibility for unemployment compensation. At the same time, notify your new employer that you are available to start work immediately. The very worst that can happen is that you will have a short period of vacation without pay.

Now, what about all that money you will be making?

MONEY

I'm rich! I'm rich!

III

Once you have a job and are bringing home some money, you need a plan. Yes a plan. Without a plan, you will find yourself living at a higher level than your earnings will support or you will never have money when you really need it.

Chapter 9 discusses the factors that reduce your earnings before you even receive your pay check. Included in the discussion are a couple of sample pay stubs and a table showing different hourly wages and the final take home pay of the employee.

Chapter 10 explores the ever important Budget. A frank analysis of the difference between wants and needs is followed by a discussion of various types of budgets. Expense items are evaluated by dollar amount rather than as a percentage of income. Jo Ann's efforts at budget making are examined along with the steps to be followed by the reader in developing his or her own budget.

Chapter 11 presents the various types of checking accounts along with a discussion of the advantages and disadvantages of each. Financial terms associated with having a checking account are defined, and suggestions for shopping for the optimum account and bank are provided.

The chapter then demonstrates the correct way to write a check followed by a discussion of the record keeping necessary to balance the checkbook. The steps to balance the checking account statement are introduced, and the reader follows these steps in balancing a sample statement.

Chapter 12 discusses the need for and proper use of credit cards. The different kinds of credit cards and what to look for when shopping for a credit card are discussed. Included is a discussion of the need to maintain a good credit history and the actions that affect credit ratings. The chapter closes with a description of the individual's credit rights and responsibilities.

Chapter 13 is devoted to the forms used, the help available and instructions for filing your income tax return. The chapter emphasizes the need for good record keeping and the simplicity of filing the Federal Form 1040EZ. The reader watches Jo Ann prepare her 1990 federal tax return. The chapter closes by discussing filing deadlines, state returns and special tax provisions.

"TAKE HOME" OR "NET" PAY
Where did it all go?

By now I am sure you realize that $5 per hour is not $200 a week for you to spend. The difference between what you make and what you take home is determined in a large part by what you did in the previous section. Taxes, state and federal, FICA, health and life insurance you signed up for, and any savings plan you may have decided to join all take a cut from your pay check. The amount left after these deductions is called "take home" or "net" pay.

IT DOESN'T ALL GO HOME

Each state or city you live in will have its own set of rules and taxes. Some, but not many, don't tax an individual's income. For the purpose of helping you compute your take home pay, I have created a state called Anywhere, USA, with a theoretical tax structure for single persons, where the first $3,500 of earnings each year is tax free.

The table below shows this theoretical tax table for salaries up to $25,000.

Anywhere, USA, State Tax Withholding Table

Salary over…	but not over…	Tax…	of excess above…
$3,500	$5,999	2%	$3,500
$6,000	$9,999	$50 + 3%	$6,000
$10,000	$14,999	$170 + 4%	$10,000
$15,000	$24,999	$370 + 5%	$15,000

Using this state tax table, the FICA percentage, and the Federal Income Tax rates in effect in 1990, the following table was developed.

Take Home Pay (THP) Table

Hourly Pay	Weekly Pay	Federal Tax	State/Local Tax	Fica Tax	Weekly (THP)	Hourly (THP)
$ 5	$200	$16	$ 3.58	$15.02	$165.40	$ 4.13
$ 6	$240	$22	$ 5.18	$18.02	$194.80	$ 4.87
$ 7	$280	$28	$ 6.78	$21.03	$224.19	$ 5.60
$ 8	$320	$34	$ 8.69	$24.03	$253.28	$ 6.33
$ 9	$360	$40	$10.69	$27.04	$282.27	$ 7.06
$10	$400	$46	$12.69	$30.04	$311.27	$ 7.78

You can easily see that in order to bring home $200 a week, you will have to earn approximately $6.25 per hour. Depending upon the tax laws of your state, you may have a take home pay amount smaller or larger than the one shown. Remember that this table does not reflect decisions you made regarding medical insurance, life insurance, savings plans and any other authorized deductions.

Variations

You can use the table for computing take home pay (THP) for less than full dollar hourly amounts. For instance, if you make $6.50 per hour your weekly THP will be $209.50. This amount is arrived at by subtracting the amount of THP for the hourly rate of $6 -- $194.80 from the amount of THP for $7 -- $224.19. Divide the difference -- 29.39 by two and add that amount -- 14.70 to the amount of THP for the $6 per hour rate -- 194.80 to arrive at the amount for a $6.50 hourly rate -- $209.50.

The formula for working with $6.25 or $6.75 an hour is similar. To figure the amount for the quarter of the dollar, simply divide the result of the subtraction by four instead of two. The rest of the steps are the same. For the 75 cent computation, after dividing by four, multiply that amount by three before completing the rest of the steps.

Let's try another example. The amount of estimated weekly THP for earnings of $5.75 an hour is $187.45. To arrive at this figure, subtract the amount for the hourly rate of $5 -- $165.40 from the amount for $6 -- $194.80. Divide the difference -- $29.40 by four and multiply this

amount -- 7.35 by three for a total of 22.05. Add this amount to $165.40 and your estimated take home pay is $187.45.

Try it yourself, using your local tax rules, it is not hard to do.

Dependents

This book is written for the single wage earner. However, I realize that some of you may be married and even have additional dependents. Each dependent will reduce the amount of the federal income tax withheld from your pay by $5.50 per week. In addition, your state tax may also be reduced by a few cents -- less than a dollar -- per dependent, per week. The FICA deduction is not affected by the number of dependents you claim.

PAY STATEMENTS

There are a number of types of pay statements or pay stubs used by companies to document, for the employee, what was withdrawn from the pay check. Two of the more common types are presented below for Jo Ann Graduate. They are very easy to read and understand, and the amounts can be verified from the table presented earlier. The major difference between the two is: the first statement shows the computation for the gross earnings, including hours worked and overtime, if any; while the second one presents all earnings as one total without separating regular and overtime earnings. In either case the net pay amount is identical.

Example 1

PERIOD ENDED	REG.	O.T.	REGULAR	OVERTIME	OTHER	TOTAL	F.I.C.A.	FEDERAL WITH. TAX	STATE TAX	A	B	C	NET PAY	NAME OR INITIALS
6/2/89	40	—	240.00	—	—	240.00	18.02	22.00	5.18				194.80	Jo Ann Graduate
	HRS. WORKED		EARNINGS				DEDUCTIONS							

PAY STATEMENT

THIS IS A STATEMENT OF YOUR EARNINGS AND DEDUCTIONS AS REPORTED TO THE FEDERAL AND STATE GOVERNMENTS. RETAIN IT PERMANENTLY FOR YOUR TAX RECORDS.

Example 2

Earnings Statement

For period ending: ___6/2___ 19_89_

Employer: GREEN TOE NURSERY

Employee: GRADUATE Dept: ___3___

Social Security No.: 254-71-2856

Gross Pay $240.00

Deductions:

F.I.C.A.	18	02
Federal Withholding Tax	22	00
State Withholding Tax	5	18
City Withholding Tax		
Insurance		
Dues		
Other		
Total Deductions	45	20
Net Pay	194	80

With the widespread use of computers, a more comprehensive pay statement has emerged that a number of large companies are now using. This statement is called the wage and earnings statement. The wage and earnings statement includes yearly cumulative totals-to-date for each of the earnings and deductible elements. Some of the wage and earnings statements from larger companies may contain retirement, leave, and other nice-to-have employee information in addition to the earnings data discussed earlier.

No matter what format is used, when you encounter an item on your pay statement that you do not understand ask for clarification from your supervisor or your employer's personnel department. For tax purposes, it is a good idea to keep your pay statements. This is especially true if you change jobs and move a number of times during the year. It is possible that your official W-2 form may not reach you and the only records you have to base your tax return on are your pay statements.

MONTHLY TAKE HOME PAY

The easiest way to compute your monthly take home pay is to multiply the weekly figure by four. This will not be a mathematically correct figure, but will serve as a rough, conservative -- low estimate. In fact, if you use this method of computing your monthly THP to develop your budget, at the end of the year you will have four weeks of pay that hasn't been spent. If you must be mathematically accurate, multiply the weekly amount of THP by 4.334. This will give you an estimate of your monthly take home pay within a few pennies of the actual amount.

For Instance

If Jo Ann is making $5 an hour, the table reflects her take home pay amount to be $165.40 per week. Multiplying this amount by four shows a monthly amount of $661.60 while multiplying by 4.334 results in $716.84. If she is paid weekly and uses the first amount to budget her expenses, every three months she will receive an extra weekly check. If she is paid every two weeks she will receive an extra two week check approximately every six months. This can be a nice, easy way to save.

EXTRA WITHHOLDING TAX

Remember, as discussed in Chapter 5, you have the option of having the Internal Revenue Service withhold extra money from your salary each pay day. If you find that when you have money you spend it, these extra withholdings can be used as a form of forced savings. I do not recommend this method of saving because you do not earn interest on the money withheld.

The extra check method, discussed above, is a superior form of forced savings because it allows you to put the money in some form of interest bearing account on a regular basis. Even more preferred may be joining a form of savings plan where not only is the money withheld from your pay, and earns interest, but is more difficult to withdraw on a whim.

Now that you have earned the money, what are you going to do with it?

NOTES

_____

_____

_____

_____

_____

_____

_____

_____

_____

_____

_____

THE BUDGET

A little for this, a little for that, a lot for rent. 10

In the last chapter it should have become very obvious that what you earn and what you get to take home are two different amounts. The take home amount being substantially less than the amount earned. Your challenge is to use the amount you take home in a way that will provide you with a comfortable and fulfilling lifestyle. Everyone is different, there is no one set of things that will make everyone comfortable and happy. You now have to look at the things that you need, want, and are interested in, and place a cost and value on each. Only by doing this will your budget stand any chance of success.

NEEDS

This is an area that has changed much in the last 20 to 30 years. Items that were considered luxuries in the 1960s are considered needs today. Medical insurance, your own car or other form of personal transportation, a telephone, and even a dishwasher now fall into the category some people call needs.

As my son, Jeff, pointed out to me during one of our discussions, needs are really determined by the individual. What he was doing was creating a gray area in the original definition. He was breaking needs up into absolute and individual necessities.

Absolute

There are some basic survival needs that everyone has. In fact, each will be discussed in detail in the remainder of this book. They are:

1. Shelter, including utilities
2. Food
3. Clothing -- basic body covering for protection from the elements

Individual

Once the basic needs are met, there remains a full set of individual needs based on work requirements, location of residence, available time, and desired lifestyle.

Examples

Jo Ann is told by her employer that a telephone is recommended for all Green Toe Nursery employees. He explains that, when the employees have a phone, the supervisors can make changes in work assignments based on weather conditions, delivery of required materials, and customer preferences. By making these changes over the phone, both the employee and employer save time and unnecessary traveling. Jo Ann takes the suggestion seriously and makes arrangements to get a phone. In this case, not only is the phone a need that moves up to the absolute category, a portion of the expense may be tax deductible. Expenses of this nature will be discussed in Chapter 22.

Jo Ann finds it easier and quicker to report directly to the job site instead of first going out to the Green Toe Nursery each morning. She checks around and discovers that no one else in the company lives close to her home and, since the Green Toe Nursery is not located in the heart of town, there is no public transportation available. This does not automatically establish a requirement for personal transportation. Jo Ann must weigh the advantages of finding living quarters closer to her place of business against the cost of purchasing and maintaining a vehicle. If she decides that the personal mode of transportation is a must, it also moves up to her absolute need category. The cost of personal transportation is discussed in Section IV.

Jo Ann's job is not the cleanest in the world. In fact, it is quite dirty. As the commercials say, her clothes have "ground in dirt and mud." She decides that she needs either her own washing machine and dryer or she must have them very close by. Doing wash for Jo Ann is going to be at least an every other night chore. Accessibility to a washing machine and dryer may still not be an absolute need but Jo Ann decides to move it from the "want" category to the individual need category.

MAKE YOUR LIST

It's your turn. Get a sheet of paper and make three columns. Starting at the left, label the columns Absolute Needs, Individual Needs, and Wants. Now divide each of the columns in two and starting at the left, label each of these sub-columns Item and Cost. Your paper should look like this:

Absolute Needs		Individual Needs		Wants	
Item	Cost	Item	Cost	Item	Cost

Keep this piece of paper, as you go through the rest of the book you will fill it in with actual costs or budgeted amounts. When you are finished reading this book you will have the data you need for the first step towards smart money management: your *budget*.

YOUR BUDGET

What It Is

The budget is a plan. It is not something new, you budget all the time. When you look in your wallet and see that you have $14 to last through the weekend, you immediately form a mental budget. You may say to yourself, "If I go to the movies with John and pay my own way, I will still have $9 left. This will leave me enough for a hamburger, fries and soda, and the $5 admission to the Rock Concert at the community center tomorrow. What I won't have is gas money for transportation."
As you work out this minor challenge, you are budgeting your funds. Making up a budget simply means that before you spend any money you first make a plan. By doing this, you greatly reduce the little unpleasant situations where you open your wallet and, just like "Old Mother Hubbord's cupboard," you find it is bare.

Even in the survival mode, a well thought out budget can result in providing funds for the things you really want, such as a vacation, a trip, a car, or new clothes.

How It Works

The Appendix provides a list of titles for a number of excellent books that cover money management and budgeting in great detail. Some of these books even show sample budgets and provide you with percentages to use as a guide for estimating how close your budget matches the "average" for people with similar income.

As you read this chapter and the recommended books, remember, only you can develop your budget. More importantly, only you can carry it out and make it work. But then, you are the one that gets to reap the benefits of your good money management.

SAMPLE AVERAGE BUDGET

Expense Item		Income		
		$5 Hour $866 mo.	$7.50 Hour $1,300 mo.	$10 Hour $1,733 mo.
Taxes & FICA	22%	$ 190	$ 286	$ 381
Rent	30%	260	390	520
Food	15%	130	195	260
Transportation	9%	78	117	156
Utilities	6%	52	78	104
Personal	4%	35	52	69
Insurance	4%	35	52	69
Contributions, Savings, and Loans Payments	10%	86	130	174
Total Outlay	100%	$866	$1,300	$1,733

This may be interesting information, however everyone's budget is different. Don't be concerned if yours is not even close to the above table, especially if your amounts are less in most categories. The above table is the kind used by financial institutions to determine the first cut when screening a new borrower's ability to pay. What they are really saying is that if you have more than 91% of your pay committed to expenses, they will have to take a very close look at how much, if any, money they will lend. This will be discussed in detail in Chapter 16.

Steps to Follow

There are six easy-to-follow steps in setting up and using a budget. They are:

(1) Identify your expense items
(2) Honestly classify them (absolute needs, individual needs, and wants)
(3) Apply cost data
(4) Re-evaluate the classifications and revise as required
(5) Execute the plan -- your budget
(6) Keep good records

List

Using a fresh sheet of paper, make another list just like you did for your resumé objective. This time list any items of expense that come to mind. When you are done, you may have items like clothing, shoes, movies, gifts, dinner, and even a new stereo. Hopefully, you also listed rent, food, phone, utilities, laundry, medical costs, contributions, and transportaion. If you have a car, you should also have listed gasoline, insurance, and maintenance. If you owe money on the car, you should have listed the loan amount. If you missed any of these items go back and complete your list. Your budget will only be as good as your list is complete.

Classify

You have already started the second step. The sheet of paper with the six columns you made up earlier will be used to form the structure for your personal budget. It is very important that you place your expense items in the correct columns. For instance, if you live in an area that has an excellent transportation system that will pick you up one block from your residence and take you to within two blocks of your place of employment, is a car really an absolute need?

Do you really need $100 a month for new clothes? Can you afford to eat out every night? Must you live alone or can you cut your rent by sharing? Can you live with your parents? When making just $5 an hour can you afford to give presents to family members that cost $50 each? Is the $700 stereo really an individual need or is it a want?

The rest of this book is devoted to helping you make these decisions by providing alternatives for your consideration. Even after reading this book from cover to cover, the final decisions are still going to be yours. Being honest with yourself is the key to this step.

Cost

To provide help with the cost element, some research using selected cities around the country was performed. As a result of this research, the following table of average cost, for each of the stated items of expense, was compiled. In all cases, the premise used was of a single individual, living alone, doing their own cooking and making use of public transportation. Since clothing, including jewelry and cosmetics is such a personal expense, it is not listed as one of the necessary expenses. You will have to provide that estimated cost based on your own tastes and needs.

Section VII is devoted to a discussion on clothing and ways of expanding your wardrobe. Whatever your estimate for clothing, remember to subtract a like amount from the item listed later called "left over cash."

MONTHLY FIXED EXPENSES

Item	Range	Average
Rent & Utilities	$250 - $300	$275
Food	110 - 150	130
Transportation	50 - 100	75
Medical Insurance	25 - 45	35
Totals	$435 - $595	$515

Contrary to most other books on budgets, I take the stand that you must allocate yourself a minimum amount of personal cash. It is true that, unlike rent, this amount is not really fixed. However, experience dictates that if you do not allow for some personal cash each month, your budget is doomed to failure. Plan on setting aside at least one dollar a day, which in today's economy may not be enough. One dollar a day will not even buy you a soda and snack cake in some areas of our country. So, unless you are including this type of expense under the item for food, consider one dollar a day the absolute minimum. The amount you budget for food, though listed as fixed, can also be adjusted, especially during lean times.

Using the average column from this table and the take home pay information from Chapter 9, you begin to get a feel for the impact that a dollar per hour increase will have on your ability to survive. The table below presents the monthly take home pay as four and one third (4.334) times the weekly amount.

SAMPLE BASIC BUDGET APPLIED AGAINST VARYING WAGES

Hourly wage	$5	$6	$7	$8	$9	$10
Monthly THP	$716	$843	$971	$1097	$1222	$1348
Rent & Utilities	275	275	275	275	275	275
Food	130	130	130	130	130	130
Transportation	75	75	75	75	75	75
Medical Insurance	35	35	35	35	35	35
Personal Expenses	30	30	30	30	30	30
Left over cash	171	298	426	552	677	803

Now wait a minute, don't start spending the excess yet. This is a basic budget. The table doesn't show anything put aside for clothing, entertainment, savings, church and other contributions, and gifts. It contains nationwide averages for the expense amounts and reflects the use of public transportation rather than a personal vehicle, as the primary method of travel. And only one dollar a day has been budgeted for personal expenses.

In addition, for some unexplained reason, as we earn more take home pay, our satisfaction with the "basics" changes and we desire more expensive places to live and even begin to spend more for food. Throw in a new or bigger car, more expensive medical insurance, and we have confirmed what the advertisement agencies have always known -- if we have it, we will spend it!

Format

It is now time to put all your data into a format that is usable as a budget. Using your list of items classified and with the cost column filled in, make a new chart. Put those needs, including your individual needs, that cost the same amount each month, under a heading called fixed, or uncontrolled expenses, and everything else under a heading called variable, or controlled expenses.

Let's take a look at how Jo Ann is doing. She has her six column list and has started doing her budget.

Her budget looks like this:

Take Home Pay   **$843**

Fixed Expenses:
Rent	$250	
Utilities	35	
Phone	20	
Food	140	
Car	50	
Medical Insurance	25	
Total Fixed		**520**

Variable Expenses:
Clothing	45	
Gifts	12	
Church	10	
Hairdresser	10	
Entertainment	45	
Personal	50	
Total Variable		**172**

Total expenses   **692**

Left over cash   **$ 151**

As you look at Jo Ann's budget, she is thinking to herself that she can save $80 and still have $71 extra each month to spend or put toward a great vacation for next year. She didn't expect her budget to look this good.

Looking at her budget, can you identify something she may have missed? Hint, it has to do with the car expense. There is no car on the road today where the owner can get by on a total of $50 per month.

Re-evaluate

Sure enough, after giving it some thought, it becomes obvious to Jo Ann that not only did she forget the car insurance, which is paid every six months, she also forgot the small items of gas, oil, and routine maintenance. The $50 she included is what she is paying back to her Mother for the loan she used to purchase the car.

For more information on this item of expense be sure to read Section IV for a detailed breakdown of the cost of owning and operating your own car. For now, Jo Ann estimates her monthly cost for gas, oil and routine maintenance at $30. She knows her insurance cost $420 every 6 months or $70 per month and to be safe, she decides to set aside $20 per month to cover long term maintenance items. She enters the $70 for insurance and $20 for long term maintenance under fixed expenses and the $30 for gas, oil, and routine maintenance under the variable expenses. Jo Ann also decides to put $30 per month into savings.

Revise

Jo Ann's revised budget is presented below.

Take Home Pay   **$843**

Fixed Expenses:
Rent	$250	
Utilities	35	
Phone	20	
Food	140	
Car: Loan	50	
Insurance	70	
Maintenance	20	
Medical Insurance		25
Total Fixed		**$610**

Variable Expenses:

Clothing	$45
Gifts	12
Church	10
Gas, Oil, etc.	30
Hairdresser	10
Entertainment	45
Savings	30
Personal	50

Total Variable	**$232**
Total expenses	**842**
Left over cash	**$ 1**

Execute

Jo Ann is not too upset at the final outcome. In the back of her mind she knew something was not right with the first budget. She also knows that with a little care controlling her expenses in clothing, entertainment and personal items she will have no problem in meeting her budget. She also gets great satisfaction in knowing that she will be saving money for both car maintenance and for future use.

By budgeting as much as she has for clothing, gifts, entertainment and personal expenses she has made the decision that those things are more important in her life than saving or investing. This means that she is very unlikely to be able to afford any large purchases in the near future, unless she buys them on credit.

Once you have established your budget, it is a good idea to check on your execution each month for at least the first three months. After that, a periodic check, like at six month intervals, is recommended.

Records

The better the records you keep, the easier it will be to verify your success. Everyone knows that most people are unable to account for each penny, or even dollar, they spend, however, if you are going to try to live by a budget, it is not only recommended, it is required.

There are three things you can do that will help:

(1)   Carry a piece of paper around with you and list all your expenses;
(2)   Always ask for receipts when making cash purchases, and
(3)   Open a checking account.

In addition to having automatic receipts, the more things you use a check to buy, the easier it is to keep track of your expenses. Each week, you will need to make a record of all your cash expenses from the piece of paper and the receipts you have collected. You will also need to keep a good checking account ledger so that each month you will be able to verify your success in following your budget.

By following these simple steps, you will know what you can or cannot afford to buy. You will know this in advance and will have the satisfaction of knowing that you are in control of your finances. You can derive some very important benefits by keeping monthly records. You will readily see if you are living within your budget. And, at the end of the year, while all your friends are searching for their income tax records, you will know exactly where yours are. In addition, since you keep monthly records, you only have the 12 separate months to deal with, not a shoe box full of little slips of paper. How sweet it is...

SUMMING IT UP

Not keeping good records of expenses, failing to develop and stick to a budget and spending money on impulse are the three major reasons why adults of all ages have financial management problems. These problems can quickly go from a lot of bills, to bills unpaid, and, in no time at all, bad credit and bankruptcy.

If you have never developed a budget, now is not too early to do so. But remember, before you can make a meaningful budget you either must have records of your expenses or a very good idea of the amounts.

The budget alone will not make you financially secure or rich, but sticking to it and executing it properly will help you to achieve your goals.

THE CHECKING ACCOUNT
I can't be out of money; I still have checks!   11

One of the best aids in keeping to your budget will be a checking account. In some cases, you can have your pay deposited directly into your account. This is called direct deposit and is a must if your bank is not close to your residence or place of employment.

CHOOSING A BANK

The very first thing you will want to do is to choose a financial institution. It can be a "full" service bank, a savings and loan institution, or a credit union. At this point in your career, they all offer the services that you will be looking for, and in this chapter the term "bank" will be used to refer to them all. The services offered by these banks include: checking accounts, savings accounts, Automatic Teller Machine (ATM) cards, and credit cards. Each of these services will be discussed in detail. It is not a requirement that all of these services be obtained from the same bank.

At this time, you should be looking for a bank close to your home or work place that offers the type of checking account you feel fits your needs, at a competitive cost. Checking accounts, unless you can meet the requirements for interest checking, which will be discussed later in this chapter, all cost money. The fees charged and services offered differ from bank to bank. It will pay you to shop around if you have more than one bank in a location convenient to your home or work place.

WHAT TYPE OF CHECKING ACCOUNT?

The customer can usually choose from three kinds of checking accounts. They are the Reg-

ular, Budget, and Interest checking accounts. Each will be discussed in some detail, but remember, the rules are set by the individual bank. You must study the rules and fees of each before making a choice. Some banks have mixtures of the three accounts as in the credit union's "share draft" account. Most large banks also offer money market accounts for the customer who can afford to deposit and leave $5,000, or even $10,000, in the account. Money Market accounts usually pay substantially higher interest than the interest account that will be discussed.

Regular Checking

If you plan to be writing more than six or eight checks a month and do not have $1,000 or more to leave in your checking account month after month, this is the account for you.

You can usually write an unlimited number of checks, and, if you keep a minimum amount -- $200 - $500 -- depending on the bank, in the account, you do not have to pay a service charge. If your balance during any one day in the month falls below the minimum, you will be charged from $2 to $6, based on the bank, for that month's service.

Budget or Special Checking

If you don't have enough money to meet the minimum daily balance and plan to write less than six to eight checks a month this is the account for you. There is usually no minimum balance required. However, there is a fee, $2.50 to $3 for which you can write, depending on the bank, up to six or eight checks per month. If, during a month, you write more than the allowed number of checks, the bank charges you an additional fee -- between 50 cents and a dollar, for each additional check.

Interest Checking

If you want unlimited check writing privileges and can keep a minimum daily balance in your checking account of $1,000 or greater, this is the checking account for you. Be careful, it is not uncommon for banks to require minimum balances in excess of $2,000 for this type of account. You draw interest on all the money in the account, but if the balance, on any one day, falls below the bottom limit, you not only stop drawing interest, you are also charged a service fee. This fee will range from $4 to $10 per month until the daily balance again exceeds the bottom limit.

A Comparison

Types of Checking Accounts

Regular	Budget	Interest
No service charge	Small Service charge	No service charge
Small minimum balance	No minimum balance	High minimum balance
Unlimited checks	Charge for extra checks over 6 or 8	Unlimited checks
No interest on $ balance	No interest on $ balance	Interest on $ balance

Note: In most cases you have to pay for the printing of your personalized checks -- $7 - $10 per 200.

Options

With each of the accounts above, you can obtain one or more of the following options:

(1) Money Card
(2) Automatic Transfers
(3) Direct Deposit
(4) Overdraft Protection

Money (ATM) Cards

Danger! Danger! Danger! There are two potential pitfalls with the frequent use of money cards. The first is that with some cards there is a charge for each withdrawal made from a nonmember bank system. These charges, which can be up to one dollar per use, add up and should be treated as a "service" or "check cashing" charge. The second pitfall is that people often forget to keep the bank slips and to post the transactions in their check book on a regular basis. If you do not have much money in your checking account and forget to post money card withdrawals, your checkbook will be impossible to balance. And, if you can't balance your checkbook, you will quickly create problems with your account.

If you write a check and do not have the funds to cover it, the bank will return it to the person you gave it to labeled "refused, not sufficient funds." The bank will then charge you a fee for returning the check. At my bank, the fee is $12 for each check returned. The place you wrote it is authorized to charge you an additional fee, which can be $15 or more for processing the collection of their money. This will quickly put you into a spiral from which it may be very difficult to recover.

If you must have a Money Card, and some people find them very convenient, be careful where you use it. Also, as discussed in the previous chapter, be sure to keep meticulous records. The careless use of this banking option has been responsible for its share of overdrawn accounts and ruined credit records.

Automatic Transfers

Most banks will transfer money from your checking account to pay fixed amount bills each month and even to move money from your checking to your savings account. This service is usually free or is provided at a very small fee -- less than 25 cents per transaction. In addition to saving you the hassle of writing a check and the postage to mail it, automatic transfer can be used as a supplement to the Budget checking account by decreasing the number of checks you need to write.

Direct Deposit

This service insures that your paycheck gets deposited in your account on the same day each pay period. You do not have to worry about getting to the bank before it closes on payday. Direct deposit is an excellent free service and can save you time and unnecessary stress, unless you have the burning desire to look at and feel each pay check.

Overdraft Protection

Unfortunately, many of us have times when we are not sure if our checking account has a sufficient balance to cover the check that is about to be written. There may be times when, no matter how hard you try, you will not post your money card withdrawals in your checkbook and a check will arrive at the bank before your deposit does. In banking, this results in an over-drawn account. That is, there is not enough money in your account to allow the bank to honor your check.

This is a serious situation and, in most states, if done intentionally, is a violation of law, and you can be charged with "theft by taking" or criminal fraud.

There are three ways to prevent this from accidently happening:

(1)   You can keep a high enough balance in your account so it will never run out.

(2)   You can cover the amount by pre-authorizing a transfer of funds from any savings you have in the bank into your checking account to cover the overdraft. In most cases, the transfer from your savings account is free; you only lose the interest the money would have earned.

(3)   You can use overdraft protection.

Arrangements for overdraft protection must be made in advance and usually requires having a credit card. When you use a credit card to cover the overdraft, it is like making a loan. You will be charged for the service, and if the transferred amount is not paid during your credit card's next billing cycle, you will be charged interest. Either the second or third choice will save you money as well as sleepless nights.

OPENING A CHECKING ACCOUNT

When you decide to open an account at the bank of your choice, you will be required to provide personal information. The information you will be asked to provide, in addition to name, address, and phone number, is previous address, employer, business phone, driver's license number, social security number, name and address of nearest relative and an additional reference. You will also be asked if you have accounts at any other banks and possibly their account numbers. This information and some money is all that is required to open your checking account.

Where's Your Money?

I strongly suggest that you request an explanation of the rules your bank uses for clearing checks you deposit into your account. This is especially true if you are going to be depositing checks from "out of town" banks. Generally, the policy is that, until you have established a good record with the bank, you will not have immediate access to these funds until the check clears. You need to know when the funds will be available for your use. The amount of time your bank can prevent your access to these funds is determined by the location of the other bank and the laws of your state. The money from payroll checks, if directly deposited, is usually available immediately, no matter what bank the checks are drawn against.

WRITING A CHECK

Don't Take Chances

You work too hard for your money to lose it because of careless check writing. Even if you have had a checking account before, chances are no one ever showed you how to correctly write a check. Your checks must be written so that they are unalterable -- can't be changed. Look at the check below.

It appears harmless enough. It was written for $4.16, to pay for some items purchased at the drug store. So, what's wrong? Because it was written quickly and without the proper care, it could just possibly clear the bank and be charged to your account as the check below for $94.16.

Surprise...Surprise...Surprise! Ninety hard earned dollars have just disappeared from your checking account and you have little hope of ever getting it back. You know you wrote the check for $4.16, but how are you going to prove it?

Sure, you are angry and will raise hell with the drugstore, but, unless the store can identify who altered the check, you have just lost $90. And it was all preventable. The check below cannot be altered, at least not without being obvious.

Be careful; write each check as if someone was waiting to change it. Your money is at stake. Writing a check that may be altered is just asking for someone to help themselves to your cash. You can't afford to give your money away.

BALANCING YOUR CHECKING ACCOUNT

Contrary to what you may have heard, balancing your checking account statement is not a difficult process. People make this simple process difficult by their attitudes and practices. For example, I have a good friend who only posts checks to his checkbook in even dollars. No matter how much the check is for, he rounds the amount, either up or down, before entering it into his check book. I have another friend who, because she has overdraft protection, does not even bother to keep track of her account balance. In both of these cases, the balancing of the checking account will be a nightmare. It doesn't have to be that way.

What You Need

You will need your checkbook and any money card slips you haven't yet posted. You will also need your current checking account statement with the cancelled checks, your previous statement, and a calculator.

Steps

Before anything else, bring your checkbook balance up to date. This is accomplished by posting, in date order, your money card slips and other withdrawals, all checks written, and any deposits you have made.

If this is not your first month's statement, get the previous month's statement and verify that the checks, if any, that were outstanding have or have not cleared the bank. This step will save you many hours when trying to balance your checkbook. If your bank returns your cancelled checks, this is a good time to put them into check number sequence.

Go through the statement and the cancelled checks and check off, in your checkbook, each item that matches an entry. Draw a line under the balance following the last entry in your checkbook. This is the figure you will balance with on your statement. Don't panic if the amount on your statement does not match this figure; it seldom will. Bringing these two figures into agreement is what is called balancing your statement.

Turn your statement over and follow the instructions. What you are trying to do is make the banks records and what you have in your checkbook reflect the same data. Simply stated, you have to add any deposits and subtract any checks and withdrawals, that the bank has not posted, to your statement balance. At the same time, you will add any interest the bank may have paid and subtract any service charges from your checkbook balance. Unless you or the bank made a mistake -- yes, they do make mistakes -- the two figures will balance.

Example

Using her checkbook, last month's statement, the current month's statement and the checking account balancing form on the back of the bank statement, Jo Ann will balance her checkbook as we watch over her shoulder.

She has already posted her money card slips and her checkbook balance is posted up to date. She has just finished putting a check mark next to each entry that cleared her account during this statement period and has drawn a dark line after her last checkbook entry.

Her last statement shows an outstanding check for $120. As she checks her new statement she notices that this check still has not cleared the bank. She looks back in her checkbook and finds that this check was made out to her father. She makes a note to talk to him about depositing the check and writes the date, amount, and number on the back of the bank statement in the column labeled "checks outstanding."

Checkbook

CHECK NO.	DATE		CHECK ISSUED TO	BAL. BR'T. F'R'D.	✓	386	15
	12/9	TO	BANK	AMOUNT OF ~~CHECK OR~~ DEPOSIT		26	84
		FOR	PAY CHECK	BALANCE		412	99
130	12/10	TO	PHONE COMPANY	AMOUNT OF CHECK ~~OR DEPOSIT~~		14	65
		FOR	NOV. TELE CHARGES	BALANCE		398	34
131	12/10	TO	POWER + LIGHT Co.	AMOUNT OF CHECK ~~OR DEPOSIT~~		10	00
		FOR	NOV. UTILITIES	BALANCE		388	34
132	12/10	TO	SINGLES Apts.	AMOUNT OF CHECK ~~OR DEPOSIT~~		226	00
		FOR	DEC. RENT	BALANCE		162	34
133	12/10	TO	WATER WORKS	AMOUNT OF CHECK ~~OR DEPOSIT~~		7	10
		FOR	NOV. WATER	BALANCE		155	24
	12/11	TO	BANK	AMOUNT OF ~~CHECK OR~~ DEPOSIT		35	59
		FOR	REFUND CHECK	BALANCE		190	83
	12/14	TO	BANK CARD	AMOUNT OF CHECK ~~OR DEPOSIT~~		10	00
		FOR	MISC. CASH	BALANCE		180	83
	12/16	TO	BANK CARD	AMOUNT OF CHECK ~~OR DEPOSIT~~		20	00
		FOR	MISC. CASH	BALANCE		160	83
	12/27	TO	BANK CARD	AMOUNT OF CHECK ~~OR DEPOSIT~~		70	00
		FOR	Christmas + New Years Party	BALANCE		90	83
	1/3	TO	BANK	AMOUNT OF ~~CHECK OR~~ DEPOSIT		194	80
		FOR	PAY CHECK	BALANCE		285	63
134	1/3	TO	Church	AMOUNT OF CHECK ~~OR DEPOSIT~~		10	00
		FOR	Contribution	BALANCE		275	63
	1/12	TO	BANK	AMOUNT OF ~~CHECK OR~~ DEPOSIT		194	80
		FOR	PAY CHECK	BALANCE		470	43
	1/13	TO	BANK	AMOUNT OF CHECK ~~OR DEPOSIT~~		4	00
		FOR	SERVICE CHARGE FOR DEC.	BALANCE		466	43

Checking account statement

OK NATIONAL BANK

642 DRY GULCH RD.

SOFT LIFE, OK 12389

Statement of Account
PAGE   1

4

Last Stmt. Date	Current Stmt. Date
12/07/88	01/06/89

For Information Call:

(405) 327-1892

Jo Ann T. Graduate
2246 Home Street
Soft Life, OK 12389

8190-4620 PERSONAL CHECKING	TAXPAYER ID 254-71-2856	1278000 03

Balance Last Statement	We Have Added			We Have Subtracted			Resulting In A Balance Of
	No.	Deposits Totaling	Interest	No.	Items Totaling	Service Chg.	
506.15	2	62.43	.00	7	367.75	4.00	196.83

* * * SEASONS GREETINGS * * *

Posting Date	Transaction Description	Reference No.	Transaction Amount	Bal. Date	Balance Amount
12-07	BEGINNING BALANCE			12-07	506.15
12-09	DEPOSIT	15326905	26.84+	12-09	532.99
12-19	DEPOSIT	11050713	35.59+	12-12	518.34
12-12	CHECK 130	11661451	14.65	12-14	498.34
12-14	CHECK 131	15455976	10.00	12-16	478.34
12-19	CHECK 132	11050711	226.00	12-19	280.83
12-19	CHECK 133	15109371	7.10	12-27	210.83
01-05	CHECK 134	11220467	10.00	01-05	200.83
12-14	LONG STREET	12130000	10.00	01-06	196.83
	CASH WITHDRAWAL	0000051			
12-16	BARRACKS RD I	12150000	20.00		
	CASH WITHDRAWAL	0000139			
12-27	LYNNHAVEN MALL	12270000	70.00		
	CASH WITHDRAWAL	0000099			

AVERAGE BALANCE FOR STATEMENT PERIOD
OF 32 DAYS IS $323

| 01-06 | MAINT CHARGE | | 4.00 | | |

Where this asterisk is shown a preceding check (or checks) is still outstanding or has been included in a previous statement.

The total(s) represents the correct amount of money you have in the bank. Please examine at once. If no error is reported within 14 days, your account(s) will be considered correct.

Checking account balancing form

For your convenience, this form is provided to help you verify your balance on this statement. Please report any errors promptly.

Checks Outstanding

DATE	DOLLARS	CENTS	
11/20	120	00	#128
TOTAL	120	00	

1. Ending BALANCE
shown on this Statement   194.80 $ 196.83
ADD
  Deposits not
  shown on   194.80 $ 389.60
  Statement

Sub Total $ 586.43

SUBTRACT $ 120.00
  → Checks Outstanding

Sub Total $ 466.43

TOTAL 1.   466.43

2. Check Book Balance $ 470.43

SUBTRACT $ 4.00
  Charges, if any

Sub Total $ 466.43

ADD $ —0—
  Earnings Paid

TOTAL 2.   466.43

Total 1 should equal Total 2

Jo Ann verifies her statement against her checkbook and notices that the last two pay checks she mailed to the bank are not reflected on this statement. She enters the amount $194.80 twice on the right hand side of the balancing form in the area marked "ADD Deposits not shown on Statement."

Next, Jo Ann enters the four dollar service charge in her checkbook and on the balancing form in the area marked "SUBTRACT Charges, if any."

Now she follows the instructions on the check balancing form. The statement has a balance of $196.83, when added to the outstanding deposits the subtotal is $586.43. Subtracting the $120 outstanding check brings the total for part 1 to $466.43.

Her checkbook balance is $470.43, which Jo Ann enters in part 2. When she subtracts the $4 service charge she gets a total of $466.43. Since she had no interest, she carries this amount to the bottom line, and, comparing the total from part 1 to the total from part 2, she notes they are identical. This is what she was hoping for, her account is in balance. She is still not finished. She must now enter and subtract the $4 service charge from her checkbook balance and date the line she put in the checkbook earlier as the point of balance. Next month, should she have a problem in balancing, she will know that her account was in balance to this point.

COMMON PROBLEMS

The nine most common reasons for not being able to balance a checkbook are:

1. Not balancing the account monthly.
2. Not using checks in numerical order.
3. Failing to enter deposits in the checkbook.
4. Guessing at the amount of a deposit or check when posting the item from memory.
5. Not keeping and recording money card transactions.
6. Forgetting about miscellaneous charges, like fees for new checks.
7. Not posting interest and service charges.
8. Errors in adding or subtracting.
9. Bank errors -- they do happen.

SUMMARY

The checking account is the perfect way to keep records of your financial transactions. You may look at your money and say, "I don't have enough to warrant a checking account." You are wrong. Start now with a good record keeping system. It makes filing your taxes easier, and later, as you earn more money, you will be glad you have a good, functioning system.

NOTES

_____

_____

_____

_____

_____

_____

CREDIT CARDS
Plastic money, a necessary evil?

12

HISTORY

The principle of the credit card, or the concept of purchasing now and paying later, has existed in the American market place for many years. It all started when this country was still very young, and the local merchant would allow a homesteader to purchase groceries and tools on the promise of payment when the first crop was harvested. In the north country, it was the promise of furs to be trapped, and, during the days of the gold fever, payment was promised when the miner struck it rich.

During the 1950s, large department stores began to issue their own charge cards. These cards could only be used at the store that issued them, and the buyer paid a small fee -- service charge -- for the privilege of buying the merchandise and paying for it later. Both the buyer and the seller benefited. The buyer got the merchandise that he/she wanted, and the seller received not only the sale of the merchandise, but also the extra money that was charged to the buyer for paying at a later date. In effect, the buyer was paying the seller for the use of the seller's money.

With the arrival of the 1960s, the banks and other financial institutions saw an opportunity to make it easier for customers to shop at whatever store they desired, and at the same time, make money. It was no longer necessary to have credit approval from each store and to carry each store's credit card. This was the humble birth of the bank card. This card was usually issued by a large regional bank and could be used at any member store.

Everyone benefitted, or did they? The buyer could shop at many stores with one card and still pay for the purchases over a period of time. The seller sold his merchandise and received immediate payment for it, minus a small fee which was charged by the bank. The bank made money both from the customer, in the form of interest, and the seller, by charging a small fee.

In the 1970s and '80s the concept matured. Now, almost all banks and other financial institutions offer one or more of the most popular credit cards, and they are always looking to increase their share of this most lucrative market. It is lucrative because some banks not only charge interest in excess of 20%, they also charge a yearly fee to customers just for owning the card.

There is no question that merchandise purchased with borrowed money will cost more when the interest charges are factored into the cost. It is also true that, as the popularity of the cards grew and the fees charged to the sellers grew, some businesses simply added the charge card fees to the price of the item. The item now costs more when it is bought, and, if the buyer doesn't pay the balance off in full each month, the buyer is also charged interest on the outstanding balance due.

THE CREDIT CARD

Need

When you try to cash or pay for a purchase with a check, you will usually be asked for two items of identification. The seller will want your driver's license in addition to a "major credit card."

If you have tried, you know it is almost impossible to rent a car without either a credit card or a very large cash deposit. If you try to make hotel or motel reservations and your arrival before a certain time is questionable, you will need a credit card to ensure that the room will be available when you arrive.

On top of this, emergencies do occur. Your car needs repairs, your dentist found two cavities, the doctor says you need to take medicine to combat the new flu virus... The stress during any of these situations can be eased by knowing you can financially handle the emergency. Credit cards do have their use. If you do not want one now, you probably will in the near future.

Acquiring a Card

The easiest way to get a credit card is to already have one. No, I'm not being funny, I am simply stating a fact. Once you have a credit card and use it wisely, by never missing a payment or paying it off each month, you will receive countless offers for additional cards from other financial institutions.

People who have lived in the same house for a number of years, have a good credit record, have worked for the same employer for over two years, and have demonstrated an ability and willingness to pay their bills on time, have no trouble acquiring a credit card.

If you are looking for your first card, the situation can be quite different. It will seem that every application you complete and send in comes back marked "disapproved, not enough credit history." If you want a credit card and not a store card, you have three choices:

(1)   Go to your bank,
(2)   Have someone co-sign, or
(3)   Get a "collateralized" card.

Your Bank

Go to the bank where you have your checking account and request overdraft protection. If you have had the account there for a little while, have had no overdrafts or bad credit history, and have lived in the same city for over two years, you will probably get a credit card with at least a $300 maximum limit. This is how most banks currently provide overdraft protection.

Since you only want the card for overdraft protection, to use as a reference when cashing a check, emergencies, car rentals, or confirming hotel and motel reservations, this is perfectly acceptable.

Co-signer

Anyone with a good credit rating may be a co-signer. However, many people will not offer to do this because a co-signer on a credit card guarantees that all bills charged will be paid. In addition, a co-signer's good rating can be harmed by co-signing for an individual who does not act responsibly.

If your parent or parents have a good credit rating, ask them to co-sign for you. Be sure to explain to them that you only want the card for emergencies and will not go on a shopping spree. Once you have demonstrated to the financial institution both an ability and desire to repay your debts, you will be able to drop the co-signer. You will then be on your own.

Collateralize

Most large banks have just started offering what is called a "collateralized" credit card. This type of card allows you to use your savings or a portion of your savings to back up your credit card. This part of your savings, say $300, is set aside and cannot be used by you until released by the bank. In return, you still earn interest on your money and after a fixed amount of time, your money with interest is released to you. No one, except you and your bank, knows that you have acquired your card by providing collateral to guarantee payment.

If you have the savings, and you really want to start a credit history by acquiring a credit card, this is an excellent way to do it without asking for outside help. Remember, if you fail to meet a payment or ignore the bill when sent to you, not only will your savings be used to make the payment, your credit history will be off to a dismal start.

Shopping For a Card

The four factors to consider when shopping for a credit card are:

(1)   yearly fee,
(2)   method of computing interest,
(3)   interest rate, and
(4)   minimum payment computation.

All of these factors have a substantial impact on what your credit card will really cost.

Yearly Fee

The credit card business has become a very competitive business. The reasons for this are many, but all stem from the fact that lending money is a very profitable business. This is especially true now that there are no federal regulations and very few state regulations that limit the amount of interest that may be charged. There are still a few states that limit the interest that can be charged on credit card purchases to 18% per year.

In addition to interest, one of the big money makers is the yearly fee. This is a fee that you pay yearly just to use your card. This fee will range from $15 to $50 per year for most financial institutions and is subject to change. You can see that, if you have a credit limit of $300 and your card has a $50 yearly fee, you are paying over 16% a year just for the privilege of having a card. This is in addition to the yearly interest charge.

However, this is one of the factors that banks use to draw in new accounts. If they really want your business, the fee for the first year may be waived or dropped. All other factors being equal, not having to pay the yearly fee has just increased your buying power. Unless you are limited to only one source for a credit card, shop around and try to minimize or eliminate this fee.

Method Of Computing Interest

Even though you want the card primarily for emergencies and identification, you need to know how the interest is computed. You do not have to have an understanding of higher math to realize that there is a big difference between computing interest starting 30 days after your purchase and starting it on the day the charge is received by the bank.

For Instance

Suppose that the muffler and tail pipe fell off Jo Ann's car. She went to her friendly mechanic and the bill was $94 which she paid with her credit card. The charge is received by the bank the next day and there are still 22 days until her next billing cycle.

If she is paying 18% and her interest charges start when the bank receives the charge slip, by the time her monthly bill is mailed, this purchase will have already cost her $1.02 in interest. Jo Ann will have to pay this interest even though she decides to pay the full amount.

If the interest does not begin until the charges remain outstanding after the billing cycle, and Jo Ann pays the bill in full, she will pay nothing in interest.

When you are shopping for a credit card, try to get an account that only charges interest on outstanding balances, instead of one that charges interest on receipt of purchase statements.

Interest Rate

You never intend to pay interest. This is commendable and you should be proud of yourself. But what if it does happen? You get sick, you need medicine, and you don't have any sick leave. You use your credit card to purchase the medicine, and when the bill comes, you can only afford the minimum payment. You will be charged interest. To learn what the interest rate means in dollars, read on.

For each one percent of interest, you will owe an additional 8.333 cents per month for each hundred dollars of balance. This means that if you owe $200 and your interest rate is 12%, your monthly interest charge will be right at $2. If your bank charges 18% and you have the same $200 balance, you will owe $3 in interest for the same period. At 21% the interest charge will be $3.50. These pennies add up quickly. Some banks now charge two or more different rates of interest, the interest percentage goes down as the amount you owe goes up. Be careful and stick with the "paying off the balance" policy. You work too hard to just give your money away, so shop around to minimize the rate of interest.

You can always minimize the interest impact by paying an amount greater than the required minimum payment.

Minimum Payment Computation

Most cards have a minimum, minimum payment per month. This is the absolute minimum payment you must make as long as you have an outstanding balance. This amount is usually stated as a flat amount in even dollars and is what the bank figures is the smallest payment they are willing to accept. Without this base amount, some credit card holders would never pay off their accounts. Computed minimums are calculated as a percentage or other factor based on the outstanding balance. For example, if the computed monthly payment was 4% of the outstanding balance and you only owed $100 the computed payment would be $4. Most banks do not want to process such small payments so they will have a set dollar minimum of from $10 to $25 per month. Anytime your computed payment falls below this minimum, you pay the set amount.

The table has been developed to demonstrate the difference in interest charges and length of pay back between a minimum payment of two and three percent. The table is based on a balance of $1000 so you do not get confused by the minimum, minimum payment.

Table of data on a $1,000 balance

Interest	12%		15%		18%		21%	
Minimum Payment	$20	$30	$20	$30	$20	$30	$20	$30
Months To Repay	70	39	78	42	93	46	120	50
Total Interest	$400	$170	$560	$260	$860	$380	$1400	$500

By glancing at the table, you can see that the interest rate charged coupled with the minimum payment computation has a great impact on the total amount of interest you will pay for using your credit card. Using the 15% columns you can see that making $30 payments not only pays off the loan amount of $1000 36 months earlier, it also saves you $300 in interest charges. This is almost one third of the amount of your original purchases.

At an interest rate of 18%, your purchases will cost you almost double their value and take 93 months -- almost eight years -- to repay. And, at 21%, your purchases will cost you almost two and a half times their value and will take 10 years to repay if you make payments of $20 a month. By making payments of just $30 per month you will save $900 and reduce the length to repay by 70 months -- almost six years. Since little or none of this interest is tax deductible, you can readily see that using someone else's money can be very expensive.

Economical Credit Card Use

The following 10 suggestions will help you to maximize the use and minimize the cost of using a credit card.

(1) Shop for the best rates and lowest yearly fee.
(2) Remember why you have the credit card.
(3) Never lend your credit card to anyone.
(4) Never charge food or meals.
(5) Never charge an item where the vendor adds a fee for not paying cash.
(6) Never charge immediate use items, such as entertainment, unless you are sure you can pay for them when the bill arrives.
(7) Never charge an item when you have the money to pay for it.
(8) Always pay the complete amount of the statement or the maximum you can spare, even if it cuts into your savings for that month.
(9) Do not use the minimum payment schedule if you can afford to pay more per month. As shown in the previous table, each additional $10 payment you make, can, over time, save you hundreds of dollars.
(10) Regardless of the offers you receive, try to have only one card at a time. You may want to switch cards after you have established a good credit history to take advantage of lower rates and yearly fees. This is good financial management. Having multiple credit cards means multiple payments each month, which is not good financial management.

Following these rules will also benefit you by helping to protect your credit rating.

YOUR CREDIT RATING

This is the report that your creditors, banks, and other financial institutions use to determine if you are a good credit risk. Since these institutions are in business to make money by providing you with cash to make purchases, they must be sure that they will receive payment. If payment is not made, not only is their profit -- the interest you are charged -- lost but so is the cash that was advanced.

You have already started building a credit record by opening a checking account. If you have any overdrafts and do not have overdraft protection, this information will eventually find its way into your credit record. This record is accumulated and maintained by one or more credit bureaus or agencies in your local area. Every time you apply for any form of credit, you authorize the lender access to your record.

Good Credit--An Investment in the Future

Without realizing it, you have already started buying items on credit. Your rent, utilities and your telephone are all provided on credit. Each of the people you have dealt with have decided to advance to you services, shelter, and items with the understanding that when the bills are presented, you will immediately pay them. Any straying from this implied agreement will result in a mark against your credit history.

You will want a new car sometime in the future. You probably will also want to own your own home. For a very large percentage of Americans, this will require a good credit rating. A good credit rating is easy to develop:

(1) Do not buy more than you can reasonably afford to repay and
(2) make all payments on time.

If you can live by these two rules, you will never want for credit as long as you have a steady income.

Protect It

As with any other investment you will have, you will want to protect your credit rating. By following the rules above, you should never have a problem.

However, this is not always possible; we all encounter emergencies and unexpected expenses. You may not want to believe this, but the credit agency and your creditor understand that this happens.

My experience has shown that the single most destructive element affecting a credit rating is lack of communication. For example, suppose that Jo Ann's mother became ill. Out of concern for her mother's health, Jo Ann makes a number of long distance phone calls during a one month period resulting in a phone bill of $76. From her budget we can see that she is going to have trouble paying this bill, especially since she also had to replace the muffler on her car. She has a few dollars saved, but remember she is just starting her new job and cannot pay the total telephone bill. What does she do?

She either picks up the phone and calls the telephone company's billing department or, even better, she writes a note with her check for partial payment. The note must include three things:

(1) a short statement explaining the situation,
(2) the amount of the partial payment and
(3) when the remainder of the charges will be paid.

Jo Ann's Note

Date

Local Phone Company

Billing Department:

Enclosed is my check for $35 as partial payment of this month's phone bill. My long distance charges were unusually high this month because of illness in my family and should not be repeated. I will pay the balance of $41 plus my regular bill and any late fees next month.

If this arrangement is not acceptable please let me know.

I thank you in advance for your consideration and understanding.

                                        Sincerely,
                                        Jo Ann Graduate

Jo Ann should keep a copy of this letter for later reference and must now make sure that the bill is completely paid next month. If she does, and these situations do not occur frequently, no notation will be made in her credit history.

If she does not write the note, a flag will be set on her account because she has a past due amount. If, when the phone company sends a past due notice, she still does not pay the balance or communicate with the company, her credit history will start to suffer.

It only takes a small number of these negative entries on an individual's credit record to result in a rejection of a credit application with the comment "rejected because of poor credit history."

Three to five years and even longer may be required to overcome some negative entries on your credit record.

Getting a Copy

You are entitled, by law, to obtain a copy of your credit file. To do so, call one of the major furniture or department stores in your area to determine which credit bureau is used. For a small fee, free if you have been turned down for credit, you will receive a copy of your credit file. If you disagree with what the file contains, you are authorized to request that statements of explanation be inserted in your file. This can be very important if the negative items in your file are the result of one time situations or items that

have been corrected.

If you feel that you have not been treated equally in your application for credit, contact your state's consumer assistance office for help.

SUMMARY

We are a debtor nation. Our economy is built on the ability to buy today and pay tomorrow. Having a credit card in itself is not bad. In fact, you will want and need to acquire one just to function in our society.

Your obligation to yourself is to get and use the card intelligently, always remembering that having and using a credit card is not free.

Money is a product in our society. It should be shopped for just like food or clothing. Care should be taken to insure the best value is received. This is accomplished by comparing different financial institutions' fees, repayment schedules, interest rates and interest computation policies to determine the most economical. All of these factors are equally important in identifying the best value.

A good credit rating is a valuable asset. It is your key to future, larger acquisitions. The ability to borrow money to purchase a new car, vacation, or house is restricted to those individuals with a good credit history.

Your credit rating is extremely fragile; guard it well! Once damaged, it is very difficult to repair.

FILING THE TAX RETURN

The price of freedom.
Or, how much do I get back?

13

Taxes are a necessary part of our society. No matter how much some people complain, the fact is that the society we live in would not be possible without taxation. On a national level, it is your taxes that provide for our governing body, the military to defend us, national law enforcement, national parks and highways, and the social programs that you and others will be entitled to at some stage in your life.

On a state level, taxes provide the money to pay for the state government, state law enforcement, schools, libraries, parks, highways, and state unemployment compensation. On the city level, the city government, police and fire protection, parks, community centers, street maintenance, sanitation services, and many forms of day care and care of the elderly would not be possible without taxation.

If nothing else, you can always use taxation as something to complain about and thereby reduce stress.

This chapter will be devoted to filing the Federal Income Tax Form 1040EZ because that is the form that fits the requirements of most of the targeted readers of this book. Remember, as discussed earlier, most states also have a requirement for you to file a state income tax return. The date for filing the state return is usually around the same time as the federal return.

If you have dependents, are married, have received dividends or unemployment compensation, or wish to claim child and dependent care expenses or earned income credit, you will use either the 1040A or the 1040. If you have adequate allowed deductions -- currently over $3,000 -- and wish to itemize them, you must use the Form 1040.

PUBLICATION 17

Each year, the Internal Revenue Service offers a free, easy to follow, set of instructions for filing your income tax. This document *Your Federal Income Tax* also known as Publication 17, may be obtained by calling the toll free number 1-800-424-FORM(3676) between the hours of 8 a.m. and 8 p.m. on weekdays, and 9 a.m. to 3 p.m. on Saturdays.

Publication 17 contains instructions for completing all the different federal income tax forms including basic instructions for all of the supporting schedules. With Pub 17 and a good set of records, the average wage earner, earning less than $50,000 a year, should be able to accurately file the required Federal Income Tax Return.

HELP

As will be discussed later in this chapter, once you have provided the basic information, the Internal Revenue Service (IRS) will even compute your tax return free of charge. If you have a refund due, the IRS will send it to you. If you owe additional tax, the IRS will bill for the amount owed. You will not be charged interest or a penalty if you pay the bill within 30 days of receipt or by the normal filing deadline, whichever is later.

If your return includes depreciation, capital gains, income averaging, or unusual adjustments to your salary, you may desire to seek professional help. Depending on the complexity of the return, you will pay from $25 to $250 or even more to have someone else prepare your return. Your local yellow pages, contains a list, under the heading Tax Return Preparation, of many individuals and professional organizations that specialize in providing paid assistance. As with everything else you pay for, shop around for reliability and price.

Having someone else prepare your tax return does not release you from any liability as to the return's accuracy and you must pay any taxes, penalties, and fees assessed by the government if an audit reveals improper preparation or errors. If you have not kept good records, no one will be able to do your return the way it should be done.

WHO MUST FILE A RETURN

Simply stated, all residents of the United States who receive any income may be required to file a tax return. The stated rules take into consideration marital status, dependent status, and amount of income earned as quick check factors for individuals to use. For example, some of the rules in effect at the time this book was written are:

(1) Single persons earning more than $5,000 during the year, who cannot be claimed as a dependent by another taxpayer, must file a tax return.
(2) Married couples making more than $9,000 in the tax year must also file a tax return.
(3) Anyone entitled to a tax refund, regardless of income, must file a return to receive their refund.

These are just a few specific rules, if in doubt of your status call your local IRS office or check Pub 17 which has a whole page devoted to the different factors that determine who must file a tax return.

YOU CAN DO IT!

You are probably already thinking that this is beyond your comprehension, but stick with me.

The IRS has performed a time and motion study on the preparation of the Form 1040EZ -- the form used by many single tax payers. The study computed the average time to read the instructions, prepare the form, copy the form, and mail it to the IRS. As a result of the study, the expected time to complete the whole process is one hour and thirty one minutes. This is not much time when you only have to do it once a year.

FORMS, FORMS, FORMS

As a beginning taxpayer, you can expect to have at least three forms, in addition to your personal records, to work with. They are:

(1) W-2 - Wage and Tax Statement
(2) Form 1099-INT - Interest Income
(3) Form 1040EZ - Income Tax Return for Single Filers with no dependents

You may have more than one W-2 if you have worked more than one job during the tax year and more than one Form 1099-INT if you have received interest from more than one financial institution.

Using Jo Ann's tax return as an example, let's take a close look at each of her forms.

W-2

First there is her W-2 Wage and Earnings Statement. This form is provided by the employer to the employee, the Social Security Administration, and the Internal Revenue Service. The employee may receive multiple copies (3 or 4) of this form and the appropriate copy must be attached with each tax return filed. Each of the copies is marked as to its distribution, one for each of the following: the taxpayer -- you, the federal return, the state return and, if needed, the city or local return.

1 Control number 6231765		OMB No. 1545-0008	Copy C For EMPLOYEE'S RECORDS		Dept. of the Treasury—IRS

2 Employer's name, address, and ZIP code	3 Employer's identification number 12-07643	4 Employer's state I.D. number

GREEN TOE NURSERY
1391 Aspen Lane
Soft Life, OK 12389

5 Statutory employee	Deceased	Pension plan	Legal rep.	942 emp.	Subtotal	Deferred compensation	Void

6 Allocated tips	7 Advance EIC payment

8 Employee's social security number 254-71-2856	9 Federal income tax withheld $704	10 Wages, tips, other compensation $7,680.00	11 Social security tax withheld $567.52

12 Employee's name, address, and ZIP code	13 Social security wages $7,680.00	14 Social security tips

Jo Ann T. Graduate

2246 Home Street
Soft Life, OK 12389

16	16a Fringe benefits incl. in Box 10

17 State income tax	18 State wages, tips, etc.	19 Name of state
20 Local income tax	21 Local wages, tips, etc.	22 Name of locality

Form **W-2 Wage and Tax Statement**   **1989**
This information is being furnished to the Internal Revenue Service.

Each of the blocks on the W-2 are clearly labeled and where amounts are entered, these amounts are the totals for the taxable year. If the form you receive is an approved computer-generated facsimile, the form may look slightly different but, the boxes will be numbered the same and contain the same information as this example.

As required by law, the W-2 form is to be mailed or given to you by the 31st of January following the end of the tax year. If you have not received the form(s) from your past employers by February 10th, you should notify the employer, verify your current mailing address, and request a copy.

If you still have not received the forms by February 15th, call the toll free number for your area listed in your tax instructions and notify the IRS of your problem.

Verify

Upon receipt of your W-2 form(s) immediately verify the following:

Name and Address
Social Security Number
Totals for Earnings
Totals for Taxes
Total of Social Security Tax withheld

If there are any errors, notify your employer immediately and request a corrected form. Do not make pen and ink changes. Your copy must exactly match the one submitted to the IRS. This verification will be very easy if you have kept your records and posted them monthly.

1 0 9 9 - I N T

This form is sent to you by your bank or other financial institution if you have been paid taxable interest during the tax year. Each institution you have an interest earning account with will send you one copy of this form. This form should be used to file your return but should not be submitted with the completed return. It is for your records and should be attached to your copy of the return.

Here is Jo Ann's 1099-INT.

PAYER'S name, street address, city, state, and ZIP code		OMB No. 1545-0112		
OK National Bank **642 Dry Gulch Rd.** **Soft Life, OK 12389**		19**89** Statement for Recipients of	**Interest Income**	
PAYER'S Federal identification number	RECIPIENT'S identification number	1 Earnings from savings and loan associations, credit unions, bank deposits, bearer certificates of deposit, etc.		**Copy B** **For Recipient**
61-23456	254-71-2856	$16.42		This is important tax information and is being furnished to the Internal Revenue Service. If you are required to file a return, a negligence penalty or other sanction will be imposed on you if this income is taxable and the IRS determines that it has not been reported.
RECIPIENT'S name, street address, city, state, and ZIP code		2 Early withdrawal penalty 0.00	3 U.S. Savings Bonds, etc. 0.00	
Jo Ann T. Graduate **2246 Home Street** **Soft Life, OK 12389**		4 Federal Income tax withheld 0.00	////////////	
		5 Foreign tax paid (if eligible for foreign tax credit) 0.00	6 Foreign country or U.S. possession 0.00	

Form **1099-INT**   Department of the Treasury-Internal Revenue Service

Like the W-2 form, the 1099-INT you receive may be an approved computer-generated facsimile of the one shown above. In case you have an interest earning account and don't receive this form, follow the same guidance as given previously for the W-2 form.

Immediately verify your name and address. In the block *RECIPIENT'S identification number* is your social security number. Make sure it is correct. The amount of interest you received that must be reported on your tax return is in block 1. Make sure that this amount agrees with your records.

1040EZ

The 1040EZ, Income Tax Return for Single Filers with no dependents, is the tax return form used for this example. If you filed a return last year, you will receive, by mail, a blank copy with instructions for the current year. If you have not filed a return before or have moved and your mail hasn't caught up with you, you can get copies of the forms and instructions from most post offices and public libraries.

The Formula

Regardless of the form you use, 1040EZ, 1040A, or 1040, the following formula and rules for computing your tax obligation apply.

(1) Your adjusted gross income -- what you earned -- minus your deductions and personal exemption equals your taxable income.
(2) Your total tax amount is then figured as a percentage of your taxable income.
(3) The total tax is subtracted from what you have already paid plus any tax credits or subsidies you are entitled to.

Form 1040EZ

Income Tax Return for Single Filers With No Dependents   **1989**

OMB No. 1545-0675

Name & address

Use the IRS mailing label. If you don't have one, please print.

L A B E L   H E R E

Print your name above (first, initial, last)

Home address (number, street, and apt. no.). (If you have a P.O. box, see back.)

City, town, or post office, state, and ZIP code

Please print your numbers like this:

9 8 7 6 5 4 3 2 1 0

Your social security number

Instructions are on the back. Also, see the Form 1040A/ 1040EZ booklet, especially the checklist on page 13.

Presidential Election Campaign Fund
Do you want $1 to go to this fund?

Note: Checking "Yes" will not change your tax or reduce your refund.   ▶

Yes No

Dollars   Cents

Report your income

1   Total wages, salaries, and tips. This should be shown in Box 10 of your W-2 form(s). (Attach your W-2 form(s).)   1

Attach Copy B of Form(s) W-2 here.

2   Taxable interest income of $400 or less. If the total is more than $400, you cannot use Form 1040EZ.   2

3   Add line 1 and line 2. This is your **adjusted gross income.**   3

4   Can your parents (or someone else) claim you on their return?

Note: You must check Yes or No.

☐ Yes. Do worksheet on back; enter amount from line E here.
☐ No. Enter 5,100. This is the total of your standard deduction and personal exemption.   4

5   Subtract line 4 from line 3. If line 4 is larger than line 3, enter 0. This is your **taxable income.**   5

Figure your tax

6   Enter your Federal income tax withheld from Box 9 of your W-2 form(s).   6

7   Tax. Use the amount on **line 5** to look up your tax in the Tax Table on pages 37-42 of the Form 1040A/1040EZ booklet. Use the **single** column in the Table. Enter the tax from the Table on this line.   7

Refund or amount you owe

8   If line 6 is larger than line 7, subtract line 7 from line 6. This is your **refund.**   8

Attach tax payment here.

9   If line 7 is larger than line 6, subtract line 6 from line 7. This is the **amount you owe.** Attach check or money order for the full amount, payable to "Internal Revenue Service."   9

Sign your return

I have read this return. Under penalties of perjury, I declare that to the best of my knowledge and belief, the return is true, correct, and complete.

Your signature   Date

X

For IRS Use Only—Please do not write in boxes below.

For Privacy Act and Paperwork Reduction Act Notice, see page 3 in the booklet.   Form 1040EZ (1989)

(4) If you have a positive answer, you get a refund for that amount.

(5) If you have negative answer, you owe the IRS that amount.

The complexity of filing an income tax return is not in the formula but in the large number of ways there are to make money, the many deductions and exemptions, and the variety of tax credits. With this formula in mind, go back and take another look at the 1040EZ. Understanding the formula will make the form even easier to work with.

Jo Ann's Return

Jo Ann has verified the amounts on her W-2 and 1099-INT forms against her records and is now ready to complete her 1040EZ. She has two copies of the 1040EZ, one is her work copy, and the other will be the smooth one submitted to the IRS. Thinking ahead, she is trying to file her return early so she will get her refund, if she is entitled to one, quickly. She knows the earlier she files her return, the quicker it will be processed, because as the date for mandatory filing approaches the work load at the IRS increases.

The first thing Jo Ann does is fill out the top of the return with her name, address, and social security number. The return does not have to be typed, but the letters and numbers must be printed clearly with no frills. Remember, someone has to read it and correctly enter your data into a computer. Do not cross sevens or slash zeros. Follow the example on the upper right hand corner of the form.

Jo Ann, as any taxpayer, has the option to have one dollar of her taxes set aside to assist in reducing the cost of qualified presidential candidates when running for election. This money is set aside and does not go toward meeting the budgeted operating expenses of the government. The objective of this option is to reduce the "outside" money required by a candidate for campaign expenses when running for the office of president. If a candidate does not need this "outside" money, the special interest groups will not be encouraged to "buy" favors and their potential power over our president is virtually eliminated. Checking the "yes" box does not increase your tax and the money is divided among the qualifying candidates without regard to political party. Jo Ann puts an "X" in the yes block.

Form 1040EZ	Income Tax Return for Single Filers With No Dependents	1989	OMB No. 1545-0675

Name & address

Use the IRS mailing label. If you don't have one, please print.

LABEL HERE

JO ANN T. GRADUATE
Print your name above (first, initial, last)

2246 HOME St.
Home address (number, street, and apt. no.). (If you have a P.O. box, see back.)

Soft Life, OK   12389
City, town, or post office, state, and ZIP code

Please print your numbers like this:

9 8 7 6 5 4 3 2 1 0

Your social security number

254 71 2856

Instructions are on the back. Also, see the Form 1040A/1040EZ booklet, especially the checklist on page 13.

Presidential Election Campaign Fund
Do you want $1 to go to this fund?   Note: Checking "Yes" will not change your tax or reduce your refund. ▶

Yes No
[X] [ ]

Dollars   Cents

Report your income

1 Total wages, salaries, and tips. This should be shown in Box 10 of your W-2 form(s). (Attach your W-2 form(s).)   1

Attach Copy B of Form(s) W-2 here.

2 Taxable interest income of $400 or less. If the total is more than $400, you cannot use Form 1040EZ.   2

Adjusted Gross Income

Now, using her W-2(s) and Form 1099-INT(s), Jo Ann is ready to complete the income portion of the form. In reading the instruction booklet that came with the form, she finds that she does not have to worry about the cents. The IRS allows her to round her entries to the nearest dollar, as long as she is consistent. She has only one W-2 and one 1099-INT, so she puts the amount from her W-2--$7,680 in line 1 and rounds the amount, $16.42, from her form 1099-INT to $16 and writes this amount in line 2.

Continuing to follow the instructions, she adds the two figures together and puts the total -- $7,696 in line 3. This, she sees, is her adjusted gross income.

Taxable Income

She can no longer be claimed as a dependent by anyone, so she puts an "X" in the "no" box and writes $5,100 in line 4. This is a combination of the $3,100 that any single taxpayer is allowed to deduct in lieu of itemizing their deductions and the $2,000 that the government allows each man, woman, and child as tax free income to provide for the absolute necessities of life.

If you have valid deductions -- interest, property and income taxes, contributions, and/or medical expenses that exceed $3,100 -- you should read PUB 17. It may be beneficial for you to itemize your deductions and use the Form 1040 with Schedule A. Since the government does not have your records or know your daily obligations, they cannot tell you what form should be used to get a larger return. This is your responsibility. The IRS is responsible for collecting all of the taxes due to the government, and you are responsible for paying only the taxes you owe to the government.

Since Jo Ann does not have deductions that exceed the $3,100 minimum, she follows the instructions and subtracts the $5,100 -- line 4 -- from line 3 and enters the result -- $2,596 -- on line 5. This is her taxable income. Of the $7,696 she received as income last year, only $2,596 is taxable. She could stop here, sign and date her return, mail it to the IRS, and the IRS would compute her taxes for her.

Jo Ann decides to complete the return herself, so she continues.

Report your income	1	Total wages, salaries, and tips. This should be shown in Box 10 of your W-2 form(s). (Attach your W-2 form(s).) 1	7,680.00
Attach Copy B of Form(s) W-2 here.	2	Taxable interest income of $400 or less. If the total is more than $400, you cannot use Form 1040EZ. 2	16.00
	3	Add line 1 and line 2. This is your **adjusted gross income.** 3	7,696.00
Note: You must check Yes or No.	4	Can your parents (or someone else) claim you on their return? ☐ Yes. Do worksheet on back; enter amount from line E here. ☒ No. Enter 5,100. This is the total of your standard deduction and personal exemption. 4	5,100.00
	5	Subtract line 4 from line 3. If line 4 is larger than line 3, enter 0. This is your **taxable income.** 5	2,596.00
Figure your tax	6	Enter your Federal income tax withheld from Box 9 of your W-2 form(s). 6	,.
	7	**Tax.** Use the amount on line 5 to look up your **tax** in the Tax Table on pages 37-42 of the Form 1040A/1040EZ booklet. Use the **single** column in the Table. Enter the **tax** from the Table on this line. 7	,.

Jo Ann's Tax

As directed by the instructions, Jo Ann now enters $704 in line 6 of her 1040EZ. This is the amount of income tax withheld and was taken from box 9 of her W-2. Still following the instructions, she looks on the appropriate page of the tax table (see below) and finds that for a single person having a taxable income of $2,596 the tax obligation is $388.

She enters that amount in line 7 of the 1040EZ.

Page 41

At least	But less than	Single (and 1040EZ filers)	Married filing jointly	Married filing separately	Head of a household
			Your tax is—		
23,200	23,250	4,092	3,484	4,491	3,484
23,250	23,300	4,106	(3,491)	4,505	3,491
23,300	23,350	4,120	3,499	4,519	3,499
23,350	23,400	4,134	3,506	4,533	3,506

Section 4—1989 Tax Table

For persons with taxable incomes of less than $50,000

Example: Mr. and Mrs. Green are filing a joint return. Their taxable income on line 19 of Form 1040A is $23,250. First, they find the $23,250-23,300 income line. Next, they find the column for married filing jointly and read down the column. The amount shown where the income line and filing status column meet is $3,491. This is the tax amount they must write on line 20 of Form 1040A.

If 1040A, line 19, OR 1040EZ, line 5 is—		And you are—				If 1040A, line 19, OR 1040EZ, line 5 is—		And you are—				If 1040A, line 19, OR 1040EZ, line 5 is—		And you are—			
At least	But less than	Single (and 1040EZ filers) *	Married filing jointly	Married filing separately *	Head of a household	At least	But less than	Single (and 1040EZ filers) *	Married filing jointly	Married filing separately *	Head of a household	At least	But less than	Single (and 1040EZ filers) *	Married filing jointly	Married filing separately *	Head of a household
			Your tax is—						Your tax is—						Your tax is—		
$0	$5	$0	$0	$0	$0	1,400	1,425	212	212	212	212	2,700	2,725	407	407	407	407
5	15	2	2	2	96	**2,000**		216	216	216	216	2,725	2,750	411	411	411	
15	25	3	3	99	99			219	219	219	219	2,750	2,775	414	414	544	544
25	50	6	6	103	103	2,000	2,025	302	302	223	223	2,775	2,800	418	418	551	551
50	75	9	9			2,025	2,050	306	306	227	227	2,800	2,825	422	559	559	559
75	100		107	107	107	2,050	2,075	309	309	309	231	2,825	2,850		566	566	566
725	750	111	111	111	111	2,075	2,100	313	313	313	313	3,800	3,850	574	574	574	574
750	775	114	114	114	114	2,100	2,125	317	317	317	317	3,850	3,900	581	581	581	581
775	800	118	118	118	118	2,125	2,150	321	321	321	321	3,900	3,950	589	589	589	589
800	825	122	122	122	122	2,150	2,175	324	324	324	324	3,950	4,000	596	596	596	596
825	850	126	126	126	126	2,175	2,200	328	328	328	328						
850	875	129	129	129	129	2,200	2,225	332	332	332	332	**4,000**					
875	900	133	133	133	133			336	336	336	336	4,000	4,050	604	604	604	604
900	925	137	137	137	137	2,425	2,450		339	339	339	4,050	4,100	611	611	611	671
925	950	141	141	141	167	2,450	2,475	369	343	343	343	4,100	4,150	619	619	679	679
950	975	144	144	144	171	2,475	2,500	373	37	347	347	4,150	4,200	626	626	686	686
975	1,000	148	148	174	174	2,500	2,525	377	377	37	351	4,200	4,250	634	694	694	694
1,000			178	178	178	2,525	2,550	381	381	381		4,250	4,300		701	701	701
1,200	1,225	182	182	182	182	2,550	2,575	384	384	384	384	4,700	4,750	709	709	709	709
1,225	1,250	186	186	186	186	2,575	2,600	388	388	388	388	4,750	4,800	716	716	716	716
1,250	1,275	189	189	189	189	2,600	2,625	392	392	392	392	4,800	4,850	724	724	724	724
1,275	1,300	193	193	193	193	2,625	2,650	396	396	396	396	4,850	4,900	731	731	731	731
1,300	1,325	197	197	197	197	2,650	2,675	399	399	399	399	4,900	4,950	739	739	739	739
1,325	1,350	201	201	201	201	2,675	2,700	403	403	403	403	4,950	5,000	746	746	746	746
1,350	1,375	204	204	204	204												
1,375	1,400	208	208	208	208												

* This column must also be used by a qualifying widow(er).

Continued on next page

Owe or Refund

She is directed to subtract line 7 from line 6 and, if the answer is positive, enter the amount in line 8 as a refund. If the answer is negative -- line 7 is larger than line 6 -- the amount is entered in line 9 and must be paid by the 15th of April. The answer to Jo Ann's subtraction is positive $316. With a smile, she enters that amount in line 8, which means she will receive a refund check from the government in the amount of $316.

Figure your tax

6 Enter your Federal income tax withheld from Box 9 of your W-2 form(s).   6

7 Tax. Use the amount on line 5 to look up your tax in the Tax Table on pages 37–42 of the Form 1040A/1040EZ booklet. Use the **single** column in the Table. Enter the tax from the Table on this line.   7

			.	
,	7 0 4	. 0 0		
,	3 8 8	. 0 0		
,	3 1 6	. 0 0		
,		.		

Refund or amount you owe

Attach tax payment here.

8 If line 6 is larger than line 7, subtract line 7 from line 6. This is your **refund.**   8

9 If line 7 is larger than line 6, subtract line 6 from line 7. This is the **amount you owe.** Attach check or money order for the full amount, payable to "Internal Revenue Service."   9

Sign your return

I have read this return. Under penalties of perjury, I declare that to the best of my knowledge and belief, the return is true, correct, and complete.

Your signature _____ Date

x *Jo Ann T. Graduate*   1/30/90

For IRS Use Only—Please do not write In boxes below.

Jo Ann checks her entries and her math. When she is satisfied that everything is correct, she copies the document onto a clean form. Since she does not have an IRS mailing label, she writes in her name, address, and social security number. If she had received her forms through the mail, she would have attached the mailing label in the appropriate area on her form. She verifies the entries on the completed form, checks the math again, and dates and signs the form.

Jo Ann attaches the appropriate copy of the W-2 to the area identified on the 1040EZ and mails it to the address specified in the instructions. Since she is early, she should receive her check in about 4 weeks. She attaches the employee copy of the W-2 to her copy of the 1040EZ and files it with her other records for the tax year.

HOW LONG?

As a general rule, the typical wage earner who does not have real estate transfers or other complex entries on their returns should keep a copy of their return for three years. The three years starts on the date the return was due or filed, whichever is later.

SUGGESTIONS

If you live in an area that requires the filing of state or local income tax returns, now is the time to complete those. Save yourself a lot of needless hassle, and get in the habit of filing your return early. Waiting in the long lines at the post office at 11:45 p.m. on April 15th of each year is a pain in the ...

Should you find, after double checking all your figures, that you owe taxes, be sure to reduce the number of dependents claimed on your W-4 form or ask for additional withholding. Go back to Chapter 5 and review the work sheet for the W-4 form. Remember, not having enough tax withheld during the year can result in additional penalty and interest charges.

Form 1040EZ

Income Tax Return for Single Filers With No Dependents

1989

OMB No. 1545-0675

Name & address

Use the IRS mailing label. If you don't have one, please print.

LABEL HERE

JoAnn T. Graduate
Print your name above (first, initial, last)

2246 Home St.
Home address (number, street, and apt. no.). (If you have a P.O. box, see back.)

Soft Life, OK 12389
City, town, or post office, state, and ZIP code

Please print your numbers like this:

9 8 7 6 5 4 3 2 1 0

Your social security number

254 71 2856

Instructions are on the back. Also, see the Form 1040A/1040EZ booklet, especially the checklist on page 13.

Presidential Election Campaign Fund
Do you want $1 to go to this fund?

Note: Checking "Yes" will not change your tax or reduce your refund. ▶

Yes [X] No [ ]

Dollars | Cents

Report your Income

Attach Copy B of Form(s) W-2 here.

Note: You must check Yes or No.

1 Total wages, salaries, and tips. This should be shown in Box 10 of your W-2 form(s). (Attach your W-2 form(s).) **1**   7,680.00

2 Taxable interest income of $400 or less. If the total is more than $400, you cannot use Form 1040EZ. **2**   16.00

3 Add line 1 and line 2. This is your **adjusted gross income.** **3**   7,696.00

4 Can your parents (or someone else) claim you on their return?
[ ] Yes. Do worksheet on back; enter amount from line E here.
[X] No. Enter 5,100. This is the total of your standard deduction and personal exemption. **4**   5,100.00

5 Subtract line 4 from line 3. If line 4 is larger than line 3, enter 0. This is your **taxable income.** **5**   2,596.00

Figure your tax

6 Enter your Federal income tax withheld from Box 9 of your W-2 form(s). **6**   704.00

7 Tax. Use the amount on line 5 to look up your tax in the Tax Table on pages 37-42 of the Form 1040A/1040EZ booklet. Use the single column in the Table. Enter the tax from the Table on this line. **7**   388.00

Refund or amount you owe

Attach tax payment here.

8 If line 6 is larger than line 7, subtract line 7 from line 6. This is your **refund.** **8**   316.00

9 If line 7 is larger than line 6, subtract line 6 from line 7. This is the **amount you owe.** Attach check or money order for the full amount, payable to "Internal Revenue Service." **9**   .

Sign your return

I have read this return. Under penalties of perjury, I declare that to the best of my knowledge and belief, the return is true, correct, and complete.

Your signature   Date

X Jo Ann T. Graduate   1/30/90

For IRS Use Only—Please do not write in boxes below.

For Privacy Act and Paperwork Reduction Act Notice, see page 3 in the booklet.

Form 1040EZ (1989)

SUMMARY

We must all pay our share of the expenses of living in this country. The process of filing your return need not be difficult or take long periods of time. In fact, if you keep good records and use Publication 17, the process will be simplified. When it's all over, there is a lot of personal satisfaction in knowing you filed your own return.

If, however, you do need help, the IRS, along with some state and private agencies, are good sources of free help. You should also watch your local newspaper for advertisements offering free tax preparation clinics and make use of these offers to improve your level of expertise.

Beware of businesses promising immediate cash refunds or loans against future refunds. In some cases, it is illegal for a business to give you immediate cash and have you sign over your federal tax refund check.

NOTES

_____

_____

_____

_____

_____

_____

_____

_____

_____

_____

_____

_____

_____

_____

_____

TRANSPORTATION

What do you mean, "*walk*"?

IV

You are going to find that next to shelter, transportation will probably be the largest expense you have. It doesn't matter which mode of transportation you use, public or your own automobile, the expense is high. If you are the most fortunate of individuals, and live close to work and everything else you do so that you can walk, you are the exception. Even then, you will have a need to supplement your walking with some other form of transportation and that form will be expensive.

Chapter 14 discusses the options for transportation and the factors to be considered in choosing one or more of these options. Needs as compared to wants, as well as evaluating the versatility and practicality of vehicle types, are included in this discussion.

Chapter 15 introduces you to the various terms that you will encounter in the new and used vehicle trade. Initial cost, operating cost, budget constraints, depreciation and maintenance expenses are all explored in depth. The chapter closes by providing a list of some of the things to look for if buying a used vehicle.

Chapter 16 delves into the world of financing. A sample commercial loan agreement is dissected with emphasis on interest computation, loan language, rights of the borrower and possible pitfalls to avoid. Two stories highlight the need for close attention to the length of the loan when compared to projected depreciation.

Chapter 17 is devoted exclusively to vehicle insurance. Requirements, types of coverage, factors affecting cost, and cost of various options are all presented. Examples are used to demonstrate the need for evaluating options by comparing benefits to cost.

Chapter 18 exposes some of the frequently forgotten expenses of owning and operating a private vehicle. Insurance, routine maintenance, corrective maintenance, tags, title, taxes and other fees are explained and assigned values. Comparisons are made between new and used vehicles, focusing on the real cost of each.

SELECTING A VEHICLE TYPE
Yes, a bicycle is a vehicle.

14

One of the key factors in today's society is that we must be very mobile. Distance, local and on an international scale, is no longer a challenge. Like never before, if we wish to go somewhere, we simply decide on the fastest, least expensive, or most exotic way of getting there and make arrangements.

What most of us fail to consider is that our physical structure differs from most other animals because we are designed to walk. Unlike other animals that are designed to run, swing from trees, and even swim, our structure is designed for moving around in an upright position on our two legs -- walking.

The next few pages are going to explore the many ways we have for getting from one place to another, not on an international scale, but on the home front. We are going to concentrate on getting you from where you live to where you work and where you have fun. Do not rule out any of the forms of transportation until you have completed this section. You will then be able to compare the costs and advantages of each of the methods and find the one that is optimum for your situation. Your choice will most likely be a combination of transportation types.

You may decide that you can get to work by walking, using a bike, or car pool. You may be fortunate enough to live in an area that provides a safe, clean, and economical public transportation system. Good public transportation systems provide an excellent method of getting from one place to another, even during periods of bad weather. When determining your options be sure to consider public transportation, if available, as a valid alternative or supplement to other methods of transportation.

TYPES OF TRANSPORTATION

There are approximately seven practical ways of getting from one place to another in most cities. They are:

(1)   Walking
(2)   Riding a bicycle
(3)   Public transportation (bus, subway, or commuter train)
(4)   Taxicab
(5)   Motor bike
(6)   Automobile (car, pickup truck, or van)
(7)   Car or van pool

In addition to the above, you could go to work on skates or a skate board. You could even hitchhike or use an ultra light aircraft, but, though these methods are not ruled out, this topic does use the word "practical" in the opening statement. Of these additional four methods of transportation, hitchhiking has, at times, been used rather successfully. However, in today's society, in addition to being very unreliable, it can also be very dangerous.

Walking

Not only is walking good for your health, it is the least expensive form of transportation. Most people do not realize that it only takes between 15 and 20 minutes for the average person to walk a mile. Given that most people today have a commuting time, between home and work, of over 30 minutes, walking two miles to work would still take you less time than the average worker spends commuting.

Time spent walking is not wasted time. In addition to the health benefits derived from walking, you get to closely observe and become aware of your surroundings. Walking, because it does not require a lot of concentration, provides excellent thinking and planning time. You can use this time to plan what you are going to do after work, mentally make up your shopping list, and, if you are really dedicated, even plan what you are going to do at work each day. By using a small, inexpensive tape recorder, most of the detailed outline of this book was composed during my daily 30 to 60 minute walks.

As a form of transportation, walking does have limitations and you will need a supplemental way to: get to distant places, assist in transporting bulky or heavy packages, and provide mobility during periods of severe weather. However, even if you own a car or other motorized vehicle, don't rule out walking. Walking is one of the most environmentally sound and healthful forms of transportation available. If you live in a city and draw a circle on your local street map that includes everything within one mile of your home, you will be surprised at the places that are quickly -- within 10 to 15 minutes -- accessible by walking.

You still need to have some form of supplemental transportation to use in times of bad weather and to reach outlying places.

Bicycle

This method of "fair weather" transportation has most of the benefits of walking, with the added advantage of greater distance and increased carrying capability. It is a clean, healthy method of getting around, and, in 30 minutes, you can travel three or more times the distance you would go if you were walking.

By adding one or more inexpensive baskets or carriers to your bicycle, you can easily carry the results of a shopping trip without wearing yourself out.

If, as suggested above, you draw a circle on your map, this time to include everything within three miles from home, you will be impressed at what you can reach on a bicycle in 30 minutes or less.

As with walking, you will still need to have supplemental transportation for those times when traveling by bicycle is not practical.

Cost

Unlike walking, where the only expense you have is for a good pair of walking shoes, using a bike does cost some money.

First you will have the cost of the bicycle which can be as low as $100 to as much as $500 or more. A new, well built and lightweight 10 speed bicycle can be purchased for under $150.

By visiting your local bicycle stores, pawn shops, and thrift stores, much more elaborate used models in excellent condition may be purchased for the same, or less, money. Once you have the bicycle, you need a good lock. There is at least one company that guarantees, if your bicycle is stolen by breaking or cutting through their lock, the full cost of the bicycle, up to $500, will be refunded. This particular lock is made of carbon steel and costs about $35. A lock of this type may be a good investment.

Most avid bicyclists recommend a lightweight helmet, knee pads, and shin guards as the minimum of safety equipment. The cost of these items is between $35 and $75. If you are using the bicycle at night, you will want good reflectors and lights, at an additional cost of $15 to $25. These items should last for the life of the bike and are considered one time expenses.

If your area requires yearly registration, expect to pay $3 to $5 per year. You should also expect to pay approximately $25 to $55 per year for routine maintenance and tire replacement. The labor charges involved with these items can be greatly reduced by learning to do your own bicycle maintenance or having a knowledgeable friend do it for you.

Public Transportation

If you are fortunate enough to live in a city that has a good, inexpensive, and reliable public transportation system, you are truly blessed. I lived in New Orleans for 28 years, and, during that time, I found the public transportation system to be outstanding. When I left in 1968, you could get around the entire city for ten cents. Costs have gone up, and the city suffers from the problems of all inner cities, but the bus and streetcar system are still inexpensive and reliable.

I have a sister-in-law who has lived in Washington D.C. for the last 10 years and has not needed or wanted a car. Between walking, her bicycle, and the Metro system, she has been able to get around the city quite satisfactorily.

New York City, along with most other large metropolitan and many smaller cities, has improved their public transportation systems to minimize the need for private motorized transportation. A number of the larger cities have even expanded the area of service to reach deep into the outlying residential areas.

However, to be considered as a supplement to walking and riding a bicycle, public transportation systems must be safe, clean, and inexpensive. They must also provide full coverage of your area and be reliable.

Cost

Most public transportation systems will cost you between 75 cents and one dollar to travel a distance of up to about 10 miles. This is one way fare so, if you are going to and from work by public transportation, allow yourself at least two dollars per work-day for fare. This computes to about $42 per month.

If it is available and fits your needs, this will be the most inexpensive mode of motorized transportation you can get. You don't have to worry about maintenance, insurance, or even operating costs. Though not as flexible as owning your own vehicle, public transportation does greatly expand your mobility over walking or riding a bicycle.

Taxicab

Possibly the most expensive form of transportation found in large towns and cities is taxicabs. They should only be used in those cases where the distance to walk is prohibitive, the weather is bad, and public transportation in the form of bus, trolley, or subway will not suffice.

Taxicabs are also useful in emergencies when you cannot wait for public transportation and for getting to airports or train stations when carrying luggage. They can be useful for special occasions, especially when the formality of dress is not suitable for bus or subway travel. In that case, you are using the taxicab as an inexpensive limousine.

In most cities, you can easily pay in excess of a dollar a mile to use a taxicab. This high cost makes the taxicab a poor form of transportation for routine shopping or getting to work.

Motorcycle

This heading includes all two wheeled motorized vehicles. They greatly expand the distance you can travel over using a bicycle or walking, and for some people this is the optimum form of transportation. However, even the people who are dedicated bikers find there are times when supplemental forms of transportation must be used.

Most people do not like to arrive at work soaking wet. This will happen if you use a motorcycle, unless you carry a complete rain suit to keep you dry. The climate you live in can make using a motorcycle, as your only means of transportation, less than desirable. For most, with the exception of the dedicated motorcyclists, the motorcycle is really a recreational vehicle that can also be used to supplement the chosen form of daily transportation.

Costs

Today, motorcycles can cost as much as some full size automobiles. A good solid street bike starts at about $3,500 and the larger bikes, with options added, can cost in excess of $10,000. Like automobiles, they can be purchased used at substantial discounts. This is because, like other motorized vehicles, they depreciate -- lose value -- rapidly the first few years after they are built. In addition to initial purchase price, you need money to purchase protective clothing: helmet, good boots, coveralls, and rain gear. These items can be purchased new from about $250 up to whatever you are willing to spend. You can also purchase these items used, for a small fraction of their original cost, either through classified ads or from thrift shops.

Once you have the bike and your safety and protective clothing, you need to purchase insurance. The insurance should cover you, your bike, and any damage that may result from an accident you may cause. The cost of this insurance depends on your place of residence, driving record, age, value of the motorcycle, and the amount of coverage you want to purchase. Chapter 17 contains a detailed explanation of the factors considered when buying vehicle insurance. If you are male, single, under 25, and have a good driving record, you can expect to pay between $800 and $1,500 annually for average coverage. If you are female with the same traits, the annual rates will be as much as 40% less, with a range between $480 and $900.

In addition, you will need to budget for state and city licenses and taxes, routine maintenance, safety inspections, and gasoline -- probably the least expensive of the costs. See chapter 18 for a detailed discussion of each of these items.

Car or Van Pool

Car or van pools offer an excellent alternative to public transportation and, in both large and small cities, are becoming more popular each year. The car pool or van pool can work many ways, however, the one that seems to be the most popular is where one person owns the vehicle and does the driving with the riders paying as they would on public transportation.

The advantages of car or van pooling over public transportation are:

(1)   You are picked up and returned either at home or other convenient location.
(2)   You are taken to your place of work.
(3)   Car and van pools are usually very reliable.
(4)   They are more comfortable and more direct than public transportation.
(5)   They frequently cost less than public transportation.

For more information about car and van pools, check the bulletin boards at work and at grocery stores. You should also check your local newspaper. Many now have a classified section called car/van pools.

Automobiles

This discussion lumps all four wheeled vehicles -- cars, pickup trucks, and vans -- together. This type of vehicle provides all weather transportation with virtually unlimited range. To make the material easier to read, I have used the terms car or vehicle to include all cars, vans, and pickup trucks. The reason the other forms of transportation were discussed first is

that a large number of young adults have placed themselves into a position where they are "car poor." They buy the most expensive car they can afford as soon as, or in some cases before, they get their first real job. Then, they must work one or even two jobs to be able to pay for and maintain the vehicle they bought.

The decision to purchase a car must be based on need, not want. You may find it hard to believe, but by using some of the alternatives discussed above, you can have more fun, with a lot more money left to spend, by not having a car.

Costs

The categories of costs associated with owning a car are the same as a motorcycle, only the amounts are larger. The next four chapters are devoted to the expenses associated with owning, driving and maintaining your own car.

SUMMARY

Most likely you will eventually own a car. Like most young adults you probably want one now. Perhaps all your friends have one, and you are tired of bumming rides. But, before you rush out to buy a car, either for the first time or for a replacement, give some thought to the alternatives discussed in this chapter.

NOTES

Use this space to make a list of why a personal car is a must.

_____

_____

_____

_____

_____

_____

NEW OR PREVIOUSLY OWNED
Did you say 20 thousand *dollars*?

15

So, after reading the previous chapter, you decide you need or want an automobile of your own. This decision opens the door to many questions and considerations you will have to address before making the purchase. Possibly, the most important question is: What will the car be used for? The answer to this question will determine the features that the vehicle must have.

MAKE A LIST

As with any other buying you do, never go car shopping before you have identified what you really need. You should also make a list of features or options that you would like. If you shop around enough you may be able to find what you need with some of the additional features you want for a price you can afford.

This is especially true of car shopping because there are so many variations of the same, or similar, vehicle on the market. Unless you have a list to use as a yardstick in measuring the value against the price, you are at the mercy of the person doing the selling.

You will only be satisfied with your selection if the item you purchase fits your needs. Remember you are identifying your transportation needs. A specific color is a want, not a need. And, in spite of the automotive ads, you can buy wrap around stereo systems without buying a car.

HELP

The Appendix contains a number of good references on both new and used vehicles. These publications are used by individual sellers, car dealers, and banks, and should be used by you -- the buyer. They list, in an easy to understand format, the pertinent data about a car.

NEW CARS

For new cars, the data includes invoice and list prices for the base vehicle as well as available options. These prices are all based on information provided by the manufacturer of the vehicle before the vehicle has options added by the dealer.

Invoice Price

The invoice price of an item is supposed to represent the seller's cost. However, in the car industry this is a farce. New car dealers receive so many discounts and "incentives" that the invoice price is no longer representative of what the dealer really paid for the car. This is why dealers can sell cars for "just $99 over invoice" or even "$1 under invoice."

What the invoice price does give you is an idea of how good a deal you are getting. If the dealer will show you the actual invoice for the car, you have a base from which to deal. If, after the dealer options are added, the price is still close to invoice, you are most likely making a good buy. This only applies to the current year models. Because of depreciation -- discussed later in this chapter -- all previous years models, even if never driven, should be treated by you as used.

List Price

The "list price" of anything is the price the manufacturer has established as the selling price of the item. For a car, this is also called the sticker price. It will list the standard and optional features and must, by law, be displayed in a new car's window.

You will find cars with two stickers, one put on by the manufacturer and a second put on by the dealer. The second starts with the total from the first and adds amounts for dealer provided options, i.e. glass etching, pin-stripping, paint, undercoating, fabric protection and "market price adjustment." Regardless of how many stickers you see, the final list, or sticker price, should never be considered firm. This is simply the price that represents the car dealer's grandest dreams. Just for fun, try offering the dealer half of the sticker price and see how quick the price drops.

Rebates

A rebate, either cash or otherwise, is just another way for the dealer and/or the manufacturer to adjust the sticker price to make their vehicles more appealing than the competitors'. Usually, the rebate is not just a gift. Either the car is not selling well, the dealer is overstocked, or the cash rebate is tied to the finance charges.

For example, you can have either 2% interest for 36 months or $1,000 rebate. In this case you should look at the next chapter and determine what the car will cost you in interest at the 2% rate and at the normal rate. You also need to find out the repayment arrangements and monthly payment amount. Once you have this information, you can decide if you want the lower interest rate or the reduction in price.

USED CARS

For used cars, the references listed in the Appendix present the original list price and the current wholesale, loan, and retail prices. Wholesale, loan, and retail prices are presented as averages and are the result of wide market analysis. You may be able to find a car in good condition that sells for less than listed in the reference. If you find one that is in unusually fine condition, the price asked may be well above the average price listed in your reference book.

Mileage

One of the major factors to consider when shopping for a used car is mileage. The "average" number of miles per year used as normal yearly distance, by most professionals in the car selling business, is 12,000. If the car shows more than this average multiplied by its age, the price asked should be less than for a similar one that shows significantly less mileage.

For example, a car with 75,000 miles that is just three years old has traveled over twice the distance that is considered normal. While one that has 24,000 miles has traveled 33% less than average normal distance. In fact, the second car may still be under manufacturer's warranty which is definitely a positive factor.

Wholesale Value

The average wholesale value of a car is sometimes called the trade-in value. This is the value that a car dealer is going to use when determining the amount offered as a trade-in for a newer car. This can also be viewed as the absolute bottom price you can expect to pay for a given make, model, and year of a car in average condition. Even though this is an average value, beware of an offer that sounds too good. Remember, the seller has access to the same reference material that you do.

Loan Value

The loan value is the amount that most financial institutions will lend you on the vehicle. This amount is usually about 80% of the wholesale price. This does not mean that you can't borrow more than this amount if, in addition to the vehicle, you also offer additional collateral. Other collateral can even be your signature. The loan value amount should be used as a gauge when considering buying a used car, especially if you are going to have to finance most of the cost.

Retail Value

The retail value is the average amount that has been paid for a specific make, model, and year of car based on a sample of recent sales. The reference books are updated at least quarterly and provide a very good guide as to the maximum price that you should have to pay for your next used car. As discussed earlier, the cars in the samples are all considered to be in good condition with the average mileage. The body should be free of rust and the interior should not show more than normal wear and tear.

Now that you understand the reference materials and a little about language, it is decision time.

NEW CARS VERSUS USED CARS

Advantages of New

The primary advantage of buying a new car is that it should be relatively free from major maintenance expense. Because of the new car warranty, when maintenance is required, the service is usually good and the cost, if any, is minimal. No matter how long the warranty is: 12,000 miles or 12 months, 24,000 miles or 24 months, or 70,000 miles or 6 years; you know for that period of time someone else will pay for the maintenance. Or will they? Extended warranties, those that exceed the bumper to bumper warranty -- first 12 months -- usually only cover selected major mechanical parts of the vehicle. These parts are usually the engine and drive train, the transmission, and the emission control system.

The brakes, tires, radio, interior, air conditioner, and even radiator are not included in these extended warranties. In addition, except for the emission control system, you may be required to pay a maintenance fee -- $25 to $75 -- every time you use the warranty. You can, of course, purchase an insurance policy -- called a supplemental warranty -- that will pay the deductible amount and even provide payment for rental car expenses for extended maintenance periods. These insurance policies are rather expensive and the need is questionable.

Preventive or routine maintenance -- scheduled oil changes, fluid checks, belt adjustments -- is still necessary and even required to keep the vehicle under warranty. The cost of this maintenance is the responsibility of the owner even during the first 12 months for most cars.

Other advantages include the pleasure and prestige of owning a new car with your choice of color and options. It is difficult to place a value on these items because their worth differs from one person to the next. Some people would not think of trading in their 15 year old "Betsy" for a new car, while others cannot imagine owning a car more than three years old.

Disadvantages of New

All of the disadvantages of owning a new car are financial. Not only is the initial cost expensive, but all of the associated expenses, with the exception of gas and oil, are higher than for an older model. Insurance rates are more expensive, not just because the vehicle is more expensive but because newer cars have more expensive options and are stolen more often than older cars. Sales and property taxes are higher because they are based on value. Repairs, outside the warranty, can be more expensive because of new technology. The list can go on and on.

The purchase price, when converted to monthly payments, is only the first budget item you must consider. The impact of buying a new or more expensive vehicle must be checked against all of the transportation items in your budget.

Depreciation

And then there is depreciation... Depreciation is the loss of value that occurs starting as soon as the item is put into use. Clothes depreciate, a second hand piece of clothing may be worth only one tenth the original price, even if used only once. A new car begins to depreciate as soon as you sign the papers to purchase it. You do not even have to drive it. Once you have the title transferred to you the vehicle is used. You may call it "gently used or lovingly used," but used it is.

Go to your library and check some of the current issues of the references on new and used automobiles listed in the appendix. Look for last year's models and note the difference between the current average retail price and the sticker price of the same model when new. Most vehicles depreciate between 10 and 20 percent the first year with some depreciating as much as 25%. The average is about 15%. The second year the average depreciation is about 25%, and, by the fourth year, the vehicle will have depreciated approximately 45%. Remember this is based on the original manufacturer's sticker price and does not include many of the dealers options which can be depreciated 100% as soon as you buy the car.

Advantages of Used

It may be hard to believe, but just as the disadvantages of buying a new car are financial, the advantages of buying a used car are the same -- financial. Not only is the cost significantly less, but insurance rates, total cost of financing, and taxes are also reduced. Remember, a new car can depreciate as much as 40% by the time it is just three years old. This means that you can purchase a three-year-old car that sold for $10,000 when new for as little as $6,000. A car this age may still be under the original manufacturer's warranty. If well kept, it will look good, drive well and give you many years of good, low maintenance, low cost service.

Following this trend of thought a little further, a seven-year-old car will be selling for 20% or less of its original price. The same $10,000 car will be selling for $2,000 or less. It should have been driven less than 85,000 miles and, if maintained properly, provide safe, dependable transportation for another three or more years.

If you are a careful and patient shopper, you may even find good, dependable cars, more than 10 years old, selling for less than $1,000.

Disadvantages of Used

I guess the old saying, "when you buy something used, you buy other people's problems," clearly explains the biggest disadvantage of buying a used car.

Face reality; the person who previously sold or traded in the car did so for a reason. If you believe the used car salesperson, every car wassold because: "The kid went to college" or "The family simply outgrew the vehicle" or "This beauty was sold because it was part of a divorce settlement" or even, "The little old lady died."

You have to be smart and wary. What about the person who sold the car because the constant maintenance nightmare created too much stress? A vehicle described this way is commonly called a "lemon." What about the car that was severely damaged, but not totaled, in an accident? Then you have the car that pulls to the right, uses as much oil as gas, or accelerates whenever the notion strikes -- usually when stopped for a light! These situations all indicate problems and should be evaluated before buying the car.

Major Defects

Below is a list of the major defects you can encounter in a used car. This is not to imply that all used cars contain any of these defects but is intended to give you an idea of the cost involved if your new used car is not closely checked before the purchase.

PROBLEM	REPAIR COST
Frame and Body - dented, bent or twisted	*
Engine - leaks oil, knocks, burns oil	$800 - 1,500
Transmission - leaks, vibrates, or clatters	400 - 1,000
Differential - leaks, vibrates, or makes noise	150 - 500
Cooling System - clogged, leaks	25 - 300
Electrical System - defective computer, shorts	100 - 500
Brakes - shoes, pads, or rotors thin; leaks	65 - 500
Steering System - alignment, binding, slippage	150 - 400
Front End - worn springs, shock absorbers, ball joints, or struts	250 - 500
Fuel system - leaks, bad fuel pump, fuel injection or carburetor faulty	100 - 1,000

* The actual amount to repair this damage is very difficult to estimate. In some cases, the damage cannot be fixed completely no matter how much money and time is spent. The straightening of the front end of a car that has jumped a high curb can easily cost between $500 and $750 or more.

In addition to the above, you may have expensive as well as annoying problems with accessories -- radio, air conditioner, power windows and door locks, faulty gauges, worn belts, tires, wheels and exhaust system. Any of these items can easily cost in excess of $100 to replace or repair.

The Vehicle Itself

In addition to the possible maintenance problems you may be buying, you have another consideration. What about the problems that a given make or model may be famous for? How many recalls has this vehicle had? What about insurance? Is this one of the vehicles that cannot be insured, or if insured, costs twice as much as other vehicles?

Then, you also have the good deals offered on used Edsels, Pintos and other discontinued models or companies that are out of business. What about...? The questions can be endless but must be asked and answered. Disadvantages must be weighed against advantages.

The Real Cost!

No matter how much we talk about taxes, interest, insurance, depreciation, and maintenance, the impact does not reach us until it is expressed in dollars. The following table presents a comparison of the price, payment, depreciation and interest of a new car, selling for $10,000, to used models of the same car. To make the monthly payments representative, 60 months financing is used for the new, 48 months for the one year old, 36 months for the three year old, and 24 months for the 5-year-old model.

REAL COST

Age of vehicle:	New	1 Year	3 year	5 year
Cost	$10,000	$8,500	$6,000	$4,400
Monthly payment	218	220	196	205
Number of payments	60	48	36	24
1st year interest	1,100	935	660	484
Depreciation	1,500	1,300	850	600
Total Interest & Depreciation	2,600	2,235	1,510	1,084

From the above table it becomes apparent that if you purchase a 5-year-old car and maintenance for the year costs $500, your total expenditure will be $1,016 less than if the car was new and cost $10,000. You arrive at this figure by adding $500 to the total interest and depreciation amount of $1,084 for the 5-year-old model and subtracting this total, $1,584, from $2,600, the real first year cost of the new car. This calculation does not take into consideration the difference in monthly payment nor the reduced costs of insurance and taxes. It is very possible that your true savings of purchasing the 5-year-old vehicle would be even greater than the amount shown.

The data presented above, when coupled with the fact that good transportation vehicles can be bought for under $2,000, should give you some food for thought.

The decision, along with the responsibility, is yours. What do you want?

Are you willing to spend the majority of your income on car payments and related expenses making yourself "car poor"? Whatever you de-

decide to do, read on for suggestions of what to do before buying any vehicle.

Before Buying a New Car

The following checklist should make buying a new car easier.

(1)   Make a list of what you need and want.
(2)   Try to identify the make and model that meets number 1.
(3)   Check the reference materials listed in the Appendix to determine invoice and list prices.
(4)   Decide what you are willing to pay and how much you will have to finance.
(5)   Shop for financing. See chapter 16.
(6)   Leave checkbook, credit cards, and cash at home.
(7)   Start your shopping with the most convenient dealer. This is where you will go for maintenance.
(8)   Insist on written copies of preliminary deals.

(9) Select your best deal and buy the vehicle.

Shopping for a Used Car

Steps (1) through (9) should also be completed before shopping for a used car. Some additional things you should do are:

(1) Go used car shopping on a clear day. Bad weather and darkness can hide a vehicle's imperfections.

(2) Check the body and interior closely. Be sure to:
    (a) Check all instruments, radio, air conditioner, etc.
    (b) Check ease of opening and fit of doors, trunk, and hood.
    (c) Check for more than normal wear and tear on seats and upholstery.
    (d) Check for damp or wet spots under the floor and trunk mats.

(3) Closely check exterior looking for:
    (a) Rust and other body damage.
    (b) Uneven or too much tire wear. A new set of tires can cost $200 or more.
    (c) Leaking or rusted exhaust system.
    (d) Too much bounce indicates worn shocks or struts.
    (e) Leaks under car -- oil, transmission fluid, gas, or water.

(4) Road test car checking for:
    (a) Loose, noisy, or stiff steering. When going straight is steering wheel turned to right or left?
    (b) While driving straight, on a level surface, carefully ease hands off steering wheel and check for drift which could inidicate an alignment problem.
    (c) Smooth running engine, good acceleration.
    (d) Excessive road or wheel noises.
    (e) Smoothness of shifting and quietness of transmission.
    (f) With engine running turn on lights and then all accessories. There should only be a slight dimming of the lights and no noticeable difference in the smooth running of the engine.
    (g) While driving about 35 miles per hour, gently apply brakes. Braking should be quiet, sure, and without drift.

(5) Ask about any existing warranties. Used car dealers usually offer something, insist on a written warranty. A verbal warranty is the same as no warranty. Individual transactions may still have the original warranty in effect. If so, read the transfer clause and be sure you understand it. Otherwise, most individual sales of used cars are "as is."

(6) Ask to see the maintenance record. If no record is available, be careful.

(7) Once you are happy with the results of the above, insist on having a professional of your choice check out the mechanical condition of the vehicle. Fifty dollars spent now can result in hundreds saved later.

SUMMARY

Wants or needs, new or used, the decision is yours. Shop carefully and smartly. Watch out for deals that seem too good or where the salesperson is too anxious to sell. Also be wary of individuals that are not agreeable to having a vehicle tested by a professional mechanic. Owning and driving a vehicle that you are happy with is a very satisfying experience. Owning one that only costs you money provides no satisfaction at all.

Good luck and happy shopping.

CAR AND OTHER LOANS
Your ad says you finance anyone!

16

So, you want to buy a car or other vehicle. You have saved some money. You have checked your budget and know that you can afford the insurance and operating costs. You have done your homework and know what you need and what monthly payment you can afford. It's time to discuss financing.

Though the focus of this chapter is on car financing, the terms, rights, pitfalls, and interest table is equally applicable to any installment purchase you may make. The discussion is also valid no matter how you are financing: bank, credit union, or seller provided credit. Even though loan agreements between two individuals may vary slightly from what is discussed, the principles are the same. Be sure any loan or financing agreement you make is in writing.

In addition to being written, the agreement must be witnessed and state clearly the amount you are borrowing, the terms of the loan, and the interest rate being charged. Be sure you know all the rules before you play the game.

THE LOAN CONTRACT

The loan contract is an agreement to use someone else's money and to pay it back over a period of time. Since even the use of money has value, the agreement contains information on the length of time to repay and the cost -- interest rate -- of using the money. This type of contract must always be in writing and may be called an installment sales contract or promissory note. Ideally, the contract will contain information that clearly states the rights and responsibilities of both the lender -- seller -- and the borrower -- buyer.

Sample

Jo Ann has decided to buy a used car from a dealer. She has shopped around for both the car and financing and has decided that the dealer's bank provides competitive rates and service. The following is the sample contract for the purchase of her used car.

The car costs $2,500 and she is putting $500 down and financing $2,000. The contract is for 24 months at an interest rate of 13%. This is a two page contract so we will look at the front and then the back.

The very top of the form has a space that the financial institution will use to identify your account. Next, the form indicates that a precomputed finance charge is used in this contract. In today's financial market place, even when the interest charged is based on a declining balance, the finance charge is still precomputed based on an agreed payment plan.

The names and addresses of the seller and buyer are entered in the space provided. This equates to the lender and borrower and the parties of the contract are explained immediately following these entries

Following the explanation of the parties, you will find a statement that identifies the primary use of the purchase. Since personal property, business property, and farm property may all be financed at different interest rates, this information is used to determine the rate that will be charged for the purchase.

Next, a full description of the property being financed is entered. It is important that you verify the accuracy of all of these entries. I know of at least one instance where an individual financed one car and drove off the dealer's lot with another. If not immediately caught, this kind of error can result in a legal, as well as a paperwork, nightmare. It only takes a minute or two to verify for yourself that an honest typing mistake has not been made. We all make mistakes. Don't take anything for granted. The cost of doing so can be staggering.

Account # _____

INSTALMENT SALES CONTRACT AND DISCLOSURE STATEMENT

☒ Precomputed Finance Charge   ☐ Finance Charge on Declining Balance

Creditor (Seller Name and Address)	Buyer (and Co-Buyer)— Name and Address (Include County and Zip Code).
ESTABAN AUTO SALES ELM & FLECITY SOFT LIFE, OK 12381	JO ANN T. GRADUATE 2246 HOME STREET SOFT LIFE, OK 12387

PARTIES: In this contract the words "I", "me", "my", "we" mean any person who signs this contract as Buyer, Co-Buyer or Co-Signer. The words "you" and "your" mean the Seller or any assignee of this contract.

PURCHASE OF GOODS: I hereby purchase from you the property described below. All of this property is called "goods" in this contract. I have received and accepted the goods, which will be used primarily for: ☒ personal, family or household purposes ☐ farm purposes ☐ business purposes.

Motor Vehicle ☐ New ☒ Used	Year, Make & Model 1983 PONTIAC J2000	Body Style STA WAG	# Cyls. 4	Serial Number JG3LF246D4JA034563	Key # A1246	Odometer Reading 78,342

☒ Auto Trans. ☐ 4/5 Speed ☒ Power Brakes ☒ Power Steering ☒ Air Cond. ☒ Other POWER WINDOWS, CRUISE CONTROL

Description of Other Goods ☐ New ☐ Used N/A	Year, Make & Model N/A	Identification Number N/A

PROMISE TO PAY: In addition to the total down payment on line 2 below, I promise to pay you the "Total of Payments" disclosed below according to the payment schedule disclosed below.

ANNUAL PERCENTAGE RATE This is what my credit purchase will cost as a yearly rate.	FINANCE CHARGE This is the dollar amount this credit purchase will cost me.	Amount Financed This is the amount of credit provided to me.	Total of Payments This is the total amount I will pay if I make all payments as scheduled.	Total Sale Price This is the total cost of my credit purchase including my down payment of.
13 %	$ 281.92	$ 2,000.00	$ 2,281.92	$ 500.00 $ 2,781.92

My payment schedule will be:

Number of payments	Amount of Payment	When payments Are Due
24	$95.08	Monthly Beginning JANUARY 14 1990

ESTIMATES: If the finance charge applicable to this contract is computed on the declining balance, the "Finance Charge" and "Total of Payments" disclosed above are estimates, as are the amount of payments disclosed. These amounts have been computed on the assumption that all payments will be received on their scheduled due dates.

LATE CHARGE: If I don't pay any payment in full within 7 days of the day it is due, I will have to pay you a late charge of 5% of the payment.

SECURITY: I am giving you a security interest in the goods or property being purchased.

ASSUMPTION: If this loan is to finance the acquisition of my principal dwelling, someone buying my dwelling may not be allowed to assume the balance due on this contract on the original terms.

PREPAYMENT: If the finance charge is computed on the declining balance, I may have to pay a prepayment penalty. If there is a precomputed Finance Charge, I may be entitled to a refund of part of this charge.

I should refer to my contract documents for any additional information about nonpayment, default, prepayment refunds, any required repayment in full before the scheduled date, and other matters pertaining to this credit purchase.

PROPERTY INSURANCE: I know that I may choose the person who sells me the required property insurance. If I purchase property insurance from you, the cost will be $ N/A for _____ months.

NO LIABILITY INSURANCE INCLUDED

This credit sale is contingent upon financing upon terms which are satisfactory to the parties. Therefore, neither Buyer nor Seller will be bound if this contract is not accepted by _____ Bank (assignee) on the terms set forth in the contract within five days of its date.

IMPORTANT: I understand that there are important provisions on the reverse side of this contract and that I should read these before I sign the contract.

I signed this contract on DECEMBER 14   19 89 ____ after all applicable blanks were filled in and I acknowledge receipt of a completed copy.

SELLER: _____   BUYER: _____

By: _____   CO-BUYER _____

Title: _____   COSIGNER: _____

The following parties are signing this contract only for the purpose of granting Seller a security interest in the goods described above:

_____   _____

NOTICE: ANY HOLDER OF THIS CONSUMER CREDIT CONTRACT IS SUBJECT TO ALL CLAIMS AND DEFENSES WHICH THE DEBTOR COULD ASSERT AGAINST THE SELLER OF GOODS OR SERVICES OBTAINED PURSUANT HERETO OR WITH THE PROCEEDS HEREOF. RECOVERY HEREUNDER BY THE DEBTOR SHALL NOT EXCEED AMOUNTS PAID BY THE DEBTOR HEREUNDER.

(OVER)

In this case, the item Jo Ann is buying is a 1983 Pontiac J2000 station wagon. The vehicle is used, has 4 cylinders, automatic transmission, air conditioning, and power brakes. The serial number is JG3LF246D4JA034563, and the odometer reading-- mileage -- is 78,342. The odometer reading, though not required in all states, is usually entered by the seller.

If this contract was for some other purchase, such as a television, furniture, or stereo, the descriptive information for that item would appear on the line titled: *Description of Other Goods*.

The BIG Statement

The promise to pay statement is usually placed at this point in the contract. The simple statement, "I promise to pay you the Total of Payments disclosed below according to the payment schedule disclosed below," along with your signature makes you legally responsible for the full amount of the contract. It is very important that you fully understand what the full amount of the contract is, and what will happen if you are late or miss a payment. Read on.

The Agreement

The next part of the contract identifies the financing agreement. It includes the amount financed, annual percentage rate, amount of finance charge -- interest, the total of payments, and, in some cases, the total cost of the purchase. This final total includes interest and down payment. This is the real "bottom line" and reflects the full cost of the purchase.

Annual Percentage Rate

Discussion of annual percentage rates of interest was included in chapter 12. But, since this is an important part of your financial life, a review is appropriate. Interest is the cost of using someone else's money and is computed as a percentage of what is owed. However, since the money you owe goes down with each payment, you cannot figure the interest by multiplying the percentage times the full amount of the loan. In this case the loan is for $2,000, the interest rate is 13%, and the length of the loan is two years. The total interest charged is $281.92, a much smaller figure than the $520 that results from multiplying 13% by $2,000 by two, for the number of years. The reason for this difference is because Jo Ann will owe $2,000 for only one month of the two years. As she makes payments, the amount owed continues to decrease and so does the interest charged, until the loan is paid off.

Payment Schedule

Below is an easy to use table of payments by var-ious percentage rates with payoffs from one to five years. The monthly payment is based on a $1,000 loan amount. Using the table you can see how Jo Ann's monthly payment shown on the contract -- $95.08 was computed. Look for the point where the 13% and the two year lines meet. The monthly payment shown is $47.54. Multiply this by 2 since the loan is for $2,000 and the answer is $95.08 which matches the amount on the contract.

PAYMENT SCHEDULE
Annual Percentage Rate

Years	10%	11%	12%	13%	14%	15%
1	87.92	88.39	88.85	89.32	89.79	90.26
2	46.15	46.61	47.08	47.54	48.01	48.49
3	32.27	32.74	33.22	33.70	34.18	34.67
4	25.36	25.85	26.34	26.83	27.33	27.84
5	21.25	21.75	22.25	22.76	23.27	23.79

Now use the table for a different example. What would be the difference between the cost of borrowing $10,000 at 12% to buy a new car financed for four years compared to financing the same car for five years. The four year and 12% lines intersect at $26.34 which indicates the monthly payment for each $1,000 borrowed. Multiplying this amount by 10, for the loan amount of $10,000, gives a total monthly payment of $263.40 for 48 months -- 4 years. The total payment will be 48 times $263.40 or $12,643.20. Subtracting the amount of the loan -

- $10,000, gives you the total interest charge which is $2,643.20.

Doing the same computations for five years results in a monthly payment of $222.50, a total payment of $13,350 -- 222.50 times 60 months -- and a total interest charge of $3,350. The conclusion, then, is that to reduce the monthly payment by $41.10 will cost $706.80 in additional interest. There is more discussion on this, later in this chapter, under "Pitfalls."

Continuing with the discussion of this part of the contract, Jo Ann sees that the annual percentage rate -- 13%, the finance charge -- $281.92, and the amount financed -- $2,000 are all stated correctly. In addition, the total of payments and total sale price are correct. For this example, $2,281.92 is the total of payments and $2,781.92 is the total sale price including Jo Ann's down payment of $500.

Checking the payment schedule, Jo Ann verifies that the number of payments is 24, the amount of payment is $95.08, and her payments start on Jan 14, 1990. Reading the fine print, she sees a clause on estimates. This statement only pertains to contracts where the "declining balance" block is checked on the top of the contract.

Grace Period

The next clause on the contract, "Late Charge," is very important. What this clause states is that, if the full payment of $95.08 is not received at the bank by the 21st of each month, the payment for that month will automatically increase to $99.83. This is the regular monthly payment plus a late charge of 5% of the payment or $4.75. This clause means that Jo Ann has a seven day payment grace period.

This grace period is provided to compensate for weekends, paydays falling on Friday, the mail system, and other situations. It does not mean that Jo Ann changes her payment to the 21st of each month. To do so will mean that she will run the risk of missing the date sooner or later and have to pay the late charge. If this happens often enough there is another clause on the back of the contract called "Default" which may be exercised. In addition to paying late fees, she can lose both her car and her good credit rating.

In addition, each $4.75 late charge is like adding 25% to the interest rate. This is not a smart thing to do.

The next clause, on security, simply means that the car being purchased is the collateral for the loan. As collateral, in the event of default, it can be repossessed -- taken back and sold to another buyer -- to pay off the loan and any costs involved in the repossession.

The clause on assumption is for houses and is not applicable to this discussion. The prepayment clause states that in a precomputed interest situation, if Jo Ann pays off the full loan amount early, she may be entitled to a refund of part of the interest.

Additional Terms and Conditions

The back of this contract contains a list of addiional terms and conditions. Some of these have already been mentioned on the front of the form, in which case there is additional clarification.

Additional Charges

The late fee has already been discussed. The additional charges clause also covers any other fees Jo Ann may be charged if she does not honor the contract as written. As with all other clauses, any questions she has on its meaning must be addressed and clarified before she signs the contract.

Prepayment

Most loan agreements can be prepaid with the buyer receiving a rebate of some of the interest computed for the full length of the agreement. For this loan, the "Rule of 78" applies. This means that the computation of refunded interest will be based on the the principle that the most interest is paid on the first month and the least on the last.

The "78" is derived by adding the first month, 1, to the second month, 2, and so on. (1+2+3+4+5...+12 = 78). For example, after making five payments to pay off a one year loan that has a total interest charge of $165, you would save $59.23 in interest. Starting at seven, the number of months still left on the contract, add the month numbers together working downward. (7+6+5+4+3+2+1 = 28). Divide 28 by 78 the total for the entire 12 months. Your answer is 0.35897. Multiply this by the total interest of $165 and the result is the saving or rebate of interest you have earned: $59.23.

This is both a valid and logical way to compute the rebate, because it closely

ADDITIONAL TERMS AND CONDITIONS

<u>ADDITIONAL CHARGES:</u> I will pay you a late charge of 5% of the amount of each payment not paid within 7 days of the date it is due. I will pay a Finance Charge (at the Annual Percentage Rate disclosed on the reverse side) on all amounts remaining unpaid at maturity or upon acceleration. If I have made a payment with a check or have authorized you to make an automatic transfer of funds from an account for such a payment, and you are unable to credit this contract because of insufficient funds, a closed account, a stop payment, or for any other reason, I may have to pay you a fee for processing and handling.

<u>PREPAYMENT:</u> If this contract is based on a precomputed finance charge and I prepay the entire balance in full, I will receive a refund of the unearned portion of the Finance Charge figured by the "Rule of 78." However, you can charge a minimum Finance Charge of the lesser of twenty-five dollars ($25.00) or the amount of Finance Charge shown on the reverse side. If the finance charge applicable to this contract is computed on the declining balance, I may prepay in advance in any amount at any time without penalty. Payments will first be applied to interest to the date of actual payment and the remainder to principal. Partial prepayments will be treated as advance payments. The effect of any such advance payment will be to defer the next required monthly payment to the payment date that would occur next if the advance payment were treated as a series of single payments, each in the scheduled payment amount.

<u>ACCELERATION AND DEFAULT:</u> If a default occurs, you have the right, at your option and without giving me prior notice or demand, to require that I pay immediately the full amount that I owe under this contract, computed as if I had made a voluntary prepayment and obtained a Finance Charge credit as of the date of acceleration. Until this amount is paid in full, I will pay interest computed at the Annual Percentage Rate disclosed on the reverse side of this contract. A default occurs if (a) I do not make a payment, together with my late charge, within 10 days of the date it is due, (b) I am in or file for bankruptcy, receivership, or an insolvency proceeding, (c) I die or any Co-signer dies, (d) any order of attachment, levy, garnishment is issued against me or any Co-signer or property, assets or income of mine or of any Co-signer, (e) I fail to perform any other promise I make in this contract or any other contract with you, (f) you deem yourself insecure.

<u>SECURITY INTEREST:</u> To secure all obligations and indebtedness under this contract and, in the case of motor vehicles, to secure payment of all other obligations of any kind that I owe you now or may owe later, **I give you a security interest** under the Uniform Commercial Code in all goods described on the reverse side and all accessions (such as accessories or equipment now or later included in or affixed to the goods), collectively referred to as "collateral". As additional security, I give you a security interest in all rebates of unearned premiums on insurance written in connection with this contract.

<u>RIGHT TO REFINANCE A BALLOON PAYMENT:</u> If any payment is more than 10% greater than the regular or recurring instalment payments, it shall be subject to my right to refinance such payment.

<u>INSURANCE ON GOODS:</u> I promise to keep the goods insured against loss or damage in the amount of the unpaid balance on this contract or the value of the goods, whichever is less. If you ask, I will make the policy payable to you and will deliver the policy to you. If I do not keep the goods insured in the amount described above or do not furnish you with satisfactory evidence of insurance, you may obtain such insurance at my expense, protecting either your or my interest, or your interest alone. I assign to you all amounts payable under the insurance, directing the insurer to make payment to you, and I appoint you my attorney-in-fact to endorse any draft. I understand the proceeds of my insurance will be applied to my indebtedness in the inverse order of the maturity of instalments. I agree to reimburse you for any insurance premium expense plus interest.

<u>CANCELLATION OF INSURANCE:</u> Any refund from a cancellation of any insurance applicable to this contract, including any applicable rebate of finance charge, will be treated as follows:
1. If the finance charge is precomputed, as a reduction of the balance on the contract, in inverse order of maturity.
2. If the finance charge is computed on the declining balance, as a partial prepayment.

<u>DOCUMENTS FOR FILING:</u> If you ask, I will sign any other document you want to have filed or recorded for the purpose of perfecting the security interest I am giving you in this contract. I hereby appoint you as my attorney-in-fact to do whatever you may deem necessary to perfect or to continue a perfected security interest in the collateral and to protect the collateral. If you choose, you may file a copy of this contract, or any other security agreement or financing statement, as a financing statement under the Uniform Commercial Code. If the goods are titled, I will do whatever is necessary to apply for, obtain, and deliver to you certificate(s) of title, properly showing the security interest created in this contract. I agree that any reproduction of this agreement or of a financing statement shall be sufficient as a financing statement. I will pay all costs required for such filings.

<u>REPOSSESSION:</u> If a default occurs, you may exercise at your option any and all of the rights and remedies on default of a secured party under the Uniform Commercial Code or other applicable law, and all rights provided in this contract including without limitation the right to take possession of the collateral without my permission and without giving me notice or demand or judicial hearing. I authorize you to enter my property lawfully with or without a court order for the purpose of taking possession of the collateral. HAVING KNOWLEDGE THAT I MAY HAVE THE RIGHT UNDER APPLICABLE LAW TO NOTICE AND A JUDICIAL HEARING PRIOR TO THE TAKING OF POSSESSION UPON DEFAULT HEREUNDER, I EXPRESSLY WAIVE ANY AND ALL SUCH RIGHTS TO PRIOR NOTICE AND JUDICIAL HEARING PRIOR TO THE TAKING OF SUCH POSSESSION BY YOU OR BY ANY OFFICER AUTHORIZED BY LAW TO EFFECT REPOSSESSION, AND RELEASE YOU FROM LIABILITY IN CONNECTION WITH SUCH REPOSSESSION.

<u>OTHER PROPERTY TAKEN:</u> You may take possession of any property not subject to your security interest which is in, on, or attached to the collateral at the time you take possession of the collateral. You may hold such other property unless:
  (a) I first demand in writing that you return such property.
  (b) The demand is sent to you by certified mail within 5 days after you take possession of such other property, and
  (c) The written demand clearly describes such other property.

<u>PAYMENT OF ATTORNEY'S FEES AND OTHER COSTS:</u> If you take collection action, I must pay all collection costs including an attorney's fee of 25% of the amount due at the time the account is referred to an attorney for collection, plus your out-of-pocket collection expenses and all court costs.

<u>MISCELLANEOUS:</u> I agree to indemnify you and any assignee against loss or damage and to hold you harmless from any and all loss or damage to persons or property, or expense, caused by the goods, or by the use of or operation of the goods.

<u>OTHER RIGHTS YOU HAVE:</u> You may waive or delay enforcing any of your rights without losing them. You may assign any rights that you have under this contract and any rights that you have to the goods may be exercised by any assignee. You may enforce this contract against my heirs and legal representatives. If any part of this contract is found to be unenforceable, this will not make any other part unenforceable.

<u>EACH PARTY RESPONSIBLE:</u> Although more than one party may sign this contract, whether as Buyer, Co-Buyer, or Co-Signer, I know that each of us is totally responsible for all promises and for paying all amounts under this contract. I AGREE THAT I WILL NOT ASSERT AGAINST YOU ANY CLAIM, DEFENSE, COUNTERCLAIM, OR SETOFF WHICH I MAY HAVE AGAINST YOU EXCEPT AS PROVIDED IN THE FOLLOWING NOTICE: NOTICE: ANY HOLDER OF THIS CONSUMER CREDIT CONTRACT IS SUBJECT TO ALL CLAIMS AND DEFENSES WHICH THE DEBTOR COULD ASSERT AGAINST THE SELLER OF GOODS OR SERVICES OBTAINED PURSUANT HERETO OR WITH THE PROCEEDS HEREOF. RECOVERY HEREUNDER BY THE DEBTOR SHALL NOT EXCEED AMOUNTS PAID BY THE DEBTOR HEREUNDER.

> <u>ENTIRE AGREEMENT:</u> The parties acknowledge that this contract represents the entire agreement and supersedes any prior or contemporaneous oral or written understanding or representation.
> <u>MODIFICATION OR WAIVER:</u> Any modification or waiver of the provisions of this contract shall not be effective unless it is in writing and signed by the parties. THERE ARE NO WARRANTIES, EXPRESSED OR IMPLIED, INCLUDING ANY IMPLIED WARRANTY OF MERCHANTABILITY OR FITNESS FOR A PARTICULAR PURPOSE OR OTHERWISE WHICH EXTEND BEYOND THOSE ON THE FACE HEREOF APPLICABLE TO THE GOODS, EXCEPT THE MANUFACTURER'S EXPRESSED WARRANTIES, IF ANY, WHICH ARE ITS EXCLUSIVELY AND NOT SELLER'S.

<u>GOVERNING LAW:</u> This contract is governed by the law of the State of Virginia.
<u>ASSIGNMENT BY SELLER:</u> The Seller may assign this contract. If the contract is assigned, the Seller will receive a portion of the Finance Charge.

approximates computing interest charges on the outstanding balance. For more detailed explanations of this and other interest computations check the references listed in the Appendix.

Any other method of computing refundable interest should be explained by the seller. Don't be shy. You are entitled by law to have this fully explained.

Acceleration and Default

As Jo Ann reads the Acceleration and Default clause, she realizes that, even though the front of the contract gives her a seven day grace period, this clause states that if she is more than 10 days late, the bank can demand full payment including interest.

The bankruptcy, death, and order of garnishment statements are self-explanatory. For a car purchase, Jo Ann should be aware that insurance covering the car, to be discussed in the next chapter, is required. Failure to purchase this insurance makes the full amount of the loan, including interest, due on demand.

Note: The final sentence in this clause is a catch all. It simply means that, if at any time Jo Ann behaves in a way that makes the bank think that she may default on the loan, they can demand full payment. This is one of the statements that only a few people pay attention to, yet it is a very important clause to understand. It gives the bank the right to determine ability to pay, and, based on this determination, make the full balance of the loan due.

For example, should the bank officers find out that Jo Ann is no longer employed at the company they used to verify her income, they can call for full payment of the loan. If she misses a couple of payments or if she overdraws her checking account, they can decide the repayment of the loan is questionable and call for full payment. In other words, any behavior or change in status by the borrower can be used to call for the full payment of the outstanding balance.

Security Interest

This clause states that the merchandise -- car -- being purchased is the collateral for the loan. In case of an accident, the insurance company will first pay the bank the balance of the loan. Any value that is remaining will then be paid to Jo Ann. It also states that Jo Ann will not offer this car as collateral for another loan.

Balloon Payment

Some loans are written in two parts. This is done primarily to reduce payments during the initial period of the loan and contains a residual amount, or lump sum, to be made as the last payment. This last payment is either paid in full, or a new financing agreement is drawn up. The balloon payment clause provides that you will be able to finance this final payment.

This type of financing is the basis used by dealers when leasing a vehicle. The dealer, for a new vehicle being leased, will compute the value of the vehicle at the end of the lease period, usually 36 months. The person leasing the car pays, as the leased amount, the difference between this value and the selling price of the car plus interest.

For example, a lease for a $9,000 car that is expected to depreciate $5,000 during the first three years may be computed as follows: the selling price of the car, $9,000, minus $5,000 of depreciation equals $4,000 residual value. The three years interest on the residual value at 11% comes to $440. The regular monthly payment on a three year loan of $5,000 at 11% interest is $163.70. This will be added to 1/36 of the interest on the residual amount which was $440 or $12.22, giving a total monthly lease payment of $175.92. This amount compares very favorably with the normal financing of the $9,000 at 11% for five years which would require a monthly loan payment of $195.75, until you realize that at the end of the lease, the dealer gets the car back.

Some dealers have found that to increase the number of new car buyers, this same type of agreement is appealing because the buyer pays less in payments. However, instead of a lease, the buyer faces two loans. The initial loan, and, then to own the car, when the balloon payment comes due, a second loan is required. There is more discussion on this later in the chapter under "Pitfalls."

Insurance on Goods

If you are going to use a vehicle as collateral for a loan, you must carry insurance covering damage by accident, theft, and fire. This is a requirement of any financing agreement and should be considered before borrowing money. It is possible that, if you have to borrow money to buy a car, you will find the extra insurance to be outside your budget. The next chapter covers insurance coverages, their meaning, and cost.

Cancellation of Insurance

You will be offered life or disability insurance to cover the loan. This insurance will provide for payment of the loan in case you are disabled or die before the loan is fully paid. The cancellation of insurance clause allows you to receive a computed rebate of the insurance and applicable interest should you pay the loan off early and cancel the insurance.

You must decide whether you need this kind of insurance by weighing the cost of the insurance against the cost to your estate and the probability of not being able to make the payments. Before you make this decision, be sure the coverage, as well as the cost, is explained. These policies will not pay if you just get sick, miss work, or can't make a payment. They are designed primarily for large loans or individuals that have family support obligations.

Documents for Filing

This clause requires Jo Ann to sign the title and any other necessary documents over to the bank to secure the car. This is normal for any loan that has property as collateral. This clause goes with the Security Interest clause.

Repossession

If Jo Ann does not make a payment and the bank decides that she is in default, the repossession clause waives her right to protect her property and grants the bank permission to repossess the car without court order. The bank does not even have to notify her of repossession action. Banks will usually do everything in their power to notify someone that they consider a loan in default and are initiating repossession action. This makes good business sense since the bank is interested in getting the money, not having a parking lot full of repossessed vehicles.

Other Property Taken

The other property taken clause paragraph gives the bank the right to keep any other property that may be in the car at time of repossession unless certain prescribed action is taken by Jo Ann.

Payment of Attorney's Fees

When Jo Ann signs this contract, she agrees to pay all attorney's fees and other collection costs associated with repaying the loan. This means that if she is in default, the amount the bank has to pay to repossess the car will be added to the balance of the loan. If they sell the car for an amount greater than this combined amount, she will receive the difference. This is not usually the case. If the car is sold for less than the combined amount, not only does she not have the car, she still owes the bank money. This is why people having financial difficulties will try to sell their vehicles to someone who is willing to just take over the payments.

Miscellaneous

The miscellaneous clause releases the bank from any liability in case you are in an accident. This is necessary because the bank will be listed on the title.

Other Rights

The other rights clause lists additional rights of the bank, not Jo Ann. For example, this clause gives the bank the option of not repossessing the vehicle if one payment is missed, but to retain the right to do so if a second or third payment is missed. This allows a little flexibility under the law for the bank to decide when the loan is considered in default.

Each Party Responsible

If Jo Ann had a co-signer or co-buyer sign for her to get the loan, the each party responsible clause notifies the co-signer/buyer that both Jo Ann and the co-signer/buyer are each responsible for the full amount of the loan. Co-signing or co-buying is not a 50/50 proposition. All signers are responsible for the full sum of the loan. This is why some people are reluctant to co-sign loans.

What's Left?

The remainder of the clauses are administrative. Included, you will find one or more of the following statements:

(1)   A statement that the contract is binding to all parties who sign.

(2)   A disclaimer that the loan contract does not in any way provide any form of warranty.

(3)   The state under whose law the contract is written.

(4)   Notification that the contract may be sold or assigned to another financial institution.

(5)   A statement prohibiting the removal of the property used as collateral from the governing state without written authorization.

This last section varies greatly by financial institution and state. It should be read and understood before signing.

Jo Ann is satisfied that she understands the contract. She has already told the salesman that she will provide her own insurance so the statement "NO LIABILITY INSURANCE INCLUDED" has been stamped on the contract. She reads the rest of the document, verifies the date, and signs the contract. The automobile and the monthly payments now belong to her.

PITFALLS

Some of the pitfalls to be aware of when buying an automobile are:

(1)   Spending more money than you can afford.

(2)   Paying unreasonable interest rates by financing with a dealer who advertises that they will finance anyone.

(3)   Buying from high pressure salespeople. Those who are more interested in how much you can afford each month than in what kind car you need.

(4)   Signing a loan contract without reading and understanding it first.

Over Spending

Everyone either knows what is affordable and fits into their budget or, by performing a few calculations, can easily determine the available monthly budget excess.

Jo Ann did her homework. She knew what she wanted, took her time shopping for both the car and the loan, and read and understood the contract before signing. By doing this, she avoided many of the pitfalls that face the first or second time car buyer when financing a car. The greatest of these pitfalls is the overwhelming desire to buy a more expensive car but, at the same time, reduce the payments.

Though it is true that the payments must fit into your budget, it is also true that the length of the loan must at least match the depreciation schedule of the vehicle. This is the major problem when financing a car with a loan that has a balloon payment or a payment schedule that is unusually long.

As demonstrated earlier in this chapter and in Chapter 18, a five year $10,000 loan on a new car will cost $217.50 per month if financed at 11% interest. The total interest paid will be $3,050, and the buyer will have clear title to the vehicle -- own it.

Unless you are purchasing a vehicle with an unusually low depreciation rate, five years is the longest you should ever finance a new car. Used cars, up to two years old, can safely be financed for three years if you are not paying above the average retail price. Cars three years old and older should not be financed for more than two years.

With some new cars and 100% financing, you can still have problems.

Carol's Story

Carol had been given a couple of raises. Because of this increased income, she found herself able to fit an inexpensive new car purchase into her budget. Her problem was that she had no credit rating. She did not have a bad rating, just no rating at all. As she was checking the papers, she noticed one of the dealers offered to finance anyone.

In fact, the ad offered 100% financing for first time new car buyers. She found the dealer unwilling to negotiate on the sticker price, but, since they would finance the total amount, she made her selection. The car listed for $7,200, was financed at 14% for five years, and her monthly payments were only $167.54.

For about two years she was very happy with her purchase. Then, she received a promotion and decided that she could now comfortably afford her "dream" car.

She shopped around for the car she wanted and for financing. With this information available, she sat down with a salesman to work up the contract on her dream car. When the salesman explained that the loan amount would have to be more than the agreed upon price of the new car, she couldn't believe her ears. The salesman explained that her outstanding payoff balance on the loan was more than the trade in value of the car. By having a five year, 100% loan, she had been caught by the numbers. She owed more on the loan than the car was worth as a trade in.

The ending to Carol's story, though not a happy one, turned out to be acceptable. She had to wait to get her dream car until she personally sold her first car for a few hundred dollars more than she owed, but not as much as she thought she had invested.

Balloon Payments

A balloon payment is usually the last payment of a loan. This payment is larger than the regular payments, and to pay it off the borrower usually has to refinance this amount. It is used by loan companies to reduce the borrower's monthly payment making it easier to buy more expensive products. Just like the financing for an extended period, the use of a balloon payment can mean disaster to the borrower.

How does it work?

The dealer or financial institution conservatively computes the vehicle's projected worth at the end of a given period, let's say four years. The buyer pays the interest on that amount for four years and the regular monthly payment needed to bring the balance down to the last payment which is the balloon payment. Since this last payment is "set aside" during the first four years, the payments are reduced, but the borrower pays a higher interest over a longer period.

Example

As discussed earlier under Payment Schedule, a new car loan of $10,000 financed at 11% for five years will cost $217.50 per month and have a total finance charge of $3,050. You tell the dealer the only reason you can't sign the contract for this new car is because you can only afford $180 per month. You are surprised when the dealer says, "No problem." He has a loan company that will write you a five year loan with a balloon payment of $4,000 at 13%, and the monthly payment is only $179.89. Don't be too quick to accept this deal. Let's take a look at the true figures.

The dealer has computed the expected value of the car at the end of five years. Having used a depreciation table for this vehicle, he found that over the first five years the vehicle could depreciate as much as 60%, or $6,000. The loan will be computed to repay this $6,000 in 60 months with a balloon payment at the end for the remaining $4,000.

The annual percentage rate of interest is 13%, this is 2% higher than the regular loan, because more of the loan company's money is at risk for a longer period of time. Using the payment schedule presented earlier, we find that the monthly payment for $1,000 over five years at 13% interest is $22.76. Multiply this by the number of thousands of dollars of the loan -- six -- and you get a monthly payment of $136.56. However, this only pays off the $6,000. The borrower still has to pay the interest on the $4,000 balloon payment which is $520 per year -- $4,000 times 13%.

Since the loan is paid monthly, the loan payments will have to include 1/12 of $520 ($43.33) to cover the interest on the $4,000 balloon payment. So the total monthly payment is $179.89, but what about the total cost of the loan?

Total Loan Cost

To compute the total cost of the loan, we first multiply the monthly payment of $179.89 by the number of payments, 60, for a total of $10,793.40. Then subtract the loan amount of $6,000 from that figure, leaving a first loan cost of $4,793.40. And the car is still not yours.

If, when the balloon payment is due, you can finance the $4,000 for two years at 13%, your payments will be $190.16 for a total repayment of $4,563.84. The second loan will then cost $563.84 -- $4,563.84 - $4,000. To save about $37 in monthly payments, you will pay approximately $2,307.24 in additional interest. This is the first loan's interest, $4,793.40 plus the second loan's interest, $563.84 minus the cost of the regular five year, $10,000, 11% loan -- $3,050. Using the balloon payment method of financing the car will also take an additional two years to repay.

Bob's Story

It all started about two years ago. It was Bob's lucky day. His boss just told him about his promotion and raise. The timing was perfect. His old clunker was ready to call it quits. With his revised budget he decided that he could afford a newer car. After considering increases in taxes and insurance, he could still make monthly payments of about $120.

He shops around for financing and finds that this amount will cover a two year loan of about $2,500. He opens his newspaper to look at the used car ads and notices a full page add that states "Why drive a used car when you can buy a new XXXXX for $110 down and just $110 a month." This is unbelievable! He can fit a new car purchase into his budget. He didn't expect to be able to do this for another two or three years.

He double checks his budget, goes to the dealer, and the dealer explains that the low monthly payment is possible because at the end of 48 months there is a balloon payment of $2,800. The dealer even agrees to take the clunker as the down payment. He reads, and feels he understands, the financing agreement.

For nothing more than the expenses of taxes and titling fees, he drives home in his new car. For 18 months all is great. The car is the answer to his dreams. He washes it weekly and even buys a good stereo cassette player. Reality strikes during the 19th month. Coming home in the rain one evening, the car skids on a turn, goes off the road, and flips over into a ditch. Fortunately, Bob, though shaken up, has no major injuries.

Bob has insurance. He calls the company, and an adjuster comes out and breaks the bad news. Unfortunately, the car did not fare as well as Bob did; it is considered totaled by the insurance company. This news is bad enough, but there was still more to come. The car had a retail value of $4,480, and, after the adjuster subtracted Bob's $250 deductible, the settlement of the insurance claim was $4,230.

Because of the extended financing of the car, the balance due the bank was $4,695. This included the rebate of interest that was computed as if he was paying the loan off early. Not only did Bob not have a car, he had to make arrangements to pay the bank the difference of $465.

There was nothing underhanded or illegal in this financing arrangement. Bob simply got caught by the numbers. Had he not had the accident, or had the accident occurred later, the scales would have eventually tipped in his favor. But, with a balloon payment, it would have taken longer than a few months.

SUMMARY

The two stories, Carol's and Bob's, are recent and true. They are presented to reinforce the need to be wary of some of the advertisement and financing deals that may be offered to entice you to buy more than you need or more than you can afford. Do your homework. Read and understand any contract you sign. Be a smart shopper, know about the expenses of owning and operating a car before you buy. Except for the monthly car payments, the largest single expense for most car owners is the next topic: Insurance.

Now that you own the car, what about insurance?

INSURANCE
My two speeding tickets cost an extra what? 17

Why do you need insurance? If you cause an auto accident, you will be responsible for the damages and losses to the other persons. The people injured, either personally or as the owners of property, can go to court to make you pay for the damages. The amount of damage that can result from an auto accident today is staggering. I was a witness to an accident in which the driver of a vehicle was responsible for an estimated $75,000 of property damage. The accident caused only minor personal injuries and only took about 30 seconds. This accident also occurred about 25 years ago when property cost a lot less.

THE NEED

Without insurance, you are responsible for the damage out of your own pocket. Anything you own, your savings, the balance in your checking account, future wages, and, if you own one, your home can all be used to satisfy this debt. Insurance that covers the damage done to others is called liability insurance. Liability insurance will also pay for a lawyer to defend you against additional claims or lawsuit.

There are other reasons to carry automobile insurance:

(1) Most states require that the owner of a vehicle prove they are covered by liability insurance or an alternate self-insurance plan before the vehicle can be registered.
(2) As discussed in Chapter 16, banks are going to require insurance on any vehicle that is used as collateral for a loan.
(3) You would expect that if someone injured you or damaged your property they would pay for the damages.

AN ALTERNATE

Some states allow for the posting of what is called Uninsured Motorist Fees or Surety bonds. This is not insurance. It is a fee paid to the state that permits you to accept all risk in case you are responsible for an accident. No one else will pay for the damage. You alone will be responsible for paying all damages and lawyers fees. In most states, failure to comply with the above rules will result in loss of registration, loss of driver's license, and even additional fines and fees. Unless you can afford to accept this financial responsibility, you should be insured.

TYPES OF COVERAGE

The types of coverage that are required by your state of residence can be determined by contacting your Department of Motor Vehicles (DMV) or similar agency. Be sure to determine the requirements before buying a vehicle, since the cost of the insurance will be a major budget item. States vary in the minimum amounts of coverage but generally agree on the mandatory types of coverage, which are liability and uninsured motorist.

Liability

All states requiring automobile insurance require liability coverage. Liability insurance does not cover you, your car, or your passengers, it covers payment for damage done to others. This coverage is usually expressed in thousands of dollars and is broken into two parts. The first part, called bodily injury, covers injury or death. Most states require a minimum of $25,000 for one person and $50,000 for two or more. The second part of the liability coverage is property damage, with today's minimum being

$10,000 in most states.

The bodily injury portion of this coverage provides payment of expenses incurred by persons injured in an automobile accident caused by you or others having your permission to drive the covered vehicle. The coverage includes payment of medical and dental bills, pain and suffering, lost wages, and other expenses directly related to the accident. If you have the coverage limits discussed above, the insurance will pay up to $25,000 for one person and up to $50,000 if two or more people are injured or killed.

The property damage portion of the coverage provides payment for any damage to the property of others caused by you or another authorized driver of your vehicle. This includes damage to another vehicle, damage to a fence, or even a road sign or light pole. This coverage does not pay for damages to your vehicle.

The coverage amounts stated above are examples of state minimums. People with a lot of assets, that could be lost in a lawsuit, can even buy liability coverage of $1,000,000 per accident. The actual amounts of coverage you decide to carry will be determined by your examination of your financial status and the cost of the coverage.

For individuals like Jo Ann, who are just starting out on their own, the amount of liability coverage that meets the state requirements is usually all that fits into their budget.

Uninsured Motorist

Uninsured motorist coverage is very important. It provides the same levels of coverage required by your state for liability. You are buying protection in case you are involved in an accident caused by someone else who is not insured. Even though automobile liability insurance is required by most states and driving without such insurance is a violation of the law, it does happen. People forget or do not renew their insurance, and insurance companies refuse to insure, or even cancel, some individuals' policies. Unfortunately, many of these uninsured people continue to drive.

Later in this chapter, under the discussion of cost, you will see that the cost of this coverage is almost nothing when compared to the cost of the coverage you are required to have to protect others. This coverage is a very good investment against loss to you caused by others.

Collision and Comprehensive

Collision and comprehensive coverage pays for the repair or replacement of your vehicle in case of an accident, vandalism, fire or theft. This coverage is sometimes called physical damage coverage and is required if the vehicle is used as collateral on a loan. Some insurance companies will charge extra for very expensive sound equipment or other expensive equipment that increases the threat of loss by theft. Your insurance company may offer discounts for having alarms or other anti-theft devices. Compare your savings on insurance to the cost of a security system before making this decision.

Medical Payments

Medical payments coverage will pay for medical and/or burial expenses if you or your passengers are injured or killed as the result of an accident. This coverage is in effect even if you are the cause of the accident. It will also pay if you are struck by a vehicle while walking or riding in another vehicle. The coverage is usually for expenses incurred within one year of the accident. This coverage is a must if you do not have hospitalization insurance or if your hospitalization insurance does not pay for automobile accident claims.

Supplementary Health and Disability

Supplementary health and disability coverage is similar to Medical Payments, in that medical and dental care, rehabilitation, and funeral expenses would be covered for up to $2,000 per person for a period of one year. In addition, you would receive up to $100 per week, for a period not to exceed 52 weeks, for loss of income. This coverage will pay regardless of who causes the accident. To have both this coverage and medical payments coverage may be a duplication and should be clarified by your agent.

Miscellaneous

Most insurance companies offer a variety of additional coverages including towing, car rental, and full glass coverage.

Towing coverage will cover the cost of towing your vehicle for repairs, even if it is not involved in an accident. This coverage usually only covers the towing to the place of repair. Towing coverage is usually very inexpensive, under $5 for six months of insurance.

Car rental coverage allows you to receive payment for renting a car while yours is being repaired as the result of an accident. The coverage is usually limited to a specified number of days at a fixed rate per day. This coverage can be expensive and should only be considered if not having your car prevents you from getting to work.

Full glass coverage allows you to receive payment for any glass damage. This means that the collision and comprehensive deductible amount is waived for damage to any of the glass in your car. The cost of full glass coverage must be weighed against the area in which you live, where you park your car,and the replacement cost of damaged glass for your vehicle. Compare rates on all of these coverages by getting quotes from various insurance companies or agents.

How Much is Enough?

Some people say they can never have enough insurance. Others look at insurance, especially automobile insurance, as an added cost, and everything over what is required is too much. The minimum amounts and types of coverage you must have are easy to determine. Your state of residence will set the minimum on liability coverage, and, if your car is financed, the bank will require you to have collision coverage.

As you can see by the types of coverage available, there is more to automobile insurance than minimum requirements. How much coverage you carry is an individual choice based on peace of mind and your ability to pay the premiums. Today, a two car accident with no one seriously injured can cause more personal and property damage than most state's minimum requirements will cover. Another thing to consider is that the larger the amount of insurance the smaller the cost per thousand dollars of coverage.

Some Cost Examples

If your state's minimum requirement for personal liability is $25,000/$50,000 and the cost is $500 a year, increasing the coverage to $50,000/$100,000 -- twice the minimum re-

quired -- will cost about $100 more each year. To raise the coverage up to $100,000/ $300,000 will cost about $720 a year, or an increase of just $220 annually.

For property damage, the increases in coverage cost even less per thousand dollars. A cost of $140 for the $10,000 minimum state coverage would be increased by only $10 a year to provide $50,000 of coverage. With the ever increasing cost of repairs for automobiles and other property, this $10 will buy you additional peace of mind.

The cost of increasing your uninsured motorist coverage falls somewhere between the above examples. If the minimun coverage for your state costs $20 per year, raising it to $100,000/$300,000/$50,000 will only cost an estimated $10 more each year.

HOW YOU CAN SAVE

The best way to save money on automobile insurance is to have a perfect driving record. The less traffic tickets and accidents you have the less expensive the insurance rate. In most states, you are given points for each traffic ticket and accident you cause. Enough points and you fall into the high risk category, and will have great difficulty finding affordable insurance. Tickets and accidents will have a negative impact on your insurance for a period of three to five years. Drive defensively and safely.

Other ways you can save money on automobile insurance include not buying a sports car -- two passenger -- or equipment that has a record of high theft. In fact, there are some states where a new, red, sports car, made by certain manufacturers, cannot be insured by regular automobile insurance companies.

Keeping a car in a garage and not using it to drive long distances to work may also help cut down on the cost of your automobile insurance.

Deductible

You also save money by buying only the coverages you feel you need, in the amounts that will provide for your peace of mind.

For collision and comprehensive coverage, you can even agree to share the costs of your claims with the insurance company. This is what you are doing when you agree to a deductible clause in your coverage. You will find that having non-deductible collision and comprehensive coverage is very costly. You can reduce this cost by selecting a deductible amount from $50 up to $1,000. This means that you will pay the deductible amount first for each claim, and the insurance company will pay the balance. It is the same as our discussion of hospitalization in Chapter 4.

The questions you must ask yourself are: How much of a deductible can I afford to pay? and How much will I save in yearly insurance costs? You then pick the deductible amount that is best for you. For some people, the yearly savings are more important than the deductible amount, and for others, the reverse is true.

For example, if the non-deductible insurance cost is $400, you can save about $52 a year by choosing a $100 deductible. You can save an additional $45 a year by raising the deductible to $200, and your cost with a $1,000 deductible would be about $165 a year -- a savings of $235. Using simple math it becomes obvious that the $100 deductible is the best buy.

The actual amount of the savings will vary from state to state and insurance company to insurance company. Shop around for the best deal.

False Savings

There are two popular beliefs, especially among first time car owners, that need a little clarification. The first is that collision and comprehensive insurance for older cars is much cheaper than for newer cars. This is only partially true. If the car is old enough and the book value is so low that the deductible amount will just about cover the cost of replacing the vehicle, this belief is true.

However, older cars can cost more to fix, parts are more difficult to find, and insurance rates are based on more than the age and value of the car. The driver's age, driving record, use of the vehicle, and area of residence all play major roles in determining the cost of insurance. This means that there may be little cost difference in insuring a three-year-old car or a six-year-old car.

The second belief is that buying a car costing under $1,000 and not carrying collision or comprehensive insurance will save money. The theory is that the money saved by not having collision and comprehensive insurance can be used to replace the vehicle in case of an accident. This does not compute. If you are a single, male driver with a reasonably clean record, it should

only cost about $350 a year to get $250 deductible coverage for the vehicle. Let's look at two cases.

Examples

Paul buys an eight-year-old car for $1,000 and decides not to get collision and comprehensive insurance. He saves $375 on insurance. He has an accident and the repairs cost him $350. He has now invested $1,350 in the car. Two months later, the car catches fire and is destroyed. His loss is $1,350 and, more importantly, he no longer has a car.

Mike buys a similar car for the same amount. He buys $250 deductible insurance for a cost of $375. His luck is as bad as Paul's. The insurance company pays $100 of his $350 accident damage and $750 when his car is stolen -- $1,000 minus his $250 deductible. His total cost is $1,625 which includes the car -- $1,000, the insurance -- $375, and his part of the accident -- $250. But what does he have? He has a check in his pocket for $750 to put towards buying another car. If he doesn't buy another automobile, he is even entitled to a refund of the remainder of the year's insurance premiums.

The check in Mike's pocket cost him a maximum of $275, which is the $375 for the insurance minus $100 they paid back in accident damages. So, he is at least $475 better off than Paul.

Be sure you really know the consequences of not carrying insurance. Before you decide not to get the coverage, be certain you can accept the possible risk.

The above figures, like all the costs and figures throughout this book, though based on extensive research, are computed as nationwide averages. These amounts may differ from what you find in your area, but the relative savings will hold true.

How Much Will Car Insurance Cost?

This question cannot be accurately answered in this or any other book. There are far too many variables and factors to consider. I can give you some estimates and some examples. According to the Bureau of Insurance, State Corporation Commission, Commonwealth of Virginia, in 1986 a sampling of the top 50 automobile insurance companies doing business in the state of Virginia revealed that a single female under 20 years of age could expect to pay from $365 to $1,678 per year.

The same report placed the average cost for an unmarried male driver under 20 somewhere between $700 and $2,738 per year. The report also revealed that even in the same state -- Virginia -- the rates could vary by as much as 20% depending on where you live within the state.

The difference in the cost of insurance for male and female drivers, though getting smaller, is still substantial. The insurance companies can fully justify these cost differences historically by using traffic and accident records. You must determine the figures in your state by making a list of the coverage and amounts of coverage you want or need and get quotes from insurance companies, agents, and your state insurance commission.

HOW TO SHOP FOR INSURANCE

As stated earlier, you shop for insurance like you shop for anything else. The first thing you do is make your list. This list includes the amount of coverage you want or need and room for entering the quoted costs of different amounts of coverage and various deductible options. Next, you collect the full information on the car -- make, model, year, number of cylinders, extra equipment, etc. In addition, you will need to provide the following information to the insurance company:

Your driving record for the last five years.
How you intend to use the car.
What special anti-theft devices you have.
The distance you drive to work.
If you successfully completed a driver education course, the insurance company may want a copy of the certificate.
Name of your previous insurance company,

even if you were covered on your parents' insurance policy.

Once you have your list and necessary information, start shopping. Start with your parents' company if you and they have been satisfied with the service. Ask friends and relatives for companies or agents they recommend. Use the telephone yellow pages. There are pages and pages of insurance companies and agents selling car insurance. Contact your state insurance commission. This is done not to get a specific company recommendation, but to get a feel for the major companies and the current rates. Once you have decided on a company and the coverage, sign the papers and pay your money.

HOW TO PAY

Many insurance companies compute their rates on a six months basis. They would like full payment when you sign the papers, however, if you ask, you will find that they will accept payment over time. The payment plan I have encountered most often is the 40,20,20,20 plan. This means that you pay 40% of the bill when you sign the contract, then 20% each month for the next three months. For this timed payment plan, you pay a service charge, usually $2 to $4 for each payment.

For example, Jo Ann finds the insurance coverage she wants for $350 every six months. The company has the payment plan mentioned above and she pays the agent 40% of $350-- $140. On this date for each of the next three months she will have a payment due of $72. This is the 20% of $350 -- $70 -- plus the $2 service charge. If you treat this service charge as interest and calculate the annual percentage rate, it computes to 11.4%. Jo Ann decides this is an acceptable cost for being able to defer the payments and better fit the expense into her budget.

Now that Jo Ann has her car and insurance, what other costs can she expect to encounter?

OPERATING COSTS
I just filled it up last month!

Some people claim that a boat is a hole in the water that people pour money into. Others say that a swimming pool is a hole in the ground that people pour money into. If these two statements are true, then an automobile is a hole on wheels that people pour money into. The fact is, that in addition to the price of a car, the interest you pay, title and tags, and sales taxes, there are many operating costs to consider. These costs must be considered before the car is bought. They must fit into the budget, and the simple truth is that each car and each owner is different.

If you want to use the nationally accepted average, the high side of operating most vehicles would be 24 cents per mile. This is what the government pays its workers for using their personal vehicle as a way of saving money over the government furnishing transportation. Another practical average though in some cases a little low, is the 15 cents per mile operating cost that the Internal Revenue Service allows self-employed persons to deduct for a vehicle used in business.

An even lower figure is the 12 cents per mile operating cost that you are allowed to deduct from your income tax return if you use your personal vehicle for religious and other charitable causes. These amounts have been presented to give you an idea of the wide range that people work with when estimating the operating cost of a car.

This chapter discusses the various kinds and frequencies of operating expenses and presents examples of applying those expenses to different types of vehicles and drivers. You, the automobile owner, will still have to balance the real cost of owning a car to its benefits.

INSURANCE

This expense, which is both a cost of buying a vehicle and a cost of operating a vehicle, has been discussed in the previous chapter. The insurance will be renewed either every six months or yearly. A single male, under 21 years of age, with a good, not high risk, driving record can estimate this cost at about $1,200 a year. A female driver with the same driving record can expect to pay between $550 and $650 a year. If the vehicle being insured is new, you can add about $200 to the estimated yearly insurance cost. If the vehicle is a sports car and carries the high rating of the insurance company, the yearly rates can increase by as much as $500.

When this cost is averaged over the miles per year you drive your car, you can see that it is the largest, per mile, operating expense that you will have. A payment of $1,200 per year for insurance on a car that is driven 12,000 miles computes to a per mile charge of ten cents. If this car is driven only 10,000 miles per year, the average cost per mile for insurance increases to 12 cents. Insurance is, without question, the largest per mile expense. Driving more miles does not really decrease the cost per mile because the amount of miles per year you drive is one of the factors that determines your insurance rates -- the more miles, the higher the rate.

GASOLINE

For most drivers, the next highest expense per mile is gasoline. If you are wondering about depreciation, that is considered, along with the interest paid on a car loan, as a cost of buying the car, not operating it. If gasoline is selling at $1.25 a gallon and your car goes 20 miles on a gallon of gas, your per mile cost is six and a quarter cents per mile. If you get 25 miles per gallon, this cost drops to five cents per mile and at 30 miles per gallon, it is down to just over four cents per mile.

This may not sound like much difference, but if you drive 12,000 miles per year, at six cents per mile you will spend $720 on gas, while at four cents per mile, you will only spend $480. Another way to explain the difference is, on a constant monthly basis, the higher mileage vehicle will save you $20 per month just in reduced gasoline expenses.

MISCELLANEOUS OPERATING EXPENSES

Scheduled Maintenance

Because of the comparatively low individual costs of the other routine maintenance items, I have grouped these together. The following table lists the expense, the frequency, and the estimated cost. Following the table, I will compute the average cost per mile for the entire table. The frequencies are based on driving the vehicle 12,000 miles per year.

Routine Maintenance

Item	Frequency	Cost	Yearly Cost
Oil, Filter, Lube	3 months, 3,000 miles	$ 20	$ 80
Tires	3 years, 36,000 miles	$210	$ 70
Brakes	3 years, 36,000 miles	$120	$ 40
Front End Alignment	yearly, 12,000 miles	$ 30	$ 30
Radiator Maintenance	yearly, 12,000 miles	$ 30	$ 30
Engine Tune Up	18 months, 18,000 miles	$ 66	$ 44
Total yearly cost for routine maintenance			$294

The total yearly cost for all of the above is about $294 which equates to an estimated per mile cost of just under two and a half cents per mile. Since the recommended maintenance schedule is based on both time and mileage, the estimated cost of $294 per year should be used if you plan to drive between 7,500 to 15,000 miles per year. If you intend to drive over 15,000 per year, you will want to increase your estimate accordingly.

Other Routine Maintenance

There are many other scheduled maintenance items that may be required for your particular vehicle, including greasing wheel bearings, changing transmission fluid, checking and adjusting belts, replacing the air filter, and rotating and balancing the tires. Because of the infrequent or inexpensive nature of these items, the total cost over the use of the automobile is less than two cents per mile, or an additional $20 per month. As with all other costs, if you are going to drive the vehicle for much more than 12,000 miles, increase your estimate accordingly. As an example, if you expect to drive your car 15,000 miles, take the costs computed for 12,000 miles and multiply them by 1.25. If the estimate for 12,000 miles was $180, your estimate for 15,000 miles will be $225 -- $180 times 1.25.

There is no savings, in fact, it will be very expensive to try to save money by not doing the recommended routine maintenance on your car. The often quoted statement "You can pay me now or pay me later" has been proven by many years of maintenance history. The closer you follow the recommended routine maintenance schedule for your car, the fewer high cost corrective maintenance items you will have.

If you do not know what the routine maintenance requirement is for the vehicle you have just bought, and you did not get the owner's manual, you can still get the information from a number of sources. The library, a good mechanic, any auto parts store, and even book stores have this information readily available.

Taxes, Tags, Inspection Fees

All states require licensing and registration. Most states also require safety inspections and charge personal property tax on automobiles. Many cities charge a tax for all vehicles that are licensed to their residents.

This tax expense is affected by many variables. The list of these variables includes, but is not limited to, the car itself, the state you live in, the use of the car, and your tax or tax exempt status. Because of these factors, placing a firm cost on this expense is practically impossible. Until you determine your actual cost, you may use $240 per year as an estimate. This estimate should work for an average three-to five-year-old car in a state with moderate taxes and licensing charges. Sales tax was discussed under buying a car in Chapter 16 and is a one time cost.

Corrective Maintenance

In Chapter 16, a table of corrective maintenance costs was presented as a factor to consider in deciding to buy a new or used vehicle. Budgeting for and performing the recommended routine maintenance will reduce the need for the large cost corrective maintenance items. Because of the varying costs of these items, it is difficult to budget enough, on a monthly basis to always be able to pay for the repair, in cash, when it is needed. I do recommend that you set aside $15 to $25 per month, in addition to your savings, to assist in

the covering of this type of expense. If you do not need this money for repairs over the life of your car, you can always use these funds to help buy another car.

It is because of these types of expenses that developing and maintaining a good credit rating is one of the most valuable things you can do. If your car is the only way you have to get to work and it needs repairs, you must get it fixed. There will be much less stress if you have been setting something aside each month. If you use your credit card or take a small loan to cover the difference between your savings and the total cost, be sure to make your payments promptly.

WHAT'S THE BOTTOM LINE?

If you plan to drive 12,000 miles or less a year, the amount you spend for gasoline is about the only expense tied directly to mileage. This also indicates the one place where you can do something about cost. The following examples include a discussion of the difference in the monthly automobile expense you can expect based on fuel economy.

Single Male Under 21

The following is a table of the expected costs of operating an automobile for one year for a single male under 21 years of age:

Expense Item	Yearly Cost	Monthly Cost
Insurance	$1,200	$ 100
Routine Maintenance	300	25
Miscellaneous	180	15
Taxes, Tags and Inspections	240	20
Corrective Maintenance	240	20
Total	$2,160	$180

Having your own automobile is not an inexpensive proposition. To the $180 per month must be added the gasoline cost. The formula for computing the monthly gasoline cost is, divide the miles per gallon into the estimated 1,000 miles per month, then multiply that number by

the cost of the gasoline. For example, a car giving 20 miles per gallon will require 50 gallons of gasoline (1,000 divided by 20 equals 50). Multiplying 50 times the estimated cost of $1.25 per gallon gives us the monthly estimate of $62.50, as shown in the following table.

The Bottom Line

	Miles per Gallon			
	15	20	25	30
Total Fixed Monthly Expenses	$180	$180	$180	$180
Gasoline expense at $1.25 per gallon	83.88	62.50	50	40
Total operating cost	$263.33	$242.50	$230	$220

You can see from the above table that a vehicle getting 30 miles to a gallon is over $40 a month cheaper to operate than one getting only 15 miles to a gallon.

Single Female Under 21

All expenses discussed for the single male apply to the single female with the one significant difference being the cost of insurance. While the single male under 21 is paying $180 per month for fixed expenses including insurance, his female counterpart, because of the lesser insurance expense, is only paying $134. This is displayed in the following table:

Expense Item	Yearly Cost	Monthly Cost
Insurance	$648	$54
Routine Maintenance	300	25
Miscellaneous	180	15
Taxes, Tags and Inspections	240	20
Corrective Maintenance	240	20
Total	$1608	$134

As with the male driver, you must still add the cost of gasoline to determine what you can expect to pay in operating expenses.

The Bottom Line

	Miles per Gallon			
	15	20	25	30
Total fixed montly expenses	$134	$134	$134	$134
Gasoline expense at $1.25 per gallon	83.33	62.50	50	40
Total operating cost	$217.33	$196.50	$184	$174

The same savings -- over $40 a month, as shown in the example for single males, can be accrued by single females by driving higher mile per gallon vehicles.

SUMMARY

Operating a vehicle, any type of vehicle, is expensive. Remember, the above tables do not include the cost of financing, depreciation or sales taxes. You must compare the cost and the advantages of having one to the disadvantages of not having one. If your decision is that you do need an automobile, it will cost you money. Your monthly expense may be as high or even higher than your rent, however, there are a number of things that you can do to reduce the expense.

1. Drive defensively and safely. Insurance is your single largest operating expense.
2. Purchase an automobile that has favorable insurance company acceptability -- no red sports car with a thousand dollar sound system.
3. Shop for the best deal on insurance.
4. Lean toward the economical models instead of the gas guzzlers.
5. Perform all of the recommended routine maintenance. The better the car runs, the better the economy.
6. Learn to perform some of the routine maintenance, i.e. checking fluid levels, adding antifreeze, checking belts and hoses, and even doing oil and filter changes. Follow good safety procedures and be careful. You can save significant dollars by not using a mechanic.
7. Be cost conscious. Only use your car when you need to. It is very expensive to use your car simply to drive down to the store in the next block.

Following some, if not all, of the above suggestions will reduce or minimize your driving cost.

NOTICE NOTICE NOTICE

The most expensive driving mistake you can make is to drive while under the influence of alcohol or drugs. In addition to the fines, court costs, and possible jail sentence, you can quickly find yourself without both automobile insurance and a driver's license.

DRIVE SAFELY!

NOTES

_____

_____

_____

_____

_____

_____

_____

_____

SHELTER

What's wrong with my car?

V

Choosing a place to call home is possibly the most important decision you will make. The only reason that shelter was not discussed first is that finding a job, knowing something about money, and developing a personal budget are necessary before thinking about new shelter. Transportation and shelter are about equal in importance, and some of the decisions made in each case are affected by the other. Transportation was placed before shelter, not to establish priority, but as a requirement for working.

Chapter 19 explores the options available to someone looking for a place to live. At the same time, the reader is encouraged to list housing needs and wants. Assigning values to wants is used as a way of setting priorities.

Chapter 20 discusses the pros and cons of sharing your shelter. Factors to be considered when making the decision to share, including individual personalities, attitudes, and values, are examined. Dual responsibilities under a shared lease are explained, followed by a short discussion of sub-leasing.

Chapter 21 dissects a sample lease. Each paragraph is explained from both the landlord and tenant point of view. Lease terminology and the need to read and understand the lease before signing is discussed. The chapter closes with a discussion of the pre-acceptance walk-through and provides a form that can be used to document any discrepancies identified.

Chapter 22 starts by presenting a list of expense categories encountered when setting up a residence. Each of the categories is expanded to identify specific items and their projected cost. The chapter concludes by presenting Jo Ann's estimate for moving into a new efficiency.

Chapter 23 discusses furniture needs and presents a list of basic furniture requirements. Non-traditional sources of free or inexpensive furniture are explored with the focus on resourcefulness in matching needs to budget.

SELECTING A PLACE
Need versus want

19

HOME SWEET HOME

Yes, you do need shelter. Sleeping in your car or van is out. In an emergency, you may be able to survive for a short period of time by doing this, but, in most states, it is illegal. If you have ever accidently gone to sleep in your car, you know how you feel when you wake up. This is not the kind of feeling you want to have as you face each day. So the question is: Where do you live?

Do you live at home? Do you rent a room somewhere? Do you rent your own apartment? Do you share an apartment? Or, do you just crash with whichever of your friends has room?

Before you answer the questions posed above, give what you are doing and where you are going some thought. You are starting out on your own as an independent adult. In order to obtain the tools that you are going to need and establish yourself as a reliable individual, you need some semblance of stability. Employers, banks, and even utility companies, desire to work with people who are reliable. This reliability equates to a permanent address, a phone where you can be reached, and a traceable record of previous employment and credit history.

You will find it very hard to establish this kind of image by living out of your car or by crashing wherever their is an open cot. You need a place you can call home. This is one of man's primary survival needs. Until this need is met, it will be very difficult to achieve any form of mental or physical well being.

This chapter discusses needs versus wants and the options and costs you will encounter when looking for a place to live. As with transportation, food, and clothing, shelter costs money. Providing shelter is the single largest expense for most working adults. When you consider rent, electricity, water, and phone costs, shelter can easily take one third to one half of your take home pay each month. Therefore, shelter should be chosen with care.

Needs

The first thing you will want to do is make a list of your needs. At this point, forget about selecting a type of shelter and don't even think about cost. Just concentrate on what you need. Get yourself a sheet of paper and make a list. To get started ask yourself the following questions.

(1)   Do I need to live close to where I work? If you do not have a car and intend to walk or use a bike to get to work, this is a valid need.

(2)   Do I need more than one room? Some people are very comfortable living in one room -- a bedroom -- reserved for them, while others require more personal space to feel comfortable.

(3)   Do I require a place to park my vehicle? If you have a motorized vehicle, you must be sure that the place you live has adequate parking space.

(4)   Do I need kitchen facilities? Some individuals are able to get along without any form of kitchen facilities except for a small refrigerator which can usually be part of any decor, even a bedroom. Unless you have made other acceptable arrangements for obtaining your meals, kitchen facilities will be a need.

(5)   Do I need laundry facilities? If your selected form of transportation is walking, riding a bike, or using public transportation, you need access to laundry facilities. It can be difficult and/or uncomfortable to carry the wash -- dirty or clean -- for any distance.

(6)   Must I live close to public transportation? If you use walking or riding a bike as your primary means of transportation, you will need to live close to public transportation. This is for those times when the distance is great or the weather is bad.

(7)   Do I need to live alone? This is a valid need for some people. If your personality is such that you are happiest and most comfortable when living alone, this is a need and should be considered as such.

(8)   Must I have first floor access? Because of physical limitations or other factors, some people must have a place to live that does not require climbing flights of stairs. If this describes your situation, no stairs is a valid need.

Wants

Once you have listed your needs, all other factors you use when shopping for a place to live should be considered wants. Keep in mind that, if, in your case, a want is so strong that you are willing to pay any amount to have it, you should move it up to the needs list.

Like needs, wants will cost money. Every option or added convenience has a cost associated with it. Just like in selecting a car, you need to apply a value to each of the options so that you can weigh the cost of the option against its value to you.

There is almost no end to the items that will show up on the wants list. These items can range from wanting your own bathroom to wanting on site racket ball courts. There is nothing wrong with dreaming. This is the way the list should be developed. Just be sure to go back and rank the list of wants by putting a value on each. For most people a fireplace will have a much lower value than a kitchen area, and location will usually be valued higher than having tennis courts.

You may also want to read Chapter 23 at this time and make some decisions on furnishings, especially if you are considering renting or leasing furniture.

WHERE OH WHERE?

Once your list is made and the assigned values have been used to put the items in a priority sequence, it is time to go back to the questions presented at the beginning of this chapter.

With Parents?

Are you now living at home? If the answer is yes, is it possible to continue to live there? Before answering this question, check what you have listed as needs against what is available at home. Does living at home provide for all your needs? Is the environment there acceptable? Will your parent(s) accept a written agreement or contract?

You are no longer planning to live at home or anywhere else as a dependent. The only way to live at home is by designing a contract or agreement that will specify the rules and responsibilities of both parties -- you and your parent -- and the amount of rent or room and board that you will pay for the services you receive.

Living at home should be treated the same as renting a room in someone else's home or boarding house. The owner has rules; you live by them or find someplace else to live. The owner has certain services, maybe one or two meals or even laundry service. These services, as with the use of utilities and telephone, must be paid for. As a wage earning adult, you are expected to carry your own weight in society. This includes paying for your space if you decide to live at home.

Plenty of young adults find this an excellent way to get started. In addition to staying in familiar surroundings, the cost is usually less than immediately striking out on your own. This allows for the saving of more money, the time to really decide on other living arrangements and an opportunity to learn something about responsibility and living costs.

Rent

If you are looking for an estimate of what to pay your parents, look in the newspaper advertisements under "rooms to rent." This will give you an idea of what a room with utilities in someone else's house will cost. Add to this a fair amount for any additional services offered, including the use of the telephone if you don't have one of your own. When living at home the amount of money that the young adult contributes for food can be a touchy matter. Everyone's eating habits are different and only you can put a value on the amount of food you eat. As a rule of thumb, you will find it difficult to buy the ingredients to prepare three meals a day for under $100 a month. You may want to read Section VI which contains a discussion of food costs.

As with renting a room, an apartment, or even a house, I strongly recommend that the rules and responsibilities involved in living at home be clearly stated in writing. These rules should be the same for you as they are, or would be, for any other tenant. Once agreed to, the agreement is binding to both parties and if either party fails to perform as agreed, the contract is voided and you look for another place to live.

Insisting on a written contract reduces stress by making living in your parents' house a business transaction. Experience will demonstrate over and over again that it is possible to love and respect someone and still not tolerate living with them. This is another reality of life.

Where else?

In most areas of the country, you can find practically any type of housing you may want or need. At one end of the scale is the single room rented in someone's home or public boarding house. At the other end is the complete house, fully furnished and including paid utilities.

The cost of housing varies from area to area and you will need to determine the fair market value for your desired area. For example, in 1989 you could rent a new, one bedroom apartment including kitchen and bath in a nice section of Houston, Texas, for only $195 a month. At the same time, in Great Neck, an area on Long Island, a one bedroom apartment rented for $1,860 a month. It is likely that in some cities or areas of the United States you can find even more expensive rental units.

Just within a large city, the cost of a one room apartment can vary by as much as $250 per month, depending on location. However, there are some laws or rules that seem to be standard. These are:

(1)   Location is a key factor in determining price.

(2)   Rooms usually rent for much less than efficiencies or full apartments.

(3)   Efficiencies usually cost less than one bedroom apartments, however the difference can be very small.

(4)   The difference between a one bedroom apartment and a three bedroom apartment is usually less than twice the one bedroom rate and sometimes as little as 50% more. Example, if a one bedroom apart-ment rents for $200 a month, a three bedroom may rent for as little as $300 but will more likely cost $400 a month.

(5)   Washers and dryers in an apartment cost more in monthly rent than having the use of a central laundry facility but may still save you money. Read Chapter 27 for a discussion of clothing care and upkeep.

(6)   Frills, including: pool, sauna, fireplace, game room, etc., all cost big bucks. The extra money you are charged is applied to the maintenance and upkeep of the equipment or, in the case of fireplaces, the extra insurance fees charged to the owners of the rental property.

HOW TO SHOP

Just like when looking for a job or locating that needed transportation, shopping for a new place to live starts with your list of needs and wants. Once the list is prepared and you have set priorities and values to your wants, the next step is to go to the advertising media. This media includes bulletin boards, at work and at local supermarkets, newspaper ads, free "Apartment Finder" or "Renter's Guides," and personal friends and family members.

It is very important that you have made your list before you start looking because your answers to the recommended questions will identify what section of the available advertisements gets your attention. For instance, if you are interested in sharing a house or apartment -- read Chapter 20 on "Sharing" -- you will focus your attention on ads that indicate others are interested in sharing. If you are looking to just rent an efficiency, you will focus on ads for efficiency rentals. And, if you are just looking for a room, you will concentrate on "Room for Rent" ads. Even your decision on furniture will have an impact by focusing your attention on "furnished" or "not furnished" ads.

REFERENCES?

Almost no one will rent you a room or apartment without personal and financial references. Your parents, family, or friends can give you personal references and your place of employment or bank can provide the financial references. Be prepared when you shop by having the names, addresses, and phone numbers of these references available. You may also be asked to provide your social security or drivers license number when you sign the agreement or lease.

If you have rented before, the new landlord will want the name, address, and phone number of your previous landlord. If there were any problems between the old landlord and yourself, explain these to the new landlord so there will be no surprises when your reference is verified.

DEPOSIT

If the kind of housing you are looking for is very scarce in your area, be prepared to give a deposit as soon as you find what you are looking for. This deposit is just to demonstrate that you are really serious and it is worth the effort for the landlord to check your references. Security deposits and paying the first month's rent is discussed in Chapters 21 and 22.

You can usually get by with just a $25 to $50 deposit. Be sure to get a receipt and verify that the amount will be refunded even if the landlord does not like your references. Sometimes rather than refund this deposit, in cash, it may be deducted from either your lease deposit or first month's rent when you sign the lease. This should not be an expense. It is a form of binder that guarantees the landlord that when your references check out, you will rent the apartment.

AND ANOTHER THING

Always be sure you have read and accepted the terms of the lease or rental agreement before you give this deposit. See Chapter 21 on reading and understanding your lease. Reading the fine print after you leave your deposit, then changing your mind, may cost you the deposit. Once you give your money to the landlord, you either rent the agreed on space or the landlord may legally keep the deposit as payment for the time and cost of verifying your references.

SUMMARY

The place you call home is where you will spend at least 50 percent of your time. True, much of it will be while you sleep, but many hours of other time will be spent there. Think about it, if you are resourceful and watching your expenses, most of your meals will be eaten there and you will participate in at least some of your recreation there.

Your shelter is also possibly the single largest expense you will have, so it is very important that it be chosen only after careful consideration of your needs and wants. If you are not comfortable in your home, for whatever reason, it will reflect in how you do your job and eventually distort your whole personality.

Be resourceful, know your needs and wants, match them to what is available, and then make your choice. If you are not really sure of what you want or need, it is better to pay a little more to rent by the month than to sign a 12 month lease.

NOTES

_____

_____

_____

_____

_____

SHARING
Less expensive, but is it worth it?

20

WHY SHARE?

There are three reasons that most people decide to live in a shared environment. The first is money, the second is convenience, and the third is company.

Money

In the previous chapter, the cost of one, two and three bedroom apartments was discussed. The cost of the three bedroom apartment or house is seldom as much as twice the cost of a one bedroom. This means that three people, who can get along and are willing to share living quarters and expenses, can acquire housing for the same, or even less money, than two people, each living in a one bedroom apartment. In addition, the costs of utilities, food and furniture can also be split three ways.

All three of my unmarried children currently share housing. Jeff shares a two bedroom apartment in Virginia Beach, Virginia, Chris shares a three bedroom house in Tuscon, Arizona, and Karen shares a three bedroom house in McLean, Virginia. All three of them are enjoying more space for less money than if they were living alone.

In many cases, only by living at home, renting a single room, or sharing can housing costs be made to fit into the budget. For example, in Virginia Beach, a one bedroom apartment starts in the $275 per month price range. By sharing a two bedroom apartment with one other person, Jeff is paying only $225 a month. He is saving at least $50 per month. Actually, his savings are substantially more when the shared cost of utilities, food, furniture, and phone are considered.

Convenience

In many cases, there will be no rooms or one bedroom apartments available where you need or want to live. Being willing and able to share an apartment or house, makes the full range of housing available for consideration.

Another convenience may be the availability of two vehicles for transportation or the use of a built in carpool. Karen and both of her roommates work at the same location. Not only do they carpool but, when one car needs servicing, there is never the worry of not having transportation. In much of our country, this may be very important.

In addition, larger residences usually have more time saving features. For example, in two or three bedroom apartments you may find dishwashers, garbage disposals and even clothes washers and dryers. These are all features not usually found in efficiencies or one bedroom apartments.

There are also the intangible -- hard to measure -- conveniences of two or more persons living together, including sharing housekeeping chores and running errands. Though the value of these conveniences is hard to measure in money, they do have value and may make sharing a good choice.

Company

Man is by nature a social animal. Most of us like to have others around. The reasons for this desire are as varied as the number of people there are. Some of us like to have people around to listen to us, while others like to listen. Some of us like to compete and others like to compliment. There are introverts who like to be around other people and extroverts, that at times, would like to be alone. Collectively we -- mankind -- like to have others around and draw comfort from knowing someone else is close by. Some of us are still scared of the dark, especially at night when the walls and floors creak.

At different times in all our lives the need for living close with someone else becomes very strong, and, at other times, it may be very weak. Some people are by nature more of the loner type and others have personalities that make sharing with them impossible.

There have been many plays and stories written on the unusual situations that can and will occur when certain people try to live together. The "Odd Couple" and "Three's Company" are only two of the more familiar ones.

For some of you, this desire to live with someone by sharing a house or apartment is so strong that you may have even listed living with someone as a need. Therefore, it is necessary to look at the disadvantages or pitfalls that you need to be aware of and may have to overcome.

PROBLEMS/PITFALLS

Webster's new unabridged dictionary defines sharing as "partaking or enjoying with others; seizing or possessing jointly or in common." This is exactly what you do when you decide to share your shelter with others. The important key words in the definition are "jointly" and "in common."

Personalities

Jo Ann possesses a great personality, she gets along with everyone, never gets into trouble, is neat, punctual and never has to diet. She may also have a very difficult time finding someone she can be happy sharing an apartment or house with. Why? Because everyone else out there is not like her. This does not mean that everyone else possesses the opposite traits, just that they don't all possess the ones that Jo Ann may be able to accept and live with.

Values

This is a perfect time to discuss value systems. We all have slightly different ideas of the meaning of right and wrong. Consider your reaction to reading about employee responsibilities in Chapter 7. If your roommate closely shares your value system, living together may not be a bed of roses, but it will be easier than if

your values differ greatly. One of the advantages we discussed was convenience which included a number of items like sharing the chores and carpooling. This list could also include swapping or lending each other clothes and other possessions. For this to work, you must know that what you share or lend, will be taken care of in the same manner that you would care for it.

Some individuals have the attitude that "what is mine is mine and what is yours is mine." This attitude breeds mistrust, which, in turn, will cause bitterness and possibly a severe financial problem for one of the individuals concerned.

Responsibility

Face reality, everyone does not have the same sense of responsibility or value system that you have. Often, it is not big things that make sharing undesirable, it is the little annoying traits that your roommate has that will seem to drive you crazy. This is why I think of sharing a house as the same as marriage, but without sex. No matter how much or how little time, each day, roommates actually spend together, the other person's presence is always there. You cannot get away from it.

You can even have individual bedrooms with private baths and still give up your privacy. Just sharing a refrigerator can be the thing that causes roommates to break up. Imagine that you like to have three meals a day, two of these at home, and your roommate either doesn't eat or eats all meals out. Your roommate thinks that the refrigerator is just for snacks and beverages and doesn't understand why there's never room to keep a full case of beer cold. Or, even though you are not a cleanliness freak, you don't like things growing in the refrigerator, while your roommate never throws anything away.

Expand the refrigerator example to include dishes, closets, furniture, and, if you share one, the bathroom, and you can see that you will get to know your roommate possibly better than anyone else, except parents or spouse. Broaden the scope by considering the differences in peoples' daily routines and tastes in choice and volume of music and TV programs.

If you split up or rotate the chores, each must be counted on to fulfill their responsibility. If one of the parties continually ignores or forgets to do their assigned chores, the other party must either live with the chore undone or do it themselves. In this type of situation, the sharing arrangement will probably dissolve quickly.

Hygiene

My children all insisted that this be included as possibly one of the most important things to look for when considering sharing a place to live. Not only must the individual be willing to do his or her part in keeping the common area neat and clean, the individual's personal hygiene must be acceptable. A bedroom that is disorderly or messy is one thing, a roommate that has an offensive odor -- stinks -- is another. Not only are people with poor personal hygiene habits offensive, they can also be unhealthy. Remember you are going to share food, dishes and eating utensils with your roommate.

Your roommate's general health condition is also a concern. You aren't interested in having to play nursemaid to a roommate who is always suffering from one ailment or another. The sharing arrangement is a joint venture, you are not planning to run a convalescent home.

Legal

In addition to the problems that may be generated by conflicting personalities, values, and concern for hygiene, there are legal concerns. The legal problems that may arise from sharing are all based on the two phrases mentioned earlier, "jointly" and "in common." Simply stated, the legal meaning of these phrases is that what one party of the sharing arrangement is liable for all other parties are equally liable for, individually and in total.

Example

Suppose that Jo Ann decides to share an apartment with two roommates. She does everything right, she has known the other two people for some time, they get along well, and they are friends. They have the lease made out in all three names; Jo Ann feels comfortable, and they settle into their new apartment. However, true love does not live by lease agreements.

One of her roommates meets her knight in shining armor, immediately falls in love, and starts making wedding plans. The wedding day is scheduled for midway through the lease. The roommate promises to continue to make her payments until a substitute can be found, very quickly she hopes.

The wedding is beautiful and time passes. One month has gone by, and, even though Jo

Ann and the remaining roommate have talked to a number of interested people, they do not seem to be able to agree on a selection. Their "ex" roommate notifies them that she can only afford to make one more monthly payment because of the expenses she and her husband are having setting up their new home. She also mentions that she does not think that Jo Ann and the remaining roommate are trying hard to replace her.

Jo Ann and her remaining roommate try to unemotionally look at the options. They can:

(1)   Sue their friend for her share of the rent, a lease is a binding, legally enforceable document,

(2)   Not be so choosy and quickly decide on a roommate,

(3)   Each pay half of their departed roommate's rent, or

(4)   default on the lease.

They decide to do a combination of options 2 and 3. They will split the rent two ways and use the extra bedroom for guests until they can find a reasonably acceptable roommate. In effect, their rent just went up by 50%. However, they both found the other options, suing their friend for her share of the rent or defaulting on the lease, distasteful.

Two more months go by, and no new roommate has been located. In fact, Jo Ann has just been told that her remaining roommate's company has given her a promotion, which means she will be transferring to another city in 60 days. Jo Ann can't believe it, what started out as the perfect sharing arrangement is a disaster. After much discussion, her roommate promises to pay one additional month's rent. This leaves Jo Ann only one month that she will have to pay the full amount of the rent -- all three shares -- if she cannot find a new roommate.

The ending could be worse, Jo Ann finds someone to room with her for the last month and share the rent. When she adds up all her expenses, she discovers that she still saved $150.00 over renting a one bedroom apartment. Her big question is: "Was it worth it?"

The Consequences

What if, when the roommate got married, Jo Ann and the remaining roommate had defaulted on the lease? First, they would have lost their deposit. Secondly, they would have received a default notice from the landlord, followed by a judgement for the full balance of the rent due under the lease. Each of the three parties involved would have received the same judgement because "jointly" and "in common" means that each party is committed to paying the full lease.

A judgement, once recorded and served, will hurt and may even ruin, your good credit history. It may not be enough for you to offer to buy out of the judgement by paying your share. The landlord can, and probably will, legally hold you responsible for the full amount of the lease.

This legal liability does not only apply to the actual rent, it applies to all aspects of the lease and any other contract that was made jointly.

Two Horror Stories

The First:

Three young men Steve, Cliff, and Leo jointly shared an apartment. They had also made arrangements with the local telephone company to have a telephone installed. For about six months everything was working out great, then Leo lost his job.

He tried to find other work but just couldn't seem to find something that suited him. Leo couldn't pay his part of the rent. The roommates started arguing, and Steve and Cliff began looking for another person to take Leo's place. One night Leo left, no goodbys, no forwarding address, no note, just no Leo. His clothes and what few possessions he owned had been loaded into his car, and he was gone.

Steve and Cliff were fortunate in finding someone to fill the void left by Leo, and they sighed with relief. Then the telephone bill arrived with over $600 in long distance calls, all made by Leo during the last five weeks he lived in the apartment. Steve and Cliff went to the phone company to explain that the calls were not theirs. The customer service person at the phone company was sympathetic but reminded them of their contract which made them equally liable.

The best the phone company would do was to allow Steve and Cliff to pay the bill over a period of six months, with the understanding that no additional long distance calls would be allowed until the bill was paid in full. Since they never saw or heard from Leo again, they chalked the experience up to an expensive lesson in joint contracts.

The Second:

Sandy and Carol shared a small furnished, two bedroom house for almost two years. Toward the end of the second year, while Sandy was visiting her parents, Carol decided to have a party. She invited a few friends, they invited a few friends, and so on, until Carol realized that her small party was getting out of hand. At best guess, the attendance was in excess of 45 people.

During the course of the party, food and drink got spilled and stained the carpet, a cigarette fell from the ashtray and burned the kitchen table, and someone accidentally sat on the end of the sofa causing the arm to fall off. In addition, the noise level got a little loud, and the landlord and the police were called.

When Sandy returned from her visit, she found a bill for $1,400 in damages and an eviction notice. Carol tried to explain to Sandy and the landlord that everything just got out of hand, and she would pay for all the damages, which she did. The problem was the landlord held fast to the eviction notice and Sandy, through no fault of her own, had to look for another place to live. In addition, she now had questionable references.

SUGGESTIONS

Here are some suggestions you may want to consider before deciding to share an apartment or house with someone.

(1)   If possible, know the person you will be sharing with.
(2)   Interview anyone you are thinking of sharing living quarters with to try to determine their personality and values.
(3)   For someone you do not know, request and verify references.
(4)   All agreements or conditions of the arrangement should be in writing and accepted by all parties.
(5)   The agreements should include a written statement as to each individual's responsibilities and contain what the arrangements will be if one party has to move out before the lease runs out. This agreement will not relieve you of responsibility for the lease but will provide you with additional basis for taking legal action to recoup your loss, if any.

(6) Make sure that all documents for the lease and any other shared commitments are signed by all parties.

CONCLUSION

Sharing an apartment or house with others can be fun as well as an economical way to provide yourself with shelter. However, the example and each of the horror stories presented earlier are true and repeated daily. Not only are the results very expensive, in terms of money, the stress and frustration can also be very damaging. They do happen, and they may happen to you, even if you try to protect yourself. If you don't protect yourself and watch for pitfalls, you can be sure they will happen.

NOTES

_____

_____

_____

_____

_____

_____

_____

_____

_____

_____

_____

_____

_____

_____

_____

_____

_____

THE LEASE
Fine print? I can hardly read the large print! 21

WHAT IS A LEASE?

A lease, sometimes called a rental agreement, is a legally binding document that identifies the parties and terms of the agreement to use, for a fee, the landlord's property. It protects the person or persons leasing the property -- the tenant or lessee -- as well as the person owning the property -- the landlord or lessor.

You, the tenant, are protected from increases in rent, from other changes in the terms of the agreement and from being evicted -- thrown out -- without just cause for the term of the lease. In addition, the lease should state both your and the landlord's rights and responsibilities.

The landlord is protected from loosing money because of damage to the property or because the tenant fails to pay the rent.

Both the tenant and landlord are protected from any misunderstanding that may exist by putting the agreement down in writing and requiring that all parties sign and date the document. In some states, the lease may be recorded in the county records just like a deed or mortgage.

Wording and Format

A lease can be a simple statement identifying the parties of the agreement, the property to be leased, the authorized use of the property, and the terms of payment. Since all states do not have detailed and explicit laws governing the rights of tenants and landlords, the lease that you may be presented with will probably be much longer than a simple statement. Some Realtors and many apartment complexes use very extensive lease forms, some containing as many as four or more pages.

For this discussion we will examine a simple "public domain" lease form.

Starting at the top, the document is identified as a "Residential Lease" between the landlord -- property owner -- and the tenant -- yourself.

Statement 1. describes the property. This description must be complete and should list all furnishings and accessories that are included as part of the lease. If your lease includes your right to a parking slot or garage space, it must be included in this statement.

Statement 2. describes the length of the lease and the starting and ending dates. If the lease is renewable, a statement addressing the time frames for renewing the lease should be stated here.

Statement 3. describes the amount of the rent, the date due, and the amount and conditions of the security deposit. If the rent is going to be paid by check, be sure to have that included, otherwise, the landlord can insist on cash or money order.

Statement 4. identifies each party's responsibilities for utilities. You will only be able to hold the landlord liable for any fees that are included in the rent if they are part of this statement. If the landlord has agreed to pay for water, gas, electricity, or garbage collection, the lease must contain that agreement. Otherwise, you have no legal right to receive those services free. This is also true for the use of laundry facilities, especially if they are provided free of charge.

Statement 5. lists the tenant's -- your -- responsibilities.

Five a. states that you will not damage or destroy any portion of the leased premises. Stains on the carpets, damaged

RESIDENTIAL LEASE

LEASE AGREEMENT, entered into between _____

(Landlord) and _____ (Tenant).

For Good consideration it is agreed between the parties as follows:

1.   Landlord hereby leases and lets to Tenant the premises described

as follows:

Parties

2.   This Lease shall be for a term of   years, commencing on

Length   19   , and terminating on   , 19

3.   Tenant shall pay Landlord the annual rent of $ during

said term, in monthly payments of $, each payable

Money   monthly on the first day of each month in advance. Tenant shall pay

a security deposit of $, to be returned upon

termination of this Lease and the payment of all rents due and

performance of all other obligations.

4.   Tenant shall, at its own expense, provide the following utilities:

Utilities

Landlord shall, at its own expense, provide the following utilities:

5.   Tenant further agrees that:

Responsibilities   a) Upon the expiration of the Lease, it will return possession of the

leased premises in its present condition, reasonable wear and tear

and fire casualty excepted. Tenant shall commit no waste to the leased

premises.

b) Tenant shall not assign or sub-let said premises or allow any other

person to occupy the leased premises without the Landlord's prior

written Consent.

c) Tenant shall not make any material or structural alterations to the leased premises without Landlord's prior written consent.

d) Tenant shall comply with all building, zoning and health codes and other applicable laws for the sue of said leased premises.

e) Tenant shall not conduct on premises any activity deemed extra hazardous, a nuisance, or requiring an increase in fire insurance premiums.

f)   Tenant shall not allow pets on the premises.

g) In the event of any breach of the payment of rent or any other allowed charge, or other breach of the Lease, Landlord shall have full rights to terminate this Lease in accordance with state law and re-enter and reclaim possession of the leased premises, in addition to such other remedies available to Landlord arising from said breach.

Binding

6.   This Lease shall be binding upon and inure to the benefit of the parties, their successors, assigns and personal representatives.

Scope

7.   This Lease shall be subordinate to all present or future mortgages against the property.

8.   Additional Lease terms:

Additional

Signed under seal this   day of   , 19 .

In the presence of :

Signature   _____   _____
                                                          Landlord

                   _____   _____
                                                          Tenant

cabinets, broken light fixtures, torn wallpaper, and scratched hardwood floors are just some of the items you could pay for under this statement. This also means that if you hang anything on the walls you are responsible for repairing the holes when you remove the hangers.

Five b. prohibits you and the other signers of this lease from sub-leasing or taking in additional tenants. If you frequently have guests that stay for more than one week at a time, you should discuss this with the landlord before signing the lease.

Five c. prohibits any altering to the property. Hanging cabinets, removing doors, and building shelves in the closets are all included in this statement. You cannot even paint a room or even a wall, your favorite color, unless you receive written permission from the landlord.

To be safe, don't make any changes that may be considered permanent without written permission of the landlord. If you make changes without permission, you could find yourself not only paying for their removal but also for repairing any damage that occurs in the removal.

Five d. requires that you conform to all local codes pertaining to the premises covered by the lease. This can include an assortment of actions ranging from no curb parking or working on your vehicle on the street to obstructing or blocking stairways. It also means that you may not be able to use property you leased as a residence as business property. Zoning laws in most states are very definite as to the use of property and this statement requires that you abide by these local laws.

Five e. prohibits unsafe or nuisance behavior. This clause could prevent you from hand-loading ammunition, using toxic or caustic chemicals, or barbecuing on the leased premises. It is this statement that allows the landlord to refuse to lease to you if you smoke. Under this clause, noise can be considered a nuisance, and you can be evicted from the premises if complaints are made because of loud music or parties.

Remember, it is the landlord's right, not yours, to decide what behavior is a nuisance. Usually a few complaints from other tenants are sufficient for the landlord to request that the objectionable behavior stop or the tenant leave.

Five f. prohibits pets. As presented, this statement needs some clarification. Does it mean just cats and dogs, all four legged animals, or all pets including fish and birds. If you want to have a pet, be sure to have this clause either removed or at least clarified. Some landlords allow pets if the tenant pays an additional pet deposit. This statement could even be expanded or another statement added prohibiting children.

Five g. gives the landlord the right to enter and reclaim the premises if the rent is late or if any of the above rules are broken by the tenant. In most states, the landlord is also entitled to take possession of whatever is found on the premises until such time as all damages and costs are paid by the tenant.

Statement 6. makes all sections of the contract binding to all parties, their successors and representatives. Simply stated, if the landlord should die, the heirs are bound by the agreement. The same is true should the landlord hire a property management agency to handle the rental property. The conditions of the lease would be unchanged.

Statement 7. states that you, the lessee, have no rights over the existing, or any future, mortgage. In other words, you cannot interfere with the sale of the property. This statement is implied even if not written in the lease.

Statement 8. is for the clarification of any of the above statements or for adding new ones. I would recommend that at least three statements be added.

The first should specify that the landlord will be responsible for repairing or replacing any appliance covered by the lease including heating and/or air conditioning. The landlord may counter with a request that an exclusion be placed in the statement covering neglect or misuse on the part of the tenant. This is a reasonable request.

The second statement would identify the landlord's responsibility for providing hazard insurance on the building and maintaining the building in a weather tight condition. You are responsible for providing insurance to protect yourself against liability and to cover the loss or damage to your personal property. See Chapter 22 for a discussion of this insurance.

The third statement I suggest adding should cover a pre-acceptance walk through of the premises and provide for a reasonable period of time -- five to 15 days from occupancy -- for the tenant to identify existing, hidden deficiencies. The walk through should be made when the premises are vacant.

Signature

The bottom of the last page of the lease is usually where the landlord, or agent, and the tenant, or tenants, sign and date the lease. No matter what other agreement you may have, only what is written in the lease that both parties have signed is binding to both parties.

OTHER FORMATS

The only differences between this sample lease and one that is four or more pages long is the degree of detail of the stipulations and the amount of time it takes to read.

Apartment complexes that have pools, clubhouses, saunas, and other recreation equipment will include the "rules of use" in the lease. By putting these rules in the lease, the landlord ties compliance with the rules directly to the right to remain a resident.

WHAT TO LOOK OUT FOR

Beware of agreements that:

(1)   Do not contain most of the sample statements.
(2)   Are not easy to understand.
(3)   Do not specifically state that the security deposit is refundable and when it will be refunded.
(4)   Make you responsible for upkeep or

damage to the exterior of the premises.
(5)   Make you responsible for maintenance and repair of appliances included in the lease.
(6)   Do not state that the landlord is responsible for keeping the residence in a livable and weather-tight condition.
(7)   Do not address walk throughs and procedures for notifying the landlord of problems.

RIGHTS

You have the right to request the deletion or change to any statement on the lease that you find unacceptable. Don't just accept the lease because it is a printed form. Your requested changes may not be accepted by the landlord, but you have nothing to lose by asking for them.

Sometimes your requested changes will cost you additional money. For example: The lease states that pets -- all pets -- are prohibited. You have a pair of Finches that you have had since you were a child, so you request that the clause be modified to allow you to keep your Finches. The landlord agrees but requests that you put up an additional $50 deposit in case they get out from their cage and do any damage. In addition, you may be required to sign a waiver releasing the landlord from any liability should they get out of their cages and get hurt or killed.

If there is anything else you want added, changed, or deleted on your lease, request the lease be changed. It is your right.

HELP

The format, content, and legality of leases vary from state to state even though the basics are very similar. To be sure that the lease you are going to sign is correct and legal, for your state, you should do one or more of the following:

(1)   Request a copy of the blank lease on your first visit. This will give you time to read, understand, and compare it with others.
(2)   Call a Realtor and request a copy of what the local Board of Realtors use as their accepted residential lease.
(3)   Go to your public library and check for state produced consumer booklets covering renting and/or leases.

(4) Contact the local Legal Aid office and request help and information.

ACCEPTANCE WALK THROUGH

There is an old warning "Don't buy a pig in a poke," which is very appropriate at this time. In pre-colonial and colonial days, a "poke" was another name for a sack. Farmers found it easy to transport small pigs to market by putting them in sacks. The warning meant, and still means, don't buy anything without seeing it first. This is true of almost anything you buy and especially true of signing a lease for an apartment or house without first checking out its condition. After all, a signed 12 month lease is a very expensive commitment.

Quite often, the apartment or house that you are agreeing to rent is occupied or under renovation, meaning that access is either not available or you must look around someone else's furniture. This is the "pig in the poke" situation and not the way to inspect your new home before making a firm contract.

Go back to the sample lease form and read *statement five a.* How do you and the landlord really know what the present condition of the premises is if you can't see it? Insist on a formal pre-acceptance walk through. Document all discrepancies that you feel you may be held liable for when your lease terminates and have the landlord sign the document. Each of you should keep a copy, and, when the lease terminates, this document establishes the initial condition of the premises.

Both of my sons, Chris and Jeff, had similar problems trying to get their security deposit refunded. Neither of them had a signed pre-acceptance walk through document and, in both cases, the apartment complex had been sold during their lease. The new owners decided that my sons were responsible for the final condition of the premises, and they were told that the deposit would be forfeited.

Fortunately, Chris had copies of notes he had written requesting repair of deficiencies and kept track of the dates he had called the landlord. He received a refund of 80% of his deposit.

Jeff's situation is a little more complicated, in that his roommates had a dog, and they did not have near the documentation that Chris had. Jeff is still waiting to hear the final outcome of his landlord's claim.

Apartment Checklist

You don't have to use the checklist provided in this book. In its place, a simple handwritten statement that identifies the problems and is signed by both parties is sufficient.

For example: Jo Ann has decided to lease a small efficiency, and, during the walk through, she discovers a few items she feels need to be documented. She writes the following:

"On December 13, 1989, I walked through Apt. 215 of the Shady Brook Apartment complex with Mr. Sharpey and discovered the following:

The front door sticks. The bathroom vanity has a gap between it and the wall. The bed/living/dining room carpet has two large (over six inches across) stains, one under the window and one against the outside wall. The tile is cracked behind the tub, and the tub and many of the tiles are discolored. "

When Jo Ann and Mr. Sharpey sign this statement, Jo Ann can rest assured that she will not be held liable for these items when her lease is terminated. In addition, she can request that the front door be fixed, and, if the carpet has not been cleaned recently, she can request it be cleaned before she accepts the apartment.

If you want to use the checklist provided, you have my permission to copy the checklist as often as needed for your personal use.

SUMMARY

Setting up your own home, either by yourself or with others, can be an exciting and fun time. However, you cannot forget that in our society the written word -- contract or lease -- is enforceable, while the spoken agreement is usually not. Your lease is not something to dread nor is it difficult to understand. It is, however, necessary to state and protect your rights.

Just as you will want references from someone you intend to share housing with, the landlord will want your personal and banking references. These references will be checked before the landlord will sign the lease with you.

If housing is in short supply -- difficult to find -- and you find something you like, you may be asked to put down a small refundable deposit. This deposit will hold the apartment until the results of your credit check are received. Be sure you get a written receipt for the deposit that states the amount and the conditions that must be met for the refund. Be sure you understand and accept these conditions before paying your money.

Always do a walk through and document all problems. Don't get caught up in the haste of moving and forget to do this most important protective step. Failure to take the time for the walk through may be costly.

Unfortunately, there is much more to establishing your own home than just paying your deposit and rent and moving in. Read on...

APARTMENT CHECKLIST

List below any items which require cleaning or repair. List any damage to the unit, such as floor or water stains, cracked windows or tiles, even if no repairs are expected. If the management has not provided this or a similar list, the tenant should complete it and submit it to the management within 5 days after moving into the unit. Management should verify entries and provide signed copy back to tenant within 5 days of receipt.

MOVE-IN

Special Remarks_____

_____

_____

_____

_____

_____

_____

General Condition_____

_____

_____

_____

_____

_____

We have inspected the apartment and have found everything in good order except as otherwise indicated. We also acknowledge receipt of the keys as listed.

Tenant:_____

Resident Manager:_____

Date:_____

MOVE-OUT

Special Remarks_____

_____

_____

_____

_____

_____

_____

General Condition_____

_____

_____

_____

_____

_____

We have inspected the apartment and have found everything in good order except as otherwise indicated. We also acknowledge receipt of the keys listed.

Tenant:_____

Resident Manager:_____

Date:_____

	MOVE	
	IN	OUT

ENTRANCE:

	IN	OUT
Door		
Knocker/Bell		
Lock(s)		
Peephole/Chain Lock		

LIVE/DINE ROOM:

	IN	OUT
Ceiling/Walls		
Floors		
Windows/Screens		
Blinds/Drapes		
Electric Fixtures		

KITCHEN:

	IN	OUT
Ceiling/Walls		
Floors		
Windows/Screens		
Blinds/Drapes		
Electric Fixtures		
Cabinets:		
Drawers/Knobs		
Shelves		
Door/Knobs		
Exhaust Fan		
Disposal		
Stove:		
Burners/Shelves		
Broiler Pan		
Refrigerator:		
Defrosted/Clean		
Freezer Door/Tray		
Ice Cube Trays		
Vegetable Drawer(s)		
Dishwasher		
Sink:		
Faucets/Stopper		
Counter Top		

KEYS:

	IN	OUT
Door/Deadbolt		
Mail Box		
Garage Card/Key		

BEDROOM(S):

	IN	OUT
Ceiling/Walls		
Floors		
Windows/Screens		
Blinds/Drapes		
Electric Fixtures		
Closet(s):		
Rod/Shelves		
Door		

BATHROOM(S):

	IN	OUT
Ceiling/Walls		
Floors		
Windows/Screens		
Electric Fixtures		
Heater/Ex Fan		
Medicine Cabinet:		
Mirror		
Shelves		
Linen Closet:		
Shelves		
Tub/Shower:		
Faucets/Stoppers		
Caulking		
Toilet Seat		
Towel/Paper Holders		
Brush/Soap Holders		
Sink:		
Faucets/Stopper		

GENERAL:

	IN	OUT
Foyer		
Patio/Balcony		
Air Conditioners		
Water Heater		
Furnace		
Yard		
Screen Door(s)		

SEPARATE LISTS:

	IN	OUT
Appliances		
Furnishings		

HIDDEN COSTS

What do you mean, doesn't include electricity or water? 22

You have a contract on your first apartment and your lease starts next week. If you didn't rent an apartment with utilities paid, and fully furnished, you have some work to do and some more money to put out. The money is for the expenses you will face as you initially set up your new home. These expenses fall into three categories: new housing, first time house-keeping and furniture. The first two groups of expenses are the topic for this chapter, while furnishings will be discussed in Chapter 23.

NEW HOUSING EXPENSES

These are expenses that you will face anytime you move from one residence to another, even if you have been on your own for a period of time. They include all or most of the following depending on the terms and conditions stated in your new lease.

(1) Rent
(2) Security deposit
(3) Application fee
(4) Utility deposits and hookup charges
(5) New phone deposit and hookup charges
(6) Insurance
(7) Moving expenses
(8) Cleaning costs
(9) Window coverings

Rent

Most landlords require payment of a full month's rent in advance. It is not unusual to have a landlord request both the first and last month's rent in advance, but, if your references and credit check are good, you may be able to get by with paying for just the first month in advance. Paying your first month's rent in advance means each month's rent will be paid in advance. You will then be able to live in the apartment 30 days after you have made the last payment.

If you are still in the planning stage and need an estimate of how much money you will need, put down the maximum you are willing to spend per month for rent.

Security Deposit

The security deposit is paid to guarantee that you will not damage the apartment or house. The landlord keeps this money, interest free, until the move-out inspection is completed. Once the landlord is convinced that the apartment is clean and there is no damage, the deposit is refunded. In some cases there may be a 30 to 60 day delay in receiving this money, so be sure the terms for the refund are written in the lease agreement.

The amount of the security deposit can vary from $50 to more than $500. A good estimate is between 50 and 75% of your monthly rent. When there are a lot of vacancies in the area, landlords have even been known to waive this requirement. Since all areas of the country have different practices, shop around.

Application Fee

Do not confuse the security deposit with an application fee. Some agents and landlords now charge an application fee. This fee is to cover the cost of the time used to verify references and conduct your credit check. Frequently this fee is non-refundable. So, you should not pay the application fee unless you are sure your refer-ences and credit are good, and you want the applied for housing. This fee should not be more than $50. You may be able to make arrangements to have it refunded if your application is approved and you accept the housing. Make this arrangement before you sign any papers or pay any money.

Utility Deposits and Hookup Charges

Unless you are renting a house or apartment with the cost of utilities included in the rent, you must apply for the utility service. If you fail to do this, you will find your new home without water, heat or lights. This can make for a few very uncomfortable days and can definitely dampen the excitement of living in your new home.

When you apply for the utility service, you will be asked to pay a hookup fee and/or place a deposit. The hookup fee is to cover the cost of establishing your account and actually turning on the service to your residence. The deposit is used to protect the utility company in case you do not pay your bills.

Deposits

Deposits for utilities can cost between $25 and $50 each and are usually based on one to two months average bill. This deposit is refundable, and in most states, even earns interest. You should insist on a written statement of the terms of the refund, including when you will receive the refund and the interest that will be paid.

Hookup charges

Hookup charges vary from utility company to utility company. Research reveals that a good estimate for water, gas, electricity and sewerage is between $10 and $35 per utility. The average total for all four utilities is approximately $100. The requirements for each apartment complex or house will be unique. Find out what your obligation is before you sign the lease. Remember, this is a charge, not a deposit, and will not be refunded.

* * * NOTE * * *

If we want to use the utility, we all have to pay hookup charges, but you may be able to get out of paying deposits. If you have previously had utilities provided in your name and paid your bills promptly, you may be eligible to waive the deposit charges. If you meet these requirements, you can request that a letter from your past utility company be provided to the new utility company. This letter will certify your good customer status, and, if the letter covers a period of at least one year, most utility companies will waive the deposit.

New Phone Deposit and Hookup Charges

Like utility companies, phone companies have both hookup charges and deposit requirements. The deposit requirements can be waived by giving your new phone company your old telephone number. They will verify that the number was listed in your name and your payment record. If your record was good, the deposit will be waived.

Telephone hookup charges vary. In 1990 the hookup cost was between $37.50 and $75, if little or no new wiring was required.

Insurance

Not only is insurance on your property a good idea, it may be required under the terms of the lease. The reason some landlords require this insurance is not because they care what happens to your property, they care about being sued. If someone accidently gets hurt while in your apartment and you do not have insurance, the person can sue the landlord as the owner of the property.

Even if the landlord does not lose the suit, the cost, in time and money for the defense, can be staggering. For this reason, more and more landlords are insisting that tenants carry what is called "Renter's Insurance."

Like automobile insurance discussed in Chapter 17, renter's insurance comes in many forms and at varying costs. The factors affecting the cost include the construction and location of the residence, the fire warning and protection devices installed, the value of your possessions, and the selected deductible amount. As with automobile insurance, you should contact your state insurance commission and shop around for the best economy and company reliability.

Do not make the mistake of underestimating the value of your possessions. When you consider all your clothing, shoes, accessories, furniture, pictures, drapes or curtains, cooking utensils, rugs, appliances (TV, radio, stereo), books, lamps and even food, the amount can easily run into the thousands of dollars to replace. When doing your planning of expenses, estimate $75 if the value of your possessions is under $5000 or check with a local insurance agent for a more precise figure.

If you already have renter's insurance, don't forget to notify the company of your move. This is not only to allow the company to adjust your insurance cost, if necessary, but to provide your new address and guarantee your coverage.

Moving Expenses

The cost of moving is based on a number of factors. They include, how much furniture, clothing and other personal possessions you have, and the distance you are moving. The expense can be as little as the cost of a few gallons of gasoline or as much as a few hundred dollars. This is one expense that you have a lot of control over, because there are many ways to move your possessions from one residence to another.

You can borrow some friends' time and a truck and/or a couple of automobiles and move across town, with the only expense being a couple of pizzas and some beverages. My daughter, Karen, and her friends have organized a loosely knit group that seem to spend a number of spring and summer weekends doing exactly that. They help fellow employees and friends move. There fee for this service is food, drink, and gas money. What they actually receive is exercise, fun, and the chance to broaden their group of friends.

When planning a move, don't forget trailer and truck rental companies. Do-it-yourself moves are on the increase because they provide flexibility, are safe and, when compared to hiring a moving company, very inexpensive.

In December 1989, my wife, Jean, our son, Jeff, and I helped my daughter, Cindy, and her husband, Mike, move to a new home about 100 miles away. They rented a 14-foot truck with a ramp, and, in one day, we moved about three rooms of furniture, including a washer and dryer, and one large motorcycle. The cost for the truck, gas, insurance, three hamburgers, four chicken sandwiches and beverages was $114.

Even if you are not going to rent a truck, you should plan for some expense. Remember boxes of chicken, pizzas, beverages and gasoline all cost money.

Cleaning Costs

The fact that you are moving to a new residence means that you are leaving an existing one. If you are leaving a leased or rented residence, the conditions of your lease should require that the vacated premises be cleaned and a move-out inspection take place. This is usually the requirement for refunding your security deposit.

You have three options.

(1) You can clean the vacated apartment or house yourself. This will be the least expensive and, unless you have allowed the dirt to build up, should not take a lot of time. The only problem is that human nature being what it is, all your interests are now focused on the new residence. Cleaning your old residence yourself takes some will power and time. But, it does save money.

(2) You can hire someone to do the cleaning for you. There are both large and small companies that will do this chore for you. Most will do it at a fixed rate and charge by the number of rooms or the size of the apartment or house. Since the residence is vacant and has no furniture, the cost will actually be less than if you were still occupying the space. For cleaning moderate to heavily soiled spaces including carpets, estimate at least $25.00 per room. A relatively small one bedroom efficiency will be computed as having three rooms, a kitchen -- all appliances have to be cleaned -- a bedroom, and a bath.

If time is a factor or if you are immediately leaving the area, this could be the easiest and least expensive way to go. Before you hire someone, be sure that the landlord agrees to accept the hired company's work as meeting the requirements for your refund.

(3) Have the landlord hire someone to clean the premises after you leave. However, this may cost you your full deposit. In fact, if the company the landlord hires charges more than the amount of your deposit, you can expect to receive a bill for the difference. This is not the best way to handle the cleaning because you lose control of the operation and put yourself at the mercy of the landlord and the cleaning company.

No matter which of the three options you

decide to use, be sure you are there for the move-out inspection, even if the apartment has not yet been cleaned. Do not leave the apartment or house without making some acceptable arrangements to get it cleaned. If you do, not only will you forfeit your entire deposit, you may damage your references.

Window Coverings

All window coverings -- drapes, shades, curtains and blinds -- are included under this category of cost because some leases specify the type and color of these items. Since what you had in the previous residence may not be usable in the new residence, this becomes a new housing expense.

Ideally, you desire a lease that does not specify what is acceptable as window coverings, but even then your old window coverings may not fit the new residence's windows. Either way, you may find yourself faced with purchasing window coverings.

It is very difficult to estimate this expense. You may be able to hang bed sheets over the windows thereby reducing the cost to almost nothing. Or you may have to buy a new set of white or beige curtains because your apartment is on the first floor facing the street, and the landlord wants all the windows to have a consistent appearance.

Window coverings are included in new housing expenses more as a consideration than to provide a specific amount. You don't need to be surprised at move-in time with an additional $100 dollar expense because you did not consider the possibility of buying window coverings.

FIRST TIME HOUSEKEEPING COSTS

If this is your first time living away from home, you must be prepared to invest or spend a sum of money in setting up your new house. These expenses are in addition to what was mentioned under New Housing Costs and what will be covered in the next chapter -- Furnishings. These expenses are primarily for items that are needed to prepare meals, serve meals, and keep your apartment or house clean. Some of the items are consumable -- you use them up, and others have a much longer life and will not be repurchased every time you move.

The expense of these items is frequently forgotten when planning to make a move and can add up to quite a surprise when establishing your independence.

Because of the number of different brands and the varying types of items you will need, you may spend less or more that the amounts estimated. The "how to" of shopping for groceries and related items is discussed in Chapter 26, and the purchasing of small appliances is included with furnishing in Chapter 23. The following lists are provided to get you thinking about and planning for these expenses. The minimum you should plan on spending to purchase these items is $100. This estimate does not include stocking the refrigerator or any other major food purchases.

Make a List

Yes, another list, and there will be more. Start by thinking of what you will need on a camping trip where you have to provide everything for your daily living except shelter. This is exactly what you are planning to do. Just as you have done before, starting with writing your resumé in Chapter 1, as you think of items, add them to your list. Try breaking your needs down into four categories: hygiene, cooking, eating and cleaning.

Let's discuss each category.

Hygiene

Start with your obvious needs for toilet paper, soap and toothpaste. Most adults, even those living with their parents, buy their own shampoo, deodorant, hair spray, shaving cream and razors. If you don't, add these items to your list. Now, consider the following:

Do you take vitamins? Do you own washcloths and towels? Do you have small bandages and antiseptic? Do you have cold medicine and other routine medications? Do you have a ventilated container for dirty clothes?

If you are living at home, look in the cabinet in the kitchen where the vitamins are kept, the medicine cabinet, and the cabinet under the sink in the bathroom. Any items you find that you use should be added to your list. Who knows, you may even be able to talk your parents out of some of these items.

Waiting until you are ready to take a shower to realize that you don't have soap, washcloth, or towel, is too late. The same is true for most of the other items that you will want to purchase when you first set up housekeeping.

Cooking

If this is your first apartment, then it is your first kitchen. Make a list of what you need to prepare basic meals. As with the hygiene category, there are some obvious needs, one or more pots, a frying pan, a couple of mixing bowls and a large spoon. These items are definitely a start, but consider the following:

(1) Coffee pot or maker -- for waking up in the morning.
(2) Toaster -- for super-quick breakfasts.
(3) Butcher knife -- for opening fast food containers and cutting meat and poultry when you can afford them.
(4) Small sharp paring knife -- for opening cardboard and plastic containers, opening mail, and finely cutting seasonings like onions and garlic.
(5) Measuring spoons and cup(s) -- a pinch of this and a pinch of that doesn't always work. Sometimes you need to be accurate.
(6) Pot holder and hot pad -- pots get hot and burns take time to heal.
(7) Wide spatula -- for prying open stubborn containers and turning pancakes, eggs and hamburgers.
(8) Long handled fork -- for stirring pasta and sticking into things too hot to get close to.
(9) Set of canisters -- coffee, tea, flour and sugar need to be stored in sealed containers in most climates. Tightly resealable coffee cans and resealable plastic containers, like the ones that peanut butter and soft margarine are packaged in, may be used as canisters. They are not as tight as some that are marketed as "airtight," but they will do the job.
(10) Glass or plastic pitcher -- used for watering the plants and to mix and serve frozen orange juice, iced tea and other beverages.
(11) Cookie sheet -- catches drippings under TV dinners and pizzas. Also good for baking refrigerator biscuits and pastries.

Many of these kitchen items can be acquired free of charge by offering to help parents, relatives, and friends clean out and organize their kitchen cabinets. Most long time cooks have two to three times the number of these items they really need. You will learn from experience that if you have a kitchen and cook, you always seem to be adding to these items.

Eating

You should be able to get by with very little expense for this category. The old camping mess kit of metal plate, pot, cup, knife, fork and spoon will suffice. However, it will suffice only if you are planning to always eat alone and like the taste of aluminum in your food. You might even be able to save on dishwashing detergents, since I have found the best way to clean these kits is sand and cold water.

Most people do not like to eat alone and have hot water and soap available. They also prefer to eat from plates and drink from glasses or cups. If this describes your likes, your list should include a couple of plates, glasses, cups, knives, forks and spoons. You may want to add to your list a couple of bowls to be used for soup, cereal or salad and a couple of tablespoons for cooking and serving.

Although a couple of each of these items is the bare minimum you will want, you will find that four of each is a much better number. Not only will you have extra settings for guests, you will not have to wash your dirty dishes and utensils twice a day. Consider buying a package of inexpensive paper plates. These are great when used with inexpensive rattan holders for snacks and meals that do not consist of very wet food.

As with the other categories of expenses discussed, these items for eating can usually be obtained from friends and family. Another good source for buying these items inexpensively is thrift stores. At one thrift store I visited, I could have bought a complete unmatched four place set of these items for under $8. The price went up to $10 if I added a small platter, two serving bowls and a large serving spoon.

At this time, the items do not have to match, you are not trying to win a "Good Housekeeping" award, only set up your kitchen.

Cleaning

You do not have to be a "cleanliness freak" or a "neatness fanatic" to need and use cleaning products. The more obvious ones are broom, sponge mop, bucket, and, if you have carpets or rugs, a small vacuum cleaner is a must. In addition, you need bathroom cleansers, kitchen and laundry detergents, sponges, general purpose disinfectant, dish towels and at least one roll of paper towels.

You will probably add to this list as you get settled, but this will give you a good start. Finding extras of these items in your friends' or parents' homes may be a little difficult. However, talk to anyone you know who has been a housekeeper for a period of time and get suggestions on what they think you will need. Ask for specifics on recommended products and brands. As with all other chemicals, be sure to read the labels for instructions on storage, use and safety precautions.

There are a couple of other ideas that may help you in obtaining some of the items in these four categories. The first applies to sharing. If you are sharing your new residence, you should share the start-up cost. The best way to do this is to share the cost of the consumables, but let each of the sharing members provide some of the utensils and larger items. These items will be used by all the sharing members but will belong to the individual who provided them. This is better than trying to compute how much of the toaster, coffee maker, plates and utensils Sally or Richard owns if or when either has to move out.

The second way to acquire these items is as "housewarming" gifts. Family and friends will frequently ask someone who is setting up an apartment or house, for the first time, what he or she needs. Do not be shy or proud, have your list ready and tell them exactly what items you need. This is similar in concept to a "wedding shower" except you don't need to get married. This gives your family and friends the satisfaction of helping and you get the items you need for starting housekeeping.

THE BOTTOM LINE

How much money are you going to need now that you are planning to lease a house or apartment? The answer to this question will vary depending on your resourcefulness, what the stipulations are in your lease, and whether or not you are sharing. This chapter has concentrated more on these items and things you will have to consider than on the dollar amount of their cost. If we use Jo Ann setting up her new efficiency as an example, we can get a rough estimate of the expenses.

List of expected expenses

First month's rent	$ 250
Security deposit	125
Utility deposits and hookup charges	100
Phone deposit ($50) and hookup fee ($35)	85
Insurance (1 year minimum coverage)	47
Do-it-herself moving expenses (gas and food)	30
Cleaning costs (Jo Ann's cleaning service)	0
Window coverings	20

Jo Ann estimates she will need a total of $657 to cover her move.

In addition, she plans to use her parents and friends to help defray the costs of getting the basic housekeeping items needed to set up her apartment. She thinks she will receive most of the items needed for cooking and eating, but she will have to buy some hygiene and cleaning supplies as well as a few food items. She adds $143 to her total, rounding off her estimate of cash required to $800.

If you are resourceful and have generous and helpful friends, you may be able to get by with less. But, for estimating and planning purposes, you will be better off using a higher figure than underestimating and finding yourself short of needed funds.

FURNISHINGS

Early American thrift shop and contemporary garage sale 23

You have leased your new residence, the utilities are turned on, and you have moved in. You look around and are impressed with how big your efficiency is, especially with only your stereo and your sleeping bag on the floor. You need some basic furniture.

WHAT DO YOU NEED?

By now you know what I am going to say. That's right, make a list. This time I am going to provide some help. In addition to the items dis-cussed in the previous chapter under cooking, cleaning and eating, you probably need some additional furnishings. The number of items you need will be greater if you are living alone than if you are sharing. The size of the residence is also a factor. Your needs are less if you have moved into a 450 to 500 square foot efficiency than if you have a 750 square foot one bedroom apartment.

We will use Jo Ann's list for the efficiency as an example. Notice that the list is separated into living zones for ease of planning. You should do the same with the list you develop.

Furnishings List

Bathroom
>   No furnishings are usually required for the bathroom

Living Area
>   Chair or chairs -- may use kitchen chairs if necessary
>   Small end or side table, for TV, lamp, etc.
>   Lamp or lamps

Sleeping Area
>   Bed -- can be "Futon" or "Day Bed" style
>   Chest of drawers, dresser, or both

Eating Area
>   Sturdy table -- will substitute as work table/desk
>   Chairs -- at least two

These are probably the basic of the basics. You may want to add additional chairs, a coffee table if you have room, possibly a TV, some rugs, posters or pictures and even bookshelves or a bookcase. If your kitchen is not equipped with a refrigerator, you will want to add that to the list, and, if you will be preparing most of your meals at home, you may want to add a small microwave oven. Consider adding a clock to the list; none of my children thought they wanted one when they were in the planning stage, but it was the first item, not on their list, that they bought.

HOW TO ACQUIRE

The five ways to *legally* acquire furniture and other furnishings are:

(1) Finding
(2) Creating
(3) Gifts
(4) Purchasing and
(5) Renting.

Finding

Finding furniture may sound strange but my son, Jeff, my daughter, Karen, and I have all added to our furnishings by using someone else's discarded furniture. Jeff picked up a set of shelves, Karen a side table, and my favorite is an oval, gold gilded, hallway mirror I have proudly called my own for over 30 years.

These items had all been discarded for the trash man or put by a dumpster to be sent to the local landfill. A little tightening, cleaning and a small amount of paint and they were all as good as new. There is a lot of truth in the idea that "one person's trash is another's treasure."

In West Germany, the residents place their unwanted items on the side of the roads on a specified day each week. Anyone and everyone is invited to drive around and select those items that may be of use. In the United States we sort of do the same thing when we have garage sales. The only difference is that at garage sales a small fee is paid for the items selected.

Creating

Be resourceful, a lot of furnishings can be created by the resourceful individual with little skill and only the simplest of tools. A couple of scrap boards and a few discarded bricks become a bookcase. Some old concrete blocks and a used hollow-core door will make a highly functional desk.

Bed sheets become attractive curtains with just a little sewing skill. Large mural beach towels and small rugs become attractive wall coverings.

For the more ambitious, the use of a hack saw, sandpaper, pvc cement and a little imagination, can turn long pieces of pvc pipe into attractive and functional furniture. You can even pick up free instructions where the pvc pipe is sold. The list of things you can create is only limited by your imagination.

Gifts

I am not talking about just "housewarming" gifts, I am suggesting that you be resourceful and generate the opportunity to be given furnishings as gifts. How do you do this? Easy, the first thing to do is make sure that your family and friends all know that you are moving into your own place. The second thing is to make sure that everyone knows what you need. The item can be something as small as a clock or a picture to something as large as a bed, bookcase or table and chairs. Lastly make sure that everyone knows that you are not proud, you're willing and able to make do with used, but functional, furnishings, and nothing will be refused.

Hint: You may want to keep track of who gives you what and remember to take the ghastly tortoise shell clock from the back of the closet if the donor ever visits.

Helping family and friends clean their garage or attic is another excellent way to end up with some nice used furniture. The key to this method is not to ask anyone for a particular item, just offer your services and advertise that your new residence is available, as a good home, for the excess treasured, but older, furnishings.

Example

Chris, my son Jeff's roommate, has a large paper route and when he was first setting up a home of his own, put a hand written flyer in all his papers. The flyer stated that he was moving into an apartment and asked for donations of unwanted furniture. Chris says the response was overwhelming. By the end of the week, he had practically furnished his apartment, including small appliances and cooking/eating utensils. His cost was under $5 which was the cost of printing the flyers.

PURCHASE

The six ways to purchase furnishings, ranked from the least expensive to the most expensive, are:

(1) Garage sales and flea markets
(2) Thrift stores and pawn shops

(3)   Classified or bulletin board ads
(4)   Used furniture stores
(5)   New
(6)   Rent to own

Garage Sales and Flea Markets

Garage sale and flea market shopping is fun if you have time and patience and don't mind getting up at the crack of dawn on Saturdays. They provide an excellent source for purchasing cooking and eating utensils, including pots, bowls, glasses and dishes. There are even some spectacular furniture and accessory buys awaiting the early shopper.

Just recently my son, Jeff, found a solid wood and leather desk chair with rollers, in excellent condition, for just $5. Over the years my family has picked up everything from complete sets of pots and pans, to end tables, chairs and even appliances. These items have really helped to outfit my children's apartments.

Unlike the merchandise found at garage sales, most of the merchandise for sale at flea markets is new. Even though you may be able to purchase this merchandise at a discount, it will cost more than if purchased used. Even the used merchandise will be priced higher because the seller must pay rent for the right to have space in the flea market. Still, most of the used items found at garage sales and flea markets are sold at a small fraction of their original cost. Depending on the item, its condition and style, the cost may be as little as 20% or less of the original price. You should treat all prices placed on merchandise at garage sales and flea markets as negotiable.

Thrift Stores and Pawn Shops

Most cities today have one or more thrift stores. They may be owned by the Salvation Army, Heart Fund, or other local non-profit charitable organizations. There are two good reasons for buying from these stores instead of garage sales and flea markets. The first is that the merchandise's condition is usually checked out before it is put on the sales floor. And the second is that the profits are used to support the charitable organization that owns the store.

Thrift stores are an excellent source of small appliances including stereo and television equipment. Furniture and even clothing can be purchased at these stores for a small fraction of the original cost. In the case of appliances, you can usually try them out in the store, and, in many cases, if they do not function properly when you get them home, you can return them for a refund.

My daughter, Karen, found a 12 cup stainless steel coffee percolator for $1.75. Except for not having an electric cord the percolator appeared brand new. In another part of the same store, she found a rack of appliance cords and matched the percolator with a cord for another 75 cents bringing the total cost to $2.50. That was four years ago, and today, after daily use, it is still working great.

Over the years, my wife, Jean, and I have used the thrift stores as reliable sources of home furnishings for helping each of our children set up housekeeping.

Pawn shops are like thrift stores in that the used merchandise can be purchased at a large reduction in price. The major difference is that the stores are private businesses and are operated to make a profit for the owner. Their merchandise is usually made up of appliances, tools, cameras, jewelry, electronic equipment and other items of value that were not redeemed when their loan payment was due.

Depending on where you live, the pawn shop selection can be very limited, but, if you have the time to wait, something you like will eventually be available. Check your yellow pages for a list of the thrift stores and pawn shops in your neighborhood. Market prices at these stores are generally not negotiable, but it will not cost anything to ask.

Classified or Bulletin Board Ads

Classified ads in your local newspaper or shopping guide, as well as ads placed on work or public bulletin boards, provide another source of merchandise at reduced prices. People normally place these ads because they are moving or have purchased new items to replace the items being sold. This is a good method of shopping for used furnishings, especially if you are looking for a limited number of items and have something specific in mind. The merchandise is usually used, and the prices are not as low as if the same items were found at garage sales.

You should consider the price advertised as negotiable even if the ad states otherwise. When you are satisfied that the item is what you want, make a reasonable offer. When someone is looking to get rid of an appliance or piece of furniture, it is difficult to pass up an offer of money unless the amount is unreasonable.

Shopping these ads can result in some real nice buys and can sometimes be as inexpensive as thrift stores, pawn shops, flea markets or even garage sales.

Used Furniture Stores

There are two kinds of stores that deal in used furniture, the first, has the furniture on consignment, and the second owns the furniture.

The company that has the furniture on consignment is simply providing a place for showing the furniture and someone to collect the money. When the furniture is sold, the owner pays the store a percentage of the selling price to cover the cost of selling the item. The selling price of the items are set by the owner and may be negotiable. The store will have to contact the owner for agreement, but reasonable offers are usually accepted. This is generally the least expensive of the two types of used furniture stores.

The second type of used furniture store functions just like any other store. The inventory is purchased, there is a markup added, and there are sales commissions to pay. This means that the prices asked for the used furniture and accessories will be higher than if you bought from an individual. Sales abound, but the prices are usually not negotiable. You pay the advertised price. These stores are usually affiliated with furniture rental companies, and the stores stock is made up of the furniture returned when the rental agreements terminate.

By careful shopping, my children have found some excellent buys at each of the two types of used furniture stores. The greatest positive factor is that used furniture stores usually have a very wide selection of both furniture and accessories.

* * * C A U T I O N * * *

When buying a mattress from a thrift or used furniture store, insist that it be steam cleaned before you make the purchase. In some states, it is against the law to sell a used mattress that has not been steamed cleaned.

New

If you can afford and desire to purchase new furniture and accessories, and we all do at some time in our lives, my only advice is to shop. Shop for quality and price. Quality is not brand name, quality is workmanship and durability. New furniture is expensive, so you want to get the best quality you can for your money.

Furniture that takes heavy use, should be made of high quality materials, reinforced in all the joints and covered in an attractive, practical and long lasting fabric. Repairing loose joints in furniture is very expensive and the recovering or reupholstering of a sofa or chair can easily cost more than the item's original purchase price.

You can find new furniture in many types of stores. Department and discount stores as well as most large retail chain stores sell furniture. In addition, there are speciality furniture stores and furniture warehouse outlets. The big four users of newspaper classified advertisements are the food, real estate, automobile, and furniture/appliance vendors. As with all other purchases, know what you want, know what you can afford, and compare different vendors offers and reputations.

Rent to Own

When you rent-to-own something, eventually that item will belong to you, so in effect you are purchasing it. I have placed this method as the most expensive for two reasons: first is because you always pay full list price for the item, and secondly, a very high interest rate is usually included in the rental agreement.

Example

Let's follow Jo Ann as she looks for a microwave oven. On her list, she has a microwave oven as a want, not a need, but she noticed an ad in the paper from a rent-to-own company offering to rent appliances for just $5 a week. The ad stated that there would be no hassle, no credit check, and only a $10 deposit.

Jo Ann calls the store and finds that they carry the same brand that has been recommended to her as being very reliable. When she arrives at the store, she sees the exact model she has been looking for and asks the salesperson for a copy of the rent-to-own contract.

The salesperson shows her the list price of the microwave -- $199 and explains that she will have a $5 charge for processing the rental agreement, and, after just one year, Jo Ann will own the microwave. The total amount of the contract will be $265 -- $5 a week for 52 weeks plus the $5 fee. The contract also guarantees service during the rental period should the microwave stop working. Jo Ann thanks the salesperson for her time and promises to think the offer over. The salesperson reminds Jo Ann that there will not be a credit check and that the contract includes one year's free service.

Upon returning home, Jo Ann decides to do some checking and, in looking through the appliance dealers' newspaper ads, notices that the same brand and model is on sale for $159. Jo Ann visits the store the next day and the salesperson explains that the store offers a one year financing plan -- 10% down, an interest rate of 18% and a minimum payment of $20 per month. The salesperson also assures her that if she has been living at the same address and working for the same company for over six months with no bad marks on her credit history, she should have no problem getting the store credit.

Jo Ann tells the salesperson she needs to think about the purchase and goes back home. At home she computes the cost of buying the microwave.

Actual cost including 5% sales tax	$167
10% Down Payment	17
Amount financed	$150
18% per year finance charge for eight months	
(Because of the $20 minimum monthly payment,	
the microwave oven will be paid for in only eight months)	10
Total to repay at $20 per month	$160

Not only will Jo Ann save $105 by buying the microwave outright, she will only have to pay $20 a month for eight months and, at the same time, be creating a credit record for herself. She also finds out that the microwave comes with a two year manufacturer's warranty. If anything goes wrong, all she has to do is return the oven to the store for repairs.

This example does not overstate the cost of rent-to-own agreements. The added costs due to the high interest rate charged and paying the full list price of the items can easily add hundreds of dollars to furniture and appliance purchases.

RENTING

Renting is the most expensive way to acquire furniture because you never own the the items. As long as you need or want the furniture, you will have to pay the rent and the total rental amount you pay is the cost. At least with a rent-to-own agreement, you pay more for the item, but the item does become yours, and you stop paying the rent at some time in the future.

About the only advantage to renting furniture is that you never have to move it. When you move or get tired of the furniture, you simply call the company you are renting from and instruct them to pick it up.

There are two ways to rent furniture. The first and usually the most inexpensive is to rent a furnished room or apartment. Furnished rooms or apartments are available because it is much more profitable for the person owning the furniture to rent it as part of the premises than it is to put it into storage. If you have not settled on a location, renting furnished living quarters can possibly be less expensive than buying furniture and then paying to have it moved.

The second way to rent furniture and accessories is from furniture rental companies. They will rent from one piece to a full house of furniture, and the only real advantage is that a lot of money is not required up front. Even though they advertise "no credit checks," most furniture rental stores will not rent anyone a substantial amount of furniture without first checking references. The quality of the rented items can range from poor through the highest of quality and most expensive of pieces, and the rental amount is adjusted accordingly.

For this type of rental, the monthly rental amount is computed by adding to the list price of the item a fixed interest charge -- your payment for using the vendor's money -- and dividing this total by a very conservative life. This is the same method used by car leasing companies discussed in Chapter 16.

Example

Walking to work one day you see a nice sofa in the showroom window of a furniture rental company. The sofa lists for $600, and you estimate a usable life expectancy of 10 years. However, the company has a table of historical data that shows that after three years of normal wear and tear as a rental item, the sofa can be sold used for only $150. The monthly rental charge for this sofa will be computed as follows:

Sofa list price	$600
Minus resale value (used)	150
Depreciation over three years	$450
Interest on $600 for three years at 18% per year	324
Total rental charge for 3 years	774
Monthly rental (Total divided by 36 months -- three years)	$21.50

The rental company will probably round this amount up to $25 to cover overhead and extra labor required for the delivery and pickup of the rental item. In one year, you will pay $300, and, at the end of the year, you have nothing. After three years and paying $900, you still have nothing, making this the most expensive method of acquiring furniture.

SUMMARY

Furnishing your first room, apartment or house can be both inexpensive and a lot of fun. Regardless of how you do it, the final outcome will reflect you. It does not make any difference if your mattress sits directly on the floor, as one of my son's does, or if you have everything matched like a professional decorator would do it; the final result is home.

Turning your new residence into a home can be inexpensive. The key to the level of expense will be your resourcefulness. The number of friends, the size of your family, and your ability to separate wants from needs will also play a role in the amount of money you spend. Take care of your needs first, then, as your budget allows, work on acquiring the wants.

Beware of impulse buying. Store managers have the promotion of impulse buying down to a science. The fast movers and expensive accessories are always attractively presented with the major item of purchase. The intent is to visually convince you that everything goes together and you must have it all to make your room look right. This will even include pictures and other wall coverings, lamps, linens and even small accent pieces. You can easily pay over $1,000 to buy a $500 sofa, if you buy all the accessories that are displayed with it on the showroom floor.

Good used furniture costs a fraction of what new furniture does and will probably give years of additional use. Remember your "new" furniture is "used" as soon as you get it home.

NOTES

_____

_____

_____

_____

FOOD

You are what you eat, or you're not what you don't eat.

VI

One very necessary requirement for surviving is eating. You must eat. But, in addition to just surviving, you must eat for good health. Eating for good health does not mean eating bland, dry unappetizing food. Nor does it mean eating the same food over and over again. Eating for good health means that you need to know some of the basic requirements of good nutrition and some of the dangers and pitfalls of always eating "fast foods."

Chapter 24 starts with a short discussion on nutrition, followed by kitchen safety and sanitation. A suggested list of appliances and utensils needed for the small kitchen, including their cost, is presented, with the chapter concluding with some hints for making cooking fun.

Chapter 25 discusses menus. The benefits of planning menus are discussed, and a sample nutritious week's menu is provided. The chapter concludes with some helpful hints and suggestions for adding variety to the menu by creating meals from leftovers.

Chapter 26 uses the menus from Chapter 25 to develop a grocery list. The do's and don'ts of grocery shopping are presented, including how to read labels, knowing your grocery store layout, and suggestions on when to shop.

COOKING
Peanut butter and jelly sandwiches get old very quickly.

24

Unless you have really struck it rich, you cannot afford to eat out three meals a day. Even with enough money, you would probably find it rather boring to eat out all the time. Most adults, both young and old, find that they not only need to cook at home but actually enjoy doing it.

This chapter focuses on nutrition, cost, utensil requirements and ideas for preparing and enjoying fast, nutritious, and delicious meals. There are a limited number of menus and no recipes in this book. There are literally thousands of cookbooks in print today, containing more information than one person can expect to absorb in 10 years. I have included a few examples of these in the back of the book under additional reading.

NUTRITION

There are many old sayings such as, "You are what you eat" and "An apple a day keeps the doctor away" that are based on sound nutritional advice. After reading over 40 books and studies on nutrition, I can safely say that what we all learned about eating, food and nutrition, in third grade health classes, is still valid.

What do we need?

Each day we should all try to eat the following:

Two servings of Protein (Meat Group)
Each serving is equal to three ounces of lean meat, poultry or fish and even includes nuts, soybeans, and cheeses -- cottage and hard -- and eggs.
Four or more servings of Fruit and Vegetables

Each serving is equal to either 1/2 cup or the typical serving size. At least one serving should be of the green leafy type.
Four or more servings of Bread and Cereal
Each serving is equal to 1 slice of bread or 1/2 English muffin, bagel, or hamburger/hot dog bun. Servings of cereal are 1/2 to 3/4 cup of cooked cereal or 1 cup of ready to eat cereal.
Two servings of Milk or Cheese (Dairy)
Each serving is measured as 1 cup milk, 3/4 cup of nonfat yogurt, 1/2 cup of ice cream or one slice, or two one inch cubes, of cheese.

Not So Good

Looking at the list, you can see that a day's menu including hot cakes, with butter and syrup, and juice for breakfast, 1/4 pound cheeseburger with fries and a shake for lunch, and a salad bar with iced tea for dinner, topped off with a brownie and milk for an evening snack seems to meet all the requirements.

The only problem is that a diet like this, if purchased already prepared, will cost about $10 per day, or $300 per month, and will probably send you to an early grave.

Eating Healthy

According to *Fast Food Facts* published by the International Diabetes Center, today's adult should be concentrating on a low fat, low sodium diet. The daily diet should consist of no more than 13 teaspoons of fat, 1 teaspoon of salt and approximately 2000 calories. More calories are acceptable if the individual is an athlete or involved in heavy manual labor. The menu described in the previous paragraph, contains about 3400 calories, 34 teaspoons of fat and 2 teaspoons of salt. This is almost three times the fat, twice the salt and almost twice the recommended calories, which is why I indicated there could be a problem in addition to the high cost.

All of us are forced by circumstances to periodically eat at fast food restaurants. When this happens, it is important to select the food we eat with great care, avoiding those items that are high in fat, sodium and cholesterol. You should make a point of reading the latest government reports on fast foods and especially *Fast Food Facts*. If at all possible, limit eating at these restaurants to once or twice a week. You will feel better, spend much less money and have more fun by cooking your own meals.

Vitamins

Most medical experts feel that if you eat a balanced diet of 2000 calories, you will get all the vitamins your body needs without taking a supplement. However, since taking more vitamins than you need has not been proven to be harmful, supplementing with a multiple vitamin will not inflict harm and may provide you some peace of mind.

Minerals

As with vitamins, except in rare cases, a balanced diet should provide all the minimum levels of the minerals suggested by the Food and Drug Adminisration. If you are concerned that your diet is not providing the minerals you need, take a multiple vitamin supplement that contains minerals. You should check with your doctor at your next visit to get a professional opinion on taking vitamin and mineral supplements.

THE KITCHEN

Safety

All the planning, shopping and cooking skills you possess will be wasted if you end up in the doctor's office or hospital emergency room. The kitchen is one of the most accident producing rooms in the house. Cuts and burns are two of the most common accidents, and both are preventable. Think safety!

My dad lost most of the skin off his back by trying to change a light bulb in the kitchen while he was frying chicken. The handle of the fry pan was not turned towards the stove, and, as he got down from the chair, his belt caught the handle and flipped the hot oil down his back.

Just recently, my daughter, Kim, accidently dropped a large pointed butcher knife. The knife dropped straight down piercing her light shoe and her foot. She spent the next six, very uncomfortable, weeks on crutches. A little more awareness, a little more thought to safety, and a little more care could have prevented both of these accidents. Remember, hot things burn, sharp things cut and moving things pinch or tear. Even the best meal in the world is not worth a visit to the doctor or the hospital.

Sanitation

Germs do not usually have a taste. Sometimes they don't even have a smell. The key to keeping yourself and others from getting very sick from eating something you cook is knowing and following the rules for safe food handling and storage.

Most packaged food contains instructions on storage, so knowing how to store the food is not really a problem if you follow the printed instructions. When the package says keep refrigerated or refrigerate after opening, don't put it on the pantry shelf. If the item does not indicate how to store or if you are in doubt about the storage instructions, put the item in a tightly sealed container and the container in the refrigerator. The exception to the tightly sealed container rule is fresh fruits and vegetables. Most have their own containers in the form of skin or peelings. Fresh potatoes and onions and most fresh fruit can be stored without refrigeration and, even if stored in the refrigerator, should not be tightly sealed.

Fresh fruits and vegetables are the exception, no other food item should ever be stored without a sealed container. An open container is not only a breeding place for germs but exposes the food to other contaminating agents, many of which can make you very very sick. Check with your local library or extension agent for additional information on storage methods and the maximum length of time you can safely store uncooked and cooked food.

Some Rules

Preparing and cooking food can make you sick. This statement need not be true if you follow some very simple kitchen rules.

(1) No pets in the kitchen, especially while food is being prepared. Animal hair and parasites don't add flavor to your meals.

(2) Never thaw frozen food at room temperature. Food does not have to get warm to spoil.

(3) Never use any plates or utensils, including your own hands, for raw and cooked meat, without first washing with hot water and soap.

(4) Cutting boards should be of high density plastic to reduce the possibility of germ growth through improper cleaning.

(5) Uneaten cooked food should be placed in the refrigerator immediately. It should not be left on the counter or stove to cool.

(6) All utensils should be clean and dry before using. Wet knives are slippery and they do cut.

(7) Wash and dry all cooking and eating utensils as soon after eating as possible.

(8) Keep the kitchen clean, it reduces the number of small critters that are unhealthy and annoying.

COOKING FOR ONE

In addition to being the most healthful and inexpensive way to feed yourself, cooking, even for one, can be fun and very rewarding. With a little imagination, planning and practice, anyone can be an acceptable cook. Add a little more imagination, daring, and more practice and nearly anyone can become a very good to excellent cook. Good meals do not have to cost a lot or take a lot of time to prepare. For example, a cup of coffee, a six ounce glass of juice, and a bowl of cold cereal will cost you less than 40 cents to have at home but more than two dollars to eat at a restaurant.

Below is a short table that compares the cost of cooking at home against buying prepared foods at a restaurant.

Some Comparisons

Item	Home Cooked	Restaurant	Savings
Sub Sandwich	$ 1.20	$ 2.75	$ 1.55
Large Salad	1.00	2.50	1.50
Baked Fish Dinner	1.25	3.75	2.50
BBQ Chicken Dinner	1.10	3.50	2.40
Hamburger	.80	1.85	1.05
Pizza 13", Sausage & Cheese	2.50	5.00	2.50
Pasta With Meat Sauce	1.10	4.50	3.40
BLT Sandwich	.50	2.50	2.00
Roast Beef Meal	1.80	6.55	4.75
French Toast (two slices)	.30	1.50	1.20
Two Eggs, Sausage & Toast	.70	2.45	1.75
Hot Cakes, Butter & Syrup	.25	2.15	1.90
Meatballs & Spaghetti	1.10	5.50	4.40
Coffee	.06	.60	.54
Iced Tea	.03	.75	.72
Ham/Cheese Omelette (two eggs)	.60	3.40	2.80
Grilled Cheese	.40	2.60	2.20
Egg Salad Sandwich	.28	1.90	1.62
Apple Pie	.50	1.45	.95
Ice Cream (one scoop)	.30	.90	.60

For all of the items in the table, I used existing prices and standard serving sizes. For instance, the omelette has two eggs, there are three hot cakes, the chicken dinner has one breast quarter, and the baked fish dinner has two large pieces. In addition, the meals all have normal vegetables and/or salad included in their cost. The cost of the home cooked pizza is based on using frozen dough and a prepackaged sauce. The bottom line is that the savings you have should be greater than those stated. The table should present you with some "food for thought," especially since none of the meals listed take very long to prepare nor do they require a high level of cooking skill.

Getting Started

Planning is the secret to eating inexpensive, nutritious and well balanced meals. Many food items cannot be purchased in small enough quantities to be used up in a single recipe. Planning allows you to take advantage of the larger size and not be faced with throwing away what is not needed. Planning also includes setting up your kitchen so that when you are trying to fix a meal, you have the utensils and other necessary items, introduced in Chapter 22 and expanded on below, close at hand.

Utensils

My son, Jeff, and his roommate, Chris, provided the following list of necessary items for the starter kitchen.

Eating -- two to eight of each of the following:

Forks, knives, teaspoons, tablespoons, ice tea spoons, plates, cups, saucers, glasses and general purpose bowls (soup/salad/cereal). If you are living by yourself start with two or three and build up as you see good deals.

Preparing -- at least one of each of the following:

Large spoon and fork, spoon with holes, metal spatula, flexible rubber spatula, egg and hot cake flipper, large plastic spoon, fork, and spaghetti server, large wooden spoon, ice cream scoop, tongs, ladle, set of measuring cups and spoons, cheese slicer and grater, large and small mixing bowls, funnel, vegetable peeler, can and bottle opener, corkscrew, scissors, and assorted sizes of plastic resealable storage containers.

Cooking--at least one of each of the following:

Large (4 quart) and small (2 quart) pots, spaghetti pot (6 or more quarts), spaghetti strainer, dutch oven, large and small frying pan, baking pan (9" X 13"), round pizza pan (13" to 18"), loaf pan, casserole dish (2 to 3 quart). All of the pots and the frying pans should be non-stick.

Nice to have --
to make cooking faster and easier, the following items are recommended:

Small toaster oven, small microwave oven and electric non-stick wok. If you have a microwave oven be sure that some of your bowls and your casserole dish are microwaveable.

Spices, etc.

In addition to the necessary utensils and appliances, no kitchen is complete without the following basic spices and condiments: salt, pepper, garlic powder, chili powder, bread crumbs, onion flakes, parsley flakes, vanilla, oregano, basil, allspice, cinnamon, catsup, mustard (brown and yellow), vegetable oil, and vinegar.

Making it Fun

Many individuals find eating alone, as with cooking for one, not much fun. In addition to not having anyone to share in your cooking endeavors and to talk to, you have to do all the work yourself. You can change all this by forming informal cooking groups among your friends. The groups don't even have to be made up of the same friends each time. The idea is not to become gourmets, but to share in the cost and labor involved in the preparation of meals and, at the same time, develop a good social atmosphere.

It works like this: each week you and possibly three friends take turns preparing, or jointly prepare a meal for four. This means that you get to shop for the larger, less expensive, per serving, packages of food and cuts of meat.

If you are taking turns preparing the meals, then you can take turns purchasing the food, meaning that you will end up paying for one meal for four, instead of four meals for one. If you are sharing in the preparation, share in the cost, with each person paying one fourth of the cost of each meal. This method can be especially fun if you actually prepare the menu as part of the socializing with the meal. Everyone pitches in to clean the table and dishes after the meal is over, so the host is not stuck with these less desirable chores. An extra benefit is that with four people con-tributing ideas for the menus, more variety will probably be added to your cooking and eating habits.

This type of arrangement can be worked with less than four people and for more than one night a week. Informal cooking groups can also add to your list of friends and acquaintances and help develop your planning, preparation and cooking skills.

NOTES

_____

_____

_____

_____

_____

_____

_____

_____

_____

_____

_____

_____

_____

_____

_____

_____

_____

MENU PLANNING
I'll eat at a different place each night.

PLANNING AHEAD

Cooking is only fun if you have the time and the necessary ingredients to turn raw food into appetizing and flavorful meals. This is as true for breakfast as it is for a full five course dinner. The key to having the time and ingredients on hand to prepare a meal is planning. You need a menu, not just for a meal, or even a day, but for at least a week. The menu is prepared for both planning and shopping efficiency. Once prepared, the menu serves as a guide, it must never be viewed as being "locked in concrete." If you decide to go bowling on Wednesday and buy a sandwich or pizza at the bowling alley, no problem. You can slip the dinner menu one day or even use that menu to start the next week's cycle.

Think of menu planning as an investment in time. Not only will you not have to go to the store each day, you will be able to minimize your shopping time by knowing what you need. In addition, the amount of time spent each day trying to decide what to prepare will be eliminated. On those days when you just don't feel like eating what's planned simply swap to another day's menu. You have a full weeks worth of ingredients already purchased so there is no need to rush to the store.

Preparing a weekly menu has three other advantages.

(1) You can look at the nutritional value of your meals and produce a much better diet for yourself than if you shop and eat on a whim.
(2) By planning a full week in advance, you can put variety into your diet so that you are not eating the same main or side dishes each day.

(3) You can plan quick meals for those days when you have scheduled an after work or evening appointment.

Breakfast

Start with breakfast. Breakfast does not have to take long to prepare nor does it have to mean a bowl of cereal each day. It only takes 10 minutes to make toast and fry an egg or two. It does not take much longer than that to fix pancakes from one of the prepared mixes or pop some canned biscuits into the oven. Bagels with cream cheese, English muffins, or cereal -- cold or hot -- take even less than 10 minutes to prepare. The truth is that you will spend more time driving to a fast food restaurant, waiting in line to give your order and picking it up than it will take to prepare and eat a breakfast at home. Most good, nutritious, and appetizing breakfasts can be prepared in the time it takes to brew a pot of coffee or a cup of tea.

Unless you are in the habit of eating a bowl of cereal and drinking a glass of juice each day, add variety. Consider the following, bagels and cream cheese, toast and jelly, or a scrambled egg sandwich -- add a slice of ham or cheese for variety. If you like cereal, try keeping a variety of the low fat, low sodium kind available or alternate between hot and cold. For hot cereal, use the quick kind but avoid the instant brands that come in envelopes -- each has 500 or more milligrams of sodium. Don't forget hot cakes, biscuits, pastries and eggs. If you add a six ounce glass of juice, milk, and coffee or tea, you have a solid breakfast.

Lunch

If you live close enough to work to go home for lunch, you are truly blessed and your choices for lunch will be unlimited. However, if you are like the rest of us and either have to take your lunch to work or buy it each day at a cafeteria, think variety. Even brown bag lunches don't have to be boring, especially if you have access to a microwave at work.

Even with no microwave, you can add variety to your brown bag lunch. Lunch each day does not have to be a slice of bologna between two pieces of white bread with a little mustard, unless that is what you like. By buying a small thermos container, you can add hot soup, chili, stew, or other hot foods to your menu. Cold chicken and other meats are good if you have access to a refrigerator or other container to keep them cold.

By alternating the snack and beverage you pack each day and making your sandwiches with different breads, fillings, and garnishings your "brown bag" lunches will have variety and still be nutritious, appetizing and inexpensive.

Dinner

How much time do you want to spend? If you are willing to spend some time, there is literally no limit to the variety that is available for a home cooked dinner. As will be discussed in Chapter 26, there are more cookbooks available in your library than you can read and use in years.

With the already prepared foods being offered by most large grocery stores, you don't have to spend a lot of time putting together a full meal for yourself or to share with someone special. To make your cooking quicker and easier, you can buy cooked roast beef, seasoned pork ribs or chops for barbecuing, frozen stuffed flounder and even frozen appetizers. When you put this assortment of entrees together with a fresh salad, from one of the grocery salad bars, it is possible to prepare an excellent meal in just minutes.

The following sample menu contains suggestions for easy, quick and nutritious meals. The dinners are not seven or even five course meals, but they do include a variety of fish, poultry, meat, vegetables and/or salads. You will want to add your favorite bread, beverage and dessert.

Sample Menu

This is a seven day sample menu, the first five days are working days and the last two are Saturday and Sunday. I have only included six dinners to allow some flexibility. The intent, of providing these menus, is to demonstrate how to use a menu to prepare a shopping list, more than to suggest that you should follow them for meal preparation.

Day One

Breakfast	Lunch	Dinner
Hot Cakes & Syrup	Submarine Sandwich	Breaded Cube Steak
Sausage Links (2)	Fruit	New Potatoes with
Juice	Chips	Butter and Parsley
Milk, Coffee, Tea	Beverage	Green Beans
	Snack Cake	Bread and Beverage
		Dessert

Day Two

Cereal	Egg Salad Sandwich(s)	Italian Meat Sauce
1/2 Grapefruit	Vegetable Soup	Pasta
Milk, Coffee, Tea	Fruit	Tossed Salad
Juice	Beverage	Garlic Bread
	Snack Cake	Beverage
		Dessert

Day Three

Breakfast	Lunch	Dinner
Ham/Cheese	Pastrami on Rye	Onion Chicken
Toast -- Butter	Chips	Rice
Juice	Fruit	Steamed Broccoli
Milk, Coffee, Tea	Candy Bar	Bread and Beverage
	Beverage	Pastry
		Coffee or Tea

Day Four

Breakfast	Lunch	Dinner
Hot Cereal	Tuna Salad Sandwich(s)	Salisbury Steaks
Bagel, Cheese	Vegetable Soup	Mashed Potatoes
Juice	Fruit	Green Peas
Milk, Coffee, Tea	Snack	Brown & Serve Roll
	Beverage	Beverage
		Dessert

Day Five

Breakfast	Lunch	Dinner
French Toast	Ham and Swiss Cheese	Broiled Fish
Juice	Sandwich(s)	Buttered Noodles
Milk, Coffee, Tea	Chips	Peas and Carrots
	Fruit	Hush Puppies
	Snack/Candy	Coleslaw
	Beverage	Beverage
		Dessert

Day Six

Breakfast	Lunch	Dinner
Bacon & Eggs	Grilled Cheese	Roast Beef & Gravy
Toast	Pickle Wedges	Baked Potato
Juice	Chips	Whole Kernel Corn
Milk, Coffee, Tea	Fruit	Tossed Green Salad
	Beverage	Brown & Serve Roll
		Beverage
		Dessert

Day Seven

Breakfast	Lunch
Toasted English Muffin	Hot Roast Beef
Butter & Jelly	Sandwich on a Sub Roll
Juice	Chips
Milk, Coffee, Tea	Fruit
	Beverage

This seven day menu will provide a full week's nutrition and the needed variety to reduce the desire to eat at restaurants. In addition, none of the meals take long to fix, and not only are they nutritious but they are satisfying and tasty.

If you have special dietary desires such as

low sodium, low cholesterol or low fat, you can find many excellent substitutions for the above menu items that will result in equally rewarding meals.

This menu will be used in the next chapter to develop a shopping list. Using a shopping list reduces impulse buying so you spend your grocery money on what you are planning to eat instead of eating what you happened to buy.

HELPFUL HINTS AND SUGGESTIONS

(1)   Adjust your menu so the items that have the shortest, safe storage time are served soonest after your shopping day.

(2)   Immediately store and refrigerate all grocery items. Your very last stop in a day of shopping should be the grocery. Freshness is important to the nutritional value as well as the taste of your meals.

(3)   Some cold cereals are excellent served hot.

(4)   Plan your menus around fruit and vegetables in season. They are both cheaper and much better tasting.

(5)   Remember that grapefruit and other citrus fruit can be either eaten or squeezed as juice.

(6)   One pound of ground meat will make four nice hamburgers or Salisbury steaks, 12 meatballs, enough meat loaf for three or four servings, enough meat for one and a half quarts of meat sauce, or any combination of the above. One person should get at least three meals from one pound of ground meat.

(7)   Loosely bagged frozen vegetables are the most convenient, however, they do require freezer space. One 15-ounce can of vegetables should be at least two servings. Refrigerate left over vegetables and mix them to provide variety or add them to soups or stews.

(8)   Sub sandwich rolls have a variety of menu uses. They make excellent sandwiches (hot or cold) and garlic bread. They can be substituted for dinner rolls or sliced bread in most recipes and when spread with your favorite salad dressing and heated, provide a real tasty compliment to any meal.

(9)   By adding an egg and some spices, cooked rice quickly becomes fried rice.

(10)   Left over boiled or baked potatoes make excellent mashed potatoes and once mashed and chilled can be used to make tasty hash browns. Instant mashed potatoes when mixed with cheese, bacon bits and spices, then reheated in an oven make great mock baked potatoes.

(11) Most delis will sell items by the slice. However, some require the purchase of at least 1/4 to 1/2 pound of each item. This can make a difference in your menu planning especially when trying to create variety in sandwiches.

SUMMARY

You need a plan. Without a plan, your shopping will be haphazard, your cooking will become a chore, and you will find yourself without any money, because you will always be eating in restaurants.

In addition to discussing the need for a plan and the factors that affect the normal three meals, a sample seven day menu has been provided which will become the basis for your shopping list in the next chapter. Use your own tastes and the material available in your library to develop a personal seven, 14, or even 30 day menu. Because of spoilage it is recommended that, no matter how many days your menu is for, you shop at least weekly unless you have adequate freezer, refrigerator and other safe storage space.

Menu planning and cooking are two excellent opportunities to be really resourceful and creative. Just reducing the amount of your leftovers or making tasteful use of what is left is a daily challenge. A few hints or tips have been provided, and, with a little imagination, you will be able to create new and interesting taste treats.

GROCERY SHOPPING
Pasta comes in many forms.

RULES

Before we go through the menus from Chapter 25 to develop a grocery list, it is important to discuss some rules of grocery shopping. Using these few simple rules will make you a quicker, more efficient shopper and help you avoid the pitfalls that plague most grocery shoppers. These rules deal with the when, where and how of shopping.

When

Knowing when to shop not only saves time but can actually reduce your food bill.

(1)   Never go grocery shopping without a list. This is possibly the single most important rule of shopping. Without a list you are a buyer not a shopper. You will be a sucker for appetizing and appealing packaging, not an organized shopper looking for the most nutrition for the least cost. In addition, you will find that for almost any meal you want to prepare you will be missing one or more ingredients and will need to return to the store daily.

(2)   Never shop for food when you are hungry. When you are hungry, your stomach and eyes do the shopping, not your mind. You are very tempted to buy more than you need, and are drawn to the impulse items -- snacks, sweets, pastries and other visually appealing food items.

(3)   Go grocery shopping when others don't. Early in the morning or late in the evening and on certain selected weekdays. Do your own research, check out your favorite or most convenient supermarkets, and adjust your shopping schedule to take advantage of slack periods. This will save time in trying to park, actually doing your shopping, and checking out with your purchases.

(4)   Find out when the weekly specials are advertised -- usually on Wednesday or Thursday, and, in some areas, on Sunday. Even if you do not get a newspaper, the ads will be posted in the front of the store. Shopping the "specials" is important even for the single shopper, and, if you are flexible or buy the paper before you plan your menu, you may save a considerable amount of money.

Where

There are basically two types of grocery shoppers, those that shop at one store and those that flit around from store to store making small purchases of sale items. Each swears that their method of shopping is the best. I believe this is a personal choice.

If you are fortunate to live in a neighborhood that has a number of large supermarkets in a very small area, shopping for sales may be just as efficient, in terms of time, and actually result in saving money. However, if there is only one large supermarket close to your home, it may cost you much more in time and gas to shop sales than to make all your purchases at the closest store.

Invest a little time in research. Some stores do have the lowest overall prices especially if you are buying the same types of products each shopping trip. Try to find a store that has a good variety of fresh fruits and vegetables, a deli section with fresh meats, and, if you like fresh bread and pastry, even an in-store bakery. Shop at a different store each week for a couple of weeks and compare your bills. Be sure to be fair when making the comparison because your grocery list will not be identical each week. For many the choice of store is based on location, cleanliness, and the friendly attitude of store personnel more than a slight difference in cost.

How

Always shop with a shopping list, especially for food. If you are not shopping from a list, you are impulse buying. Whatever strikes your fancy as you pass it in the store, you will buy. Weeks, even months later, as you find these purchases in the back of your pantry or cabinets, you will wonder how they got there. You won't even remember buying them, much less remember why you bought them.

Having a list that will allow you to prepare meals for a week is one thing, organizing that list for efficiency in shopping is another. All supermarkets are organized so that similar or complimentary items are grouped together. Group the items on your list the same way, and, as you get familiar with your favorite store, you can even put the groups in the order that matches the store.

Your objective is to save time by going through the store once. No backtracking and no going through the same section or aisle more than once. Ideally, try to get your refrigerated items last so they do not sit in the basket and get warm. In some supermarkets, this presents a challenge because the deli, the dairy and the meat and frozen food sections are spread throughout the store.

FROM MENU TO GROCERY LIST

Some of the cookbooks listed in the appendix contain shopping lists for each of the menu items. These are great for the beginning shopper, however, you should be able to take any recipe and put together a shopping list. First, you break down the menu into dishes and the dishes into ingredients. Each of the main ingredients becomes an item on the shopping list. When the list is finished, you start at the top and consolidate the list to take advantage of package size and leftovers. Even though you look at each meal separately to come up with a list of ingredients, you shop for the entire week's menu as a whole by matching your requirements to available packaging size.

For instance, if you eat cereal, drink milk with meals or do any amount of cooking with milk, you will probably buy a gallon of milk for the week. The same is true for cereal; you will buy a box of your favorite cereal, and it will last as long as two or three weeks. Remember, when shopping, your objective is to consolidate your requirements so that you minimize leftovers while taking advantage of normal size packaging.

Items such as spices, butter, sandwich bags, napkins, paper towels, sugar, pickles, sandwich spreads, salad dressings and other essentials are definitely part of your grocery list. However, these and other items such as soap, toothpaste, toilet tissue, etc., are "never out" items, not directly tied to your menus, and are reviewed for need each time you go grocery shopping. You can add them at the end of your list based on your current level of stock.

The Process

The first day's menu from Chapter 25 is:

Breakfast	Lunch	Dinner
Hot Cakes & Syrup	Submarine Sandwich	Breaded Cube Steak
Sausage Links (2)	Fruit	New Potatoes with
Juice	Chips	Butter and Parsley
Milk, Coffee, Tea	Beverage	Green Beans
	Snack Cake	Bread and
		Beverage
		Dessert

Starting with Breakfast the shopping list develops as follows:

Pancake mix, milk, eggs, syrup, sausage links, juice, sub rolls, deli meats and cheeses, fruit, large bag of chips, package of snack cakes, beverages, 1/3 lb. cube steak, can of new potatoes, can of green peas, dessert, coffee and tea.

The ingredients for the second day's menu:

Breakfast	Lunch	Dinner
Cereal	Egg Salad Sandwich(s)	Italian Meat Sauce
1/2 Grapefruit	Vegetable Soup	Pasta
Milk, Coffee,Tea	Fruit	Tossed Salad
Juice	Beverage	Garlic Bread
	Snack Cake	Beverage
		Dessert

only add between six and ten items to our shopping list. Cereal, grapefruit, can of vegetable soup, meat sauce, pasta and salad vegetables (lettuce, tomatoes, radishes, celery, carrots, etc.). You may want to add your choice of sliced bread if you do not want your egg salad sandwich on a sub roll. You will also add the makings for a meat sauce -- tomato sauce, tomato paste, ground meat and your favorite spices -- if you do not want to use one of the prepared meat sauces.

The third day's menu:

Ham/Cheese Omelet	Pastrami on Rye	Onion Chicken
Toast -- Butter	Chips	Rice
Juice	Fruit	Steamed Broccoli
Milk, Coffee, Tea	Candy Bar	Bread and Beverage
	Beverage	Pastry
		Coffee or Tea

adds: sliced ham or turkey ham, rye bread, sliced pastrami, candy bars, chicken (whole or pieces), onion soup (can or mix), rice, broccoli (fresh or frozen), and pastry. Everything else is already on the list.

Doing the same thing for the fourth through the seventh day results in the following list of groceries.

pancake mix	sub rolls (6)	1/3 lb. cube steak
syrup	fruit	can of new potatoes
milk	large bag of chips	can of green beans
sausage links	package snack cakes	dessert
juice	beverages	coffee
cereal	grapefruit	can of vegetable soup
meat sauce	pasta	salad vegetables
ham or turkey ham	rye bread	sliced pastrami
candy bars	chicken(whole or pieces)	can of onion soup
rice	tea	quick hot cereal
bagels	can of tuna	1 lb. ground beef
can of green peas	swiss cheese	1/2 lb. fish filets
noodles	frozen hush puppies	1/2 pint coleslaw
bacon	1/2 lb. roast beef	can of corn
potatoes	english muffins	pickles
jelly	colas	eggs
salad dressing	frozen broccoli	pastry
gravy mix	butter/margarine	rolls

In March of 1990, the above groceries cost approximately $54.00 when purchased at a large supermarket. However, less than $24.00 worth of these groceries would be used to prepare the sample week's menus. The rest of the groceries are stock items generated by buying the optimum package size, even if the full amount is not needed for a given meal.

Some obvious items that you would not be buying each week are: coffee, tea, pancake mix, cereal (hot and cold), syrup, dressing, broccoli, noodles, rice, bacon, pasta, bagels, butter/ margarine and english muffins. This means that after you have selected your week's menus and made up your grocery list, you will want to bounce it against what you have in stock before you go shopping. This is when you will add those items (detergent, toothpaste, paper towels,

etc.) not directly related to your menu.

Organize

As I mentioned earlier, all stores have their stock arranged by some common factors. Though individual stores will differ somewhat on certain items, they all follow a general classification. To make your shopping as efficient as possible and to benefit the most from your list, you need to organize your list the way the store is stocked.

To give you an idea of the general classifications, I have grouped the items into the categories you will find in most stores. Your final shopping list should be grouped as follows, but you really don't need the group headings.

Dairy and Bread
milk
sub rolls
rye bread
bagels
english muffins
pastry
margarine
eggs

Fruit/Vegetables
assorted fruit
grapefruit
salad vegetables
potatoes

Canned Foods
new potatoes
green beans
vegetable soup
onion soup
tuna
green peas
corn

Snacks/Colas
chips
snack cakes
beverages

Condiments
jelly
pickles
salad dressing

Deli
sliced ham
pastrami
swiss cheese
coleslaw
roast beef

Pasta/Rice
pasta
rice
noodles
meat sauce

Hot Beverages
coffee
tea

Frozen Foods
sausage links
juice
broccoli
hush puppies

Meat/Poultry
cubed steak
chicken
ground beef
fish
bacon

Flour/Cereal
pancake mix
syrup
cold cereal
hot cereal

You will have to place candy bars, gravy mix, and dessert in the grouping that matches your favorite store. These items are some that are not easily classified with a given group.

As the final step in preparing your grocery list, the groupings should be sequenced in the order that matches your favorite store. Remember, your goal is to make only one trip down the aisles and through the store. Backtracking only wastes time.

READING PACKAGES

Ingredients

This chapter would not be complete without some discussion on the reading of ingredients lists and other information contained on food packages.

In November of 1966, Public Law 89-755-- Fair Packing and Labeling Law -- was passed requiring all food packagers to list the ingredients in the package by percentage of volume. This means that when you see the first item listed on a can of New England clam chowder is water, you can be sure that the soup contains more water than any other item. On the other hand, a can of onion soup whose list of ingredients starts with onions tells you that you will find more onions than any other ingredient, including water.

By making it a point of reading the ingredients lists, you also get a good idea of how many and what kind of additives are included in the package. All natural products will have very few ingredients. If a box of oat bran cereal has only one ingredient -- oat bran -- then there are no additives or preservatives, only the bran.

By contrast, a popular rice mix has the following ingredients list:

Rice, enriched vermicelli, salt, dried broccoli, natural flavors, dextrose, sugar, chicken fat, dried carrots, dried onions, dried parsley, monosodium glutamate, dried chicken broth, dried yeast, dried chicken, soy flour, dried garlic, spice, partially hydrogenated vegetable oil, disodium inosinate, disodium guanylate, bha and propyl gallate to preserve freshness.

Based on the the requirements of P.L. (89-755), the above mix has, as the third highest volume item, salt. This is verified by looking at the nutrition information, per serving, for this dish where you find that for each 1.23 ounce serving, there is 670 milligrams of sodium. However, if you continue to read the fine print at the bottom of the package, you find that if the rice mixture is prepared according to instructions, each serving will contain 710 milligrams of sodium. This is more than half the recommended daily intake as discussed in Chapter 24. All this from one small serving of prepackaged rice mix.

The good news is that more packagers now include the nutritional information on their packages providing you with important health related information.

Package Size

It is almost impossible to buy a packaged pound of coffee anymore. In doing research for this book, I found that you can now buy 10, 11.5, 12, and 13 ounce packages of coffee, but only in the vacuum cans did I find 16 ounces -- 1 pound -- of coffee. These packages are all intermixed on the shelves and all have different prices. As strange as it may seem, some coffee vendors sell both 11.5 and 13 ounce packages, and, except for the weight being printed at the very bottom of the package, the packages look identical. This is not only true of coffee, until recently, sugar has been sold in either 2 or 5 pound bags. Guess what size bags you can find sugar sold in now? Sugar is sold in 2, 4, 4.4 -- two kilo -- and 5 pound bags. Yes, they are all on the same shelf. Be careful, paying $1.79 for a 4.4 pound bag of sugar is more expensive than paying $1.99 for a five pound bag.

Your store should have stickers on the shelves, by each of the products, that gives the equivalent price per unit of measure -- pound, pint, gallon, etc. Learn to, and take the time to read these stickers. Being a good shopper means getting the most for your hard earned money.

*** NOTE ***
Instead of raising prices some vendors of packaged foods have taken to changing the contents of the packages. Instead of raising the price 10%, the packager of the item will reduce the contents by 10 or more percent. The package appearance and size do not change. What changes is the weight or volume amount printed on the box, the number of servings and the cooking instructions. This means that the box of cereal that made 15 one ounce servings may now only make 13. The box is the same size, the picture is the same, the price is the same, but the difference is very real; you are now getting almost 10% less food for the same amount of money.

Serving Size

All of the members in my family eat different size servings, with the smaller servings not always being eaten by the females. The one thing that we all have in common is that seldom do we eat as little as the amount used by the manufacturer in computing the nutritional information printed on the package. This is true for almost all food items including cereal, soups, vegetables, and especially desserts.

This is not to challenge the information printed on the packages. What I suggest you do is compare the serving size printed on the package with the picture that shows the prepared dish and the serving size you normally eat. Most cold cereals use a serving size of about 1 ounce. One ounce of cold cereal will be between 1/2 and 1 cup of cereal. Compare what 1/2 cup of cereal looks like with the huge bowl shown on the cover of the box. If the box says there are 15 servings at 1/2 cup per serving, and you use one or more cups per serving, you will get only half the number of servings.

BE A SMART SHOPPER

It is not difficult to be a smart shopper, and the rewards are great. Some rules to follow have been given at the beginning of this chapter. They are not much different from the shopping rules for insurance, transportation, shelter, and credit. Know what you need, organize and list your needs, determine the place you are going to shop, know the details of what you want -- package size, servings, nutritional value, and cost -- and remember your time is money.

If you are well prepared, know your supermarket, and shop at non-peak times, shopping for a week's supply of groceries should not take more than 30 to 45 minutes.

When you first venture into the "Supermarket Jungle," be sure to read those labels. Pay close attention to ingredients, size of package, serving size, number of servings and price.

Unless you have great self-control, never, never go shopping without a list or on an empty stomach. To do so courts financial disaster and is dangerous to your health.

NOTES

_____

_____

_____

_____

_____

_____

_____

_____

_____

_____

_____

_____

_____

CLOTHING

Creativity stretches the dollar.

VII

If you are not careful, clothing expense can quickly get out of control. It seems that for every holiday, the clothing stores have fantastic sales. In fact, if there are no holidays handy, the stores make up some. How many times have you seen the following sales, "Back to School," "Middle of Summer," "Pre-Thanksgiving," "After Thanksgiving"? The list goes on and on. This section not only addresses the need for clothing, the types of and the expense of clothing, but it also looks at the many ways there are of acquiring clothing.

Chapter 27 opens this section with an in-depth look at style versus functionality. Wardrobe needs for men and women are discussed including a short overview of wardrobe planning. The chapter not only addresses fabric, cost, and style but expands into the true cost of a wardrobe by considering cleaning costs and usability.

Chapter 28 explores the need for wardrobe planning. Starting with an inventory of existing clothing, the reader is asked to analyze needs and wants to match optimum wardrobe buys with budget amounts. Mixing and matching existing items as an alternative to new purchases is discussed as a method of reducing costs.

Chapter 29 exposes the reader to the many and varied alternate sources of clothing available to the truly innovative shopper. From making one's own clothing, to shopping at thrift and used clothing boutiques are all evaluated and discussed as valid sources of clothing purchases. The concept of renting clothing for one time use is evaluated as a possible alternative to making expensive purchases. The chapter concludes with a discussion of selling and trading clothing as an inexpensive method of adding variety to the wardrobe.

STYLE VERSUS FUNCTIONALITY
Dry cleaning costs bundles.

DRESSING WITHIN YOUR BUDGET

It is easy to spend more on clothing in one month than on food or rent. This section is written to provide some thoughts and discussion on the factors that should be considered before you set out to spend your whole month's clothing budget on a new sweater or shirt.

Now that you are on your own and living on a budget, you need to take a serious look at your clothing needs. What you need to wear for work may be totally unacceptable for after work or social activities, meaning that you may need two separate wardrobes. Some employers, including large corporations, require that employees wear a uniform or meet a dictated dress code. This uniform is not always provided by the company with the company's name on the back and your name on the pocket. Often, the uniform is much more subtle. It can be a dark suit, white shirt, and maroon tie or, if in the blue collar field, gray work pants and matching work shirt. In many professions, the required dress is the same for both men and women.

To make matters worse, if the Internal Revenue Service finds that the required clothing is suitable for wear other than as a uniform, you can not deduct the cost of the purchase or cleaning of the prescribed clothing from your income tax. Both of the outfits described above fall into this class. The dark suit and the gray pants and shirt fall into the IRS's classification as suitable for other use and, therefore, are non-deductible.

Deductible or non-deductible, the fact is that you may be faced with providing yourself with two separate wardrobes, one for work and one for social use. In most cases, the two sets of clothing will have some common areas where some of the clothing falling into one grouping will also be suitable for the other. For example, both men's and women's dark suits, with the

right accessories, are appropriate for after five social events. Gray or khaki work pants and shirts can be appropriate dress for hiking, backpacking, and other sports related outings.

NEEDS

As with the other expenses we have discussed, the first step to providing yourself with an appropriate wardrobe is to identify your needs. These needs are different for each person and are influenced by many factors. Some of the factors that must be considered are: type of work, dress code, hobbies, activities, and importance of clothing to you as a person. All of these factors, especially the last one, will affect the type and expense of your wardrobe and the impact of clothing costs on your budget.

Since you presently have a wardrobe, your immediate expenditures for clothing will most likely be focused on meeting the needs generated by your new job. Let's use Jo Ann, with her new job at the landscaping company, as an example.

Example

When Jo Ann was informed that she had the job, she was advised to dress for outdoor work when she reported for her first day of work. Luckily, most of her first day was in preparing paperwork and getting around to familiarize herself with the layout of the Green Toe Nursery and its organization. She dressed for work in one of her older pairs of designer jeans, tennis shoes, and a light shirt. As she met her co-workers, she realized that what she was wearing might be acceptable for working in her garden at home but was totally unacceptable for doing commercial landscape work.

Her co-workers, both male and female, all had on steel toed high top work shoes, heavy denim jeans or work pants, tee shirts or work shirts, and all had work gloves. She also noticed that everyone had short hair, or else was wearing their hair in a pony tail, or otherwise had it pulled up off the neck. Everyone seemed to be wearing baseball caps that were provided free by one of the fertilizer companies.

At lunch she talked to some of her fellow workers and made the following list of immediate clothing needs:

Two or more pair of heavy work pants or jeans
Steel toed high top work shoes
Two or more pair of heavy socks
Leather or other heavy duty work gloves
Two or more plain tee shirts or tank tops
Two or more large bandana type handkerchiefs

On her way home she stopped at one of the larger clothing stores and was pleased to find that all of her requirements could be found in sizes and styles for females, even the steel toed high top shoes.

This is only one example of special clothing requirements. Every job, company, and individual is different. There are many jobs where specific clothing is not prescribed, so long as it is clean and in good repair. Keep in mind that the really successful employee will evaluate the dress requirements of the job and dress appropriately.

STYLE AND FADS

Another important consideration, when trying to stay within your wardrobe budget, is the difference between styles and fads. As with most words in our language, the dictionary does not do an adequate job of defining these words in practical terms. In *The New American WEBSTER Handy College Dictionary*, style is defined as "the prevalent fashion" while fad is defined as "a passing style or interest." From these definitions, we can reason that the difference between style and fad is the period of time a particular fashion is accepted. The difficulty with this premise is, nowhere has it been stated how long a fad must be accepted before it is considered style. From a practical standpoint, the number of people accepting the style change also has an impact on whether we are discussing styles or fads.

We also have to take into consideration that if today's fad lasts long enough and is accepted by enough people it is likely to be considered style in the future. Long hair on men and men wearing earrings are a couple of examples of this evolution. Peer pressure can also add complexity to this issue. It is important that we be accepted by others, but, unfortunately, this acceptance is frequently based on our appearance, rather than our values and personalities, making it harder for us not to give in to fads.

In this country, the male population is a little better off than the female population because the styles of men's clothing do not change frequently or drastically. This is not true for women. Styles do change frequently and some of them, according to my wife and daughters, are drastic. What was purchased last year when in style may be totally unacceptable this year. The importance of always being in style is a personal trait, and one that is usually stronger when choosing social wear than when choosing clothing for the job. It is quite possible that what was considered acceptable for social wear last year is acceptable for work this year. This really doesn't help much in understanding the problem of following fads. When trying to survive on a limited budget, the following of fads and even style changes can be very costly.

Good Taste

Perhaps the salvation of those who want to be style conscious but have to live within a small fixed budget is "good taste." Regardless of the current style or fad, individuals that have a well coordinated wardrobe that flatters their figure and personality will transcend fads and styles. They do this by dressing in "good taste." It is obvious to others when what you are wearing is well coordinated, looks good, and makes you feel good. People are much more likely to remember your overall presence than whether or not you were dressed in the latest style. This goes back to Chapter 2 when we discussed "packaging" yourself for the job interview. The rules are the same: select clothing that looks well on you, makes you feel good, and presents your best image. Concentrating on yourself and the image you create can help you avoid the high cost associated with fads and changes in style.

FUNCTIONALITY AND MAINTENANCE

Major factors to be considered when living on a budget are both the functionality and the maintenance costs of clothing purchases. Work clothing, either for heavy labor or for use in an office, should be very durable, while not requiring professional care.

Functionality

If you have an outdoor job requiring heavy labor, the most rugged and safest clothing you buy is not an expense but an investment. The investment is in your continued good health. Do not pinch pennies when buying gloves, shoes, and other protective clothing. Good gloves protect your hands from blisters and burns, goggles protect your eyes from flying objects, and high topped, steel toed, shoes protect you from ankle sprains and crushed toes. It is hard to work in the construction or other related labor fields with damaged eyes or hands, or while trying to get around on crutches.

During the late 1970s I took a part-time job as a welder, building wood burning stoves. I took the job primarily to improve my proficiency as a welder, not for the $5 per hour wage. I clearly remember spending over $100.00 in special clothing purchases. I had to have a leather apron, steel toed shoes, long leather gloves, and a head and face shield before I could report for work. I worked at this part time job regularly for over three years and never had to replace these items, nor did I miss a day of work because of injury. From a personal standpoint, this places the cost of purchasing the items in the investment category, not the expense category.

Many companies that have jobs that require special tools or safety equipment will make some form of arrangement to assist their employees in getting outfitted. Even if the company does not provide the items outright, they may provide a salary advance or have an arrangement that permits you to purchase the items at a discount, or even pay for them over a period of time, three months or more.

Wear and Tear

You do not have to work at a construction site to exert heavy wear and tear on your clothing. I have worked in an office and classroom environment for more than 30 years, and the number of times I have snagged, stained, or otherwise ruined good suits is beyond calculation. This is in addition to the ties, shirts, and even shoes that have been made unfit for wear because of sharp edges on furniture, oil or grease from desk drawers and equipment, and ink from pens and markers.

And I am not the world's greatest klutz. Just the other day, I heard one of the women in my office discussing with a fellow worker the fact that she had just put on the third pair of pantyhose that day because the first two had been ruined by pulls or snags. The work environment that caused this destruction was not a run down old building or warehouse but a modern 18-month old building with new office furniture. Living with a wife and raising three daughters, I know that pantyhose, though not really expensive, when used three-a-day, will break the budget of the average office worker.

Maintenance

Paying for the use of a washer and dryer is not cheap. Washing, drying, and ironing clothes requires valuable time, your time. These and other maintenance factors must be considered before purchasing new clothing.

Fabrics and Labels

New clothing is expensive. It doesn't make any difference if it is the latest style or just work clothes. You cannot afford to only wear a new article of clothing once. Before buying an item of clothing, read the label so you will know what care is required and be sure to read the label again before you attempt the first cleaning. A $40 dollar sweater, once improperly cleaned, will only fit a doll. A pair of jeans, washed in hot water and dried in a hot clothes dryer, will only fit a juvenile. Pants that say dry clean only, if washed, will probably only be useful as rags. The labels are there to help you get the maximum life from the article of clothing. Be smart, read and follow the instructions. Look closely for, and follow to the letter, the instructions on clothing made with "special care" fabrics.

Permanent Press

The label "permanent press" does not mean the same as "easy care" or "wash and wear."

Because of the different fabric mixes used today, it is getting more and more difficult to find real "permanent press" clothing. This is clothing that, if washed and dried properly, does not need any ironing. A new shirt I was given in February 1990 has a "permanent press" label, but on the back of the label in very small print is the statement, "some ironing may be necessary." Because of the time, equipment -- iron and board -- and skill required for ironing, try to purchase really "permanent press" items whenever possible.

For people adept at ironing as my daughters are, it doesn't take more than five minutes to iron a blouse or shirt after the iron has heated, while for someone with all thumbs as I am, it may take a half hour or more.

A few years ago, between 1984 and 1987, I purchased five really "permanent press" men's suits. These suits have been truly amazing. I have thrown them into washers and dryers at Laundromats, using the permanent press cycle, and when they were dried they looked like they just returned from a commercial cleaner. Even though they were three different brands, I have been informed they are no longer available. It seems that the material now used by suit makers for lining the coats can no longer be washed because of the fabric mix.

For anyone required to wear suits and travel a lot, this is a real blow. Not counting the time saved by not having to visit the cleaners, I estimate that I have saved over $200 a year in cleaning costs by having the "permanent press" suits.

Safety

Another factor that must be considered in fabric choice is safety. There are some fabrics such as double knits and other synthetic fabrics that are highly flammable. If you are going to be working around any form of open flame or heat source, stay away from these fabrics. The thickness of the fabric is another safety consideration. For example, because of sparks in a machine or welding shop, you will want to wear long sleeve tops that are non-flammable and thick enough to protect you from flying pieces of hot metal. This is true even if you are going to wear leather gloves and apron. The gloves and apron do not protect your neck, shoulders, and arms.

Dry Cleaning

Most commercial dry cleaners provide from one hour to two day service, so being without a piece of clothing for a week or more while it is being cleaned is not a problem. The problem with clothes that must be commercially cleaned is twofold: first, the time it takes to deliver and pick up the items and second, the cost. The more important of these two problems is cost; dry cleaning costs have skyrocketed in recent years. Remember, you are on a budget, a limited budget at that, and money spent for cleaning clothes must be taken from money set aside for personal expenses and/or entertainment.

Looking at today's cost in that light, cleaning a suit or dress for about $6.40 costs more than three movie video rentals, one admission and a medium soda at your favorite first run movie, the cover charge at your favorite night spot, four games of bowling, or five gallons of gas for your car. In fact, if you cook at home, you can feed yourself for two days on what it costs to get your suit or dress dry cleaned. You may not get a suit or dress cleaned after every wearing, so to be more realistic, let's look at the cost of cleaning a shirt or blouse. The cost of dry cleaning a shirt or blouse, items usually cleaned after one wearing, is about $1.25. What can you buy with $1.25? If you are resourceful, you can buy lots of things including one gallon of gas, one game of bowling, a large to super size soda or other beverage, a trip across town on public transportation, a movie rental at one of the budget rental stores, and many other more personally fulfilling items.

If you compute your cleaning costs over a period of time, you will find that it will be easy to spend $12 to $15 per week, and, for a month, the costs may quickly add up to $50 or more. If you go back to the discussion of the budget in Chapter 10, you can readily see that you may not be able to afford this expense. Even the sample budget we worked up for Jo Ann would have difficulty absorbing this additional expense.

Laundry Facilities

In addition to dry cleaning expenses, you also have to consider the cost of washing and drying your other clothes. If you are fortunate to have a washer and dryer in your apartment or one that is provided free of charge by the landlord, this expense is minimum. All you have to figure is the cost of your time, detergent, and possibly softening or anti-static additives.

If these facilities are not free, you will have an additional expense of about $6 per week for washing and drying three loads of laundry. Three loads of laundry per week is based on an office type job where each day's complete outfit does not require daily washing. The average of three loads a week takes into consideration periodic washing of bed linens, bath towels, and other miscellaneous items. Your requirements may be greater than this if you work in an environment requiring a complete change of clothes every day or if your work clothes are not wearable for social use.

If you have the room and the inclination, you can cut this cost in half by hang drying your clothes either indoors or, when possible, outdoors. If you must pay to use the washer and dryer, you are looking at a minimum monthly cost of about $30 just for the use of the machines. Because of this expense, having a free laundry facility either in your apartment or in the apartment complex is easily worth an additional $25 or more in rent.

Time

No matter how convenient the cleaners or laundry facility is to your work or home, you have an additional expense in time. Even if you walk or pass by the dry cleaners every day, it takes time to stop, have the ticket written up, pick up, and pay for the service. You will want to keep these visits to a minimum. Try for only one drop off and pick up every two weeks. If that is not adequate, you probably have too many items that need dry cleaning and as a consequence will have to increase the frequency of your visits to the cleaners.

Visiting the laundromat and/or laundry facilities also takes time. To wash and dry a load of clothes takes about one and a half to two hours. However, it is possible to do a full week's worth of laundry in the same time as one load by using multiple machines. To make use of multiple machines, however, you must have a way of transporting your full week's worth of laundry. If you can only transport one load at a time, either because you walk or ride a bicycle, you can estimate two hours per load of laundry. The time you wait for the machines to finish your wash need not be wasted. You can read the newspaper, a book or magazine, write letters,

work on your grocery list, or even meet new and interesting people.

When the laundry facilities are in the apartment complex but not in your apartment, you will have to decide if you need to stay with your wash or if it is safe to leave it. My children have mixed opinions on this. Some have left their clothes only to come back later and find that someone had removed them from the washer or dryer and piled them on the top of the machines or on a table. The others have not encountered this problem though they all agree that it could happen. At the same time, they have all complained about people hogging the machines by leaving their wash sitting in the machines all day. To save yourself time, try timing the machines. Once you know how long it takes to wash or dry a load of laundry, if you leave, you will be able to time your return so that you arrive before or just as the machine stops. Be aware, good clothing is expensive, and people have been known to steal clothing from laundry facilities. This is especially true if access to the laundry facility is not secured from outsiders or is available to many users.

If you have a washer and dryer at home, the time it takes to do a load of laundry is reduced to about 12 minutes: three minutes to load the washer, two minutes to transfer the clothes to the dryer, and seven minutes to remove the clothes from the dryer, fold them and put them away. You are then free to do whatever you want during the time the washer and dryer are actually working, and you don't have to worry about theft.

SUGGESTIONS

(1) Choose functionality over styles and fads, especially for workclothes.
(2) If protective items are needed, buy the best.
(3) Read the fabric care labels carefully.
(4) Select clothing made from fabrics requiring the minimum of care.
(5) Always clean clothing in accordance with their labels.
(6) Locate a commercial dry cleaner and laundromat close to your home or work.
(7) Try to have enough clothing so you do not have to make twice-a-week trips to the laundromat.
(8) If the facilities are available consider hang drying to save money.

(9) If you have a friend who has a washer and dryer in their apartment, consider swapping "home cooked meals" or "cleaning services" for use of their laundry facilities. The same holds true for using parent's laundry facilities.

NOTES

_____
_____
_____
_____
_____
_____
_____
_____
_____
_____
_____
_____
_____
_____
_____
_____
_____

HOW MUCH IS ENOUGH?
But I wore that last year.

If we are not careful, it doesn't take long before we have more clothes and shoes than we can comfortably store. Some of the over purchasing of clothes is caused by changing seasons, changing jobs, and changing fads and styles. However, for most people with a job and steady income -- even if small -- the cause is lack of planning and self-indulgence.

We all like to look good because looking good is an ego booster. We feel better when we think we look good. These are all true statements, and I don't think we should change our way of thinking. What I do believe is necessary, especially for the survival of our budget, is to give the same degree of thought and planning to our wardrobe as we give to buying a car, leasing a place to live, or shopping for food.

Chapters 25 and 26 discussed the pitfalls of "impulse shopping" in a grocery store. The same pitfalls exist when shopping for clothing, only the fall can be deeper. To bypass or leap the pitfalls, you need a plan. Without a plan, you will be subject to the will of the marketing and advertising industries and find yourself "clothes poor."

CLOTHES POOR

Clothes poor is the term used for when you find yourself with a closet full of the finest, hottest, latest styled clothing and shoes and no money left to go out and enjoy wearing them. I am not suggesting that you should never buy nice looking, in style, or designer clothing. I am suggesting that you purchase clothing with the same care and planning that you make all purchases. Each purchase should be based on need (the need to look good is a valid need), and the need should be compared to and balanced against all other needs.

For example, Jo Ann needs a new pair of jeans and light sweater to round out her wardrobe. She shops around and finds that she can buy a pair of designer jeans for $47 and a sweater in the latest style for $30. By doing some comparison shopping, she finds that she can get the same cut jeans, without the designer label, for $25 and a similar sweater for $18. Both sets look great on her and she feels good wearing them. Now, her decision is which to buy. Are the labels worth the extra $34? One way for her to determine the answer to this question is to go back to her budget in Chapter 10 and look at the monthly items. She estimated $45 a month for clothes, $30 a month for gas and other transportation expenses, $50 for entertainment, and $50 for personal expenses. What will be the impact of her decision on this month's budget?

Options

Jo Ann doesn't have anything left over from last month, and she doesn't want to touch the budget amounts for gifts, savings, hairdresser, and church, so she has about $175 of variable expenses to play with. If she buys the less expensive outfit, the cost will not exceed her clothing budget for this month, and she does not really have a problem. If she spends the $77 for the designer outfit, the excess $32 over her budget has to come from somewhere. What is the impact?

If it is the beginning of the month and she hasn't used up her budget amounts, she may choose to take the whole amount of the excess from entertainment, leaving herself with $16 for the month. This may not create a hardship, and she may decide it is worth the expense to have the labels. The same is true if she decides to charge it against the amount she has budgeted for personal expenses. She may even decide to charge the excess against a combination of the two. But suppose it is the middle of the month and she has already spent $30 for personal expenses, $20 for transportation, and $18 for entertainment. She has a total of only $62 left in her budget for these variable expenses to cover the remaining two weeks of the month. If she spends the extra $34 for the designer set, she will have only $28 left to cover the costs of two weeks of transportation, entertainment, and personal expenses. If labels are that important to her, she may decide the purchase is still workable. It is her decision to make, just as in real life it is yours.

The budget itself is a plan. It is based on average monthly expenditures. In any month you can spend less or even more than you budget as long as you have the cash, and over a 6 to 12 month period, you stay very close to your estimates. Your budget can and should allow you some flexibility, but you must discipline yourself to live within its limits. The important thing is to consider the costs of your purchases and options before making your decision, because, once made, you will have to live with its impact.

PLANNING

As with other purchases discussed in previous chapters, you need a plan. This time the plan is for clothes shopping. Your plan should be based on the result of answering the following questions:

(1)   What types of clothing do you need?
(2)   How much do you have?
(3)   How much do you need?
(4)   When do you need the items?

In addition to the above, the "when," "where," and "how" of shopping for your clothing needs will be discussed in Chapter 29.

What Types of Clothing Do You Need?

It's time to brainstorm and compile another list. Sit down and, with no restrictions or considerations as to money or the present contents of your dressers or closets, seriously identify your clothing needs. Be sure to include needs for work, hobbies, sports, socializing, and just hanging around the house. Include undergarments, shoes, socks and/or stockings, robe,

night wear, rain wear, accessories and any other special clothing items you need.

Do not worry about quantities of items at this time, as we will get to that later. If necessary take a week or more to develop this list; every time you think of something you need add it to the list. The time used to prepare the list is less important than the completeness of its contents. To give yourself the motivation to complete the list, don't allow yourself to buy any new clothes until the list is complete. Don't be surprised if your list is rather lengthy.

Once you have this long list, go back through and consolidate it, asking yourself if the same clothing can be used for dual purposes. For instance, if you work in an office, many of the clothes you buy for work can also be used for socializing simply by changing some of the accent items. The reverse is also true; clothes you buy for social wear may be acceptable in the office if the appropriate accessories are used. At the same time, athletic shoes may not be appropriate for office work but are needed for sports. If you have a construction job, steel toed boots may be required for work, but you will not want to wear them for jogging or hanging around the house.

The objective of this review of your list is to come up with a base line of needs. When you are finished, you should have a list of the minimum items of clothing you require and know how they will be used.

The next step is to compare the list to what is in your present wardrobe. Even the items that you do not presently have don't have to be bought all at once. We will discuss prioritizing your needs under "When do you need the items?" later in this chapter.

How Much Do You Have?

It's inventory time! That's right, dump the contents of all your dresser drawers on the bed, empty the closets of all hanging clothes and shoes and take a clothing inventory. It doesn't hurt, it can even be very exciting and fun. Who knows what surprises wait in the back corner of the middle drawer on the left side of the dresser? What about the shoe boxes that haven't been opened since your last move. You may actually have more acceptable clothes that meet your needs than you think. Regardless of whether the surprises in store for you are good or not so good, the inventory should be done.

Give yourself sufficient time to take this

inventory. This is the kind of job that is perfect for a rainy weekend. Turn on some good music, roll up your sleeves and dive in. As you take inventory, try the items on to see if they fit and if the styles are acceptable. This is an excellent time to try mixing and matching to get a good feel for the number of "different" outfits you own.

The results of this fun weekend are threefold. First, you now have a complete list -- inventory -- of the clothes that fit and have been put back in the drawers and closets. Second, you also have a list of what you have kept but returned to storage in an organized manner for use at a later date. And, third, you have a stack of clothes that don't fit or you no longer want. Set these aside, we will come back to them in Chapter 29.

Back to your two lists. The difference between the list of your needs and your inventory list is what you require to fill out your wardrobe.

How Much Do You Need?

In order to really determine your needs from the lists you have, you must add the quantity required of each item to your original list of needs. The number of factors affecting the quantity can be almost limitless, however some of the factors everyone should consider are:

> Location and availability of laundry facilities.
> Type of work.
> Type of hobbies, including sports.
> Type of fabric in the clothing.

Location of Laundry Facilities

The location and availability of the laundry facilities will determine how much time and money you will spend doing your laundry. The quantity of clothing needed will be much greater if you plan to clean clothes only weekly than it will be if you have a washer and dryer in your apartment.

For example, you may be able to get by with four sets of underclothing if you plan to wash two or three times a week, but will require seven or even eight sets if you plan to visit the laundromat only weekly. The same is true for work clothes that have to be cleaned each day. You will need at least three sets for twice-weekly washing and at least five sets if you plan to wash only weekly. Even sweat pants and jogging clothes can only be worn so often before your "aura" announces your arrival.

Type of Work

The type of work you do also impacts your clothing requirements by mandating the number of outfits you need. This is true even if you work in an office or at some other "white collar" type job. If you are required to wear a shirt and tie but not required to wear a suit, you may find that it is easy to have a dual use wardrobe. The same is true for the female employee that may wear a blouse and skirt or pants to work. If your job is one of the "blue collar" types that require work clothes, the amount of dual usage you will be able to build into your wardrobe will be limited. Some professions, such as nurse, postal worker, and other service related jobs, require uniforms, eliminating the dual use wardrobe completely.

Hobbies

Your hobbies definitely have an impact on the amount of clothing you will need, as well as the expense. If you like to party, you may be able to get by with mostly a dual use wardrobe, using basically the same clothing for work as you use socially. If your hobby is mountain climbing, you are going to need special clothing that will probably not be suitable for work. There are many hobbies, i.e. reading, sewing, cooking, attending sporting events, etc. that do not require any form of special clothing.

With the possible exception of specialized shoes, hobbies such as jogging, walking, bowling, skating, sailing, playing golf, tennis, softball or even touch football do not have a requirement for special or expensive clothing. Usually jeans and a top, shorts and a tee shirt, or sweat pants and sweat shirt are all that is required. For many of these hobbies even the specialized shoes may be optional. This does not mean that these sports do not cost a lot of money, only that the expense is not in the clothing but in the equipment. Be careful, a designer jogging outfit can easily cost $50 or more. Consider your budget and other uses for the money before buying one of these outfits, especially since shorts or sweat pants and a top will usually suffice.

If, however, you lean toward mountain climbing, scuba diving, or snow skiing as your hobby, the cost of dressing for your hobby can rise rapidly. Mountain climbing boots alone can cost over $150, a wet suit can easily run over $180, and a complete skiing outfit $250 or more. Fortunately, you can usually keep the cost down by buying only one, or at the most two, of these outfits. Chapter 29 discusses other ways to help make this expense even smaller.

Fabric Type

As discussed in Chapter 27, fabric type can add significantly to the amount of clothes you need. Easy care or wash-and-wear fabrics may even be washed by hand in your bathroom sink or tub in an emergency, so the number of items required is more a matter of personal desire than necessity. If you choose special care fabrics and cannot care for them at home, you will need to consider the time needed to get the care and the frequency you will be wearing the item. If the item is made from a fabric that requires dry cleaning, you will need a sufficient quantity to allow for the soiled items to be brought to the cleaners and returned.

When Do You Need the Items?

Now you have a complete list of clothing needs or at a least a good attempt at one. Each item of clothing you expect to need is listed, including the quantities of each you must or would like to have. You have subtracted your inventory from your list and now know what is needed to complete your wardrobe. It is time to separate the list by season.

Some of the clothing you need will not be usable in the dead of winter or the middle of summer, so separate the items that can be identified this way. Separating the items this way will save you money in the long run, as will be discussed in Chapter 29 under "When to Shop." The other reason for separating the clothing needs by season is to help you pinpoint what you need now. You do not want to spend your time and money shopping for and buying clothes for next winter or summer when you may have more immediate needs.

If you are like most people, you need more than one of some items and none of others. This is as it should be and allows you some flex-

ibility in getting the most for your money. Look at your list and prioritize your needs. Ask yourself some questions, like:

> If I only buy one sweater now, how many shirts can I buy?
>
> Do I really need two new pairs of jeans now?
>
> Do I really need a suit, or can I get by with another pair of pants or a co-ordinating jacket?
>
> Is the new evening outfit more important than a couple of outfits for work?
>
> Do I really need a new pair of jogging shoes, or can I use some sole rebuilder and get another 50 to 100 miles out of the old pair?

SUMMARY

Your clothing is a very important and personal part of you. It is your expression to others of yourself and what's important. Only you can make the final decision on the type and extent of your wardrobe. These few pages contain some things to consider in identifying and establishing your needs, so each purchase results in a planned addition to your wardrobe.

The start of the plan is to identify your needs. This must be followed by the ever important inventory and the prioritizing of the needed items. The intended outcome is a planned, coordinated wardrobe that not only makes you look and feel great but also fits your budget.

Being clothes poor, like being car poor, does not provide any lasting pleasure. You may get a high or feel exhilarated when you spot and purchase an item, but, later, after you leave the store, you may have second thoughts about what you might have done with the money if you hadn't made the purchase. By planning your wardrobe and your purchases ahead, you will be in the position to get the most for your hard earned money -- long lasting satisfaction.

NEW OR NEARLY NEW
Stretching your dollars.

29

Good, attractive clothing need not be a large budget item. This is especially true if you live in or near a college town or a city with 35,000 or more residents. Most larger cities and college towns have, in addition to a wide assortment of stores that sell new clothing items, many sources of used or second hand clothing. Not only that, if you are resourceful, you may be able to use one or more of the suggestions covered later and fill some of your clothing needs without paying a penny.

This is a chapter of ideas on shopping for and acquiring clothing. The chapter discusses the when, where, and how of shopping for clothing and, at the end, presents some ideas on acquiring clothing free. Yes, free.

WHEN

Timing can be very important if you want to maximize your purchasing power in clothing. First, don't try to buy anything until you have read and followed the suggestions in Chapter 27. Once you have developed your plan, you have met the first requirement of timing and are ready to shop for your new clothes.

Seasonal Sales

The second factor to consider in choosing the time to buy is called the pre- or post seasonal sale. The pre-seasonal sale is one that is held by stores before the need for the clothing exists. For instance, a pre-summer sale of swim wear or beach wear in April is an example of a pre-seasonal sale. Post-seasonal sales are the stores' attempts to get rid of leftover seasonal merchandise. For example, now that winter is over, the store management wants to get rid of the leftover winter stock to make room for spring and summer fashions. Very possibly, the store will have a post-winter sale at the same time the pre-summer sale is in progress.

The prices for the post-seasonal sales are usually lower than for the pre-seasonal ones. The reason for this is that the store is really trying to get rid of last years' fashions. They do not want to have to keep the clothing in storage over the year because storage costs money and fashions and fads may change, making the items difficult to sell next year. However, the individual who can tell the difference between fads and style can pick up some excellent buys during these sales if they choose those items not likely to change drastically. Sweaters, overcoats, long pants, wool skirts, long sleeve blouses and shirts can all be found at post-winter sales and, for the most part, are safe buys for the next year.

The real problem with the post-seasonal sales is staying within your budget. You may have more immediate needs to spend your budgeted amount on than clothes for next year. This is part of your decision making process. Look at your list and decide if you can take advantage of these sales while at the same time filling your immediate wardrobe needs.

If you cannot make use of the post-seasonal sales, your next best deal is the pre-seasonal sales. These sales are intended to start the new seasons' merchandise moving from the store racks to your closet and dresser drawers as soon as possible. The store is trying to generate a continuing cash flow to overcome the sales slump generated by the last weeks of one season and the first weeks of the next one. Not only does this benefit the store management, it also has benefits for you. Frequently, you get the first shot at the new styles and designs, with lots of selection and all at a good price. Knowing what you need from your plan allows you to take the fullest advantage of both types of seasonal sales.

Other Sales

Stores, even the highest priced ones, look for an excuse, any excuse, to have a sale. The markup on clothing is so high in most stores that a sale of up to 30% still results in a substantial profit for the store. This is not your concern, you are only interested in what you can save over what you will pay if the item is not on sale. Therefore, one of your rules for shopping for clothing is not to buy anything that is not on sale. It's easy. You know what you need now and what you will need in the future, so except for purchases like stockings, socks, underwear and other items that you must have immediately, everything else can and should be purchased when available at a discount.

There is no stigma attached to shopping for sales. You do not wear a brand across your forehead that identifies you as a person who buys clothing on sale. Even the clothing is not marked in permanent marker: "bought at 30% off." You might even say that if you do not shop for the best buys in everything, you are missing the first rule of surviving in today's marketplace: "Thou shalt get the most for thy hard earned dollar."

Give Yourself Enough Time

The third and final consideration under timing is to give yourself enough time to carefully shop for and select your purchases. Remember from the last chapter that you want time to read the labels and care instructions. You also need time to find and match accent pieces and accessories, in addition to the time required to try on your perspective purchases. You even need time to stand in line and pay for your purchases.

Shopping for clothes should not be used to kill time because you arrived at the mall too early for your dinner or show engagement. Nor should you be shopping at 5:30 p.m. today for what you intend to wear this evening. Shop for your needs with the same attention you put into developing your plan by watching for sales and setting aside enough time to carefully make your purchases. This time is as much an investment in your enjoyment of your wardrobe as the time spent in developing your plan.

WHERE

Obviously, the where to shop is also important. As with furniture, when shopping for clothing you have two choices, you can buy new or you can buy used. Before you reject the thought of buying used clothing read on.

New

New clothing may be purchased at many types of stores, not just clothing stores. There are stores that sell only clothing and accessories of the latest style and fad and carry only the most expensive and exclusive labels. There are also stores that cater to just men's or just women's fashions and may carry only the expensive labels or a variety of labels that range from very expensive to moderately expensive. You can find a wide selection of clothes at large department chain stores like Sears, Montgomery Wards, J. C. Penny's, and others. Clothes are available at discount stores and you will even find some items of clothing at large grocery and drug stores. Good quality, functional, and attractive clothing, in the latest styles, can even be successfully purchased through mail order catalogues. There are also many excellent tailors and seamstresses that will be happy to make one-of-a-kind, made-to-fit clothing. Even hardware, lumber, and equipment outlets now carry complete lines of work clothes.

From the above, and your own experience, you are now aware that new clothing can be purchased from many sources. What you may not know is that there is also a large and growing number of sources for good, never or slightly worn, clothing.

Used

In some cases the sources of used clothing are the same ones we discussed for purchasing furniture in Chapter 23 and fall into three categories: garage sales/flea markets, thrift stores and Almost New clothing stores. Not only are these excellent sources for routine clothing needs, they are also excellent sources for speciality sports clothing. By shopping around, you can find a good selection of skiing, diving, and even hiking clothing and equipment.

Garage Sales/Flea Markets

Shopping garage sales and flea markets can be an excellent way to fill your wardrobe needs, especially in the area of day or work wear. They are also excellent sources of accent and accessory items. They tend to have more children's and women's clothing, but you can frequently find great buys in men's sports coats, overcoats, work clothes, and work shoes. The prices range from about 40% to 10% or even less of the original retail price depending on style and condition. Over the years my wife and I have sold and bought clothing for ourselves and our children for as little as 25 cents an item. At the last garage sale I attended, I saw approximately 30 pairs of women's shoes selling for 50 cents a pair. They were in all sizes and styles and were in excellent, hardly worn, condition. I have bought sweaters, coats, and speciality clothing for sports and hobbies from garage sales at a small fraction of what the same item would cost if bought new. Another plus about shopping the garage sales is that the prices marked are all negotiable. Any clothing item purchased at a garage sale should be thoroughly cleaned, and shoes should be disinfected before wearing.

Thrift Stores

Thrift stores have racks and racks of clothing and shoes for sale. Though all of the clothing is donated and most of it is used, a large portion is definitely not junk. Name brand and designer dresses, coats, sweaters, and even sportswear can be purchased from the larger thrift stores. In many cities, thrift stores are found in very affluent areas and receive donations of clothing from all segments of our society, including the very rich.

Thrift stores also carry a wide selection of accessories, jewelry, and accent items. Prices are usually higher than garage sales because employees are paid to sort, clean, and stock the merchandise. Unlike garage sales, thrift store prices are set by the store and are not negotiable. However, the advantage of buying from thrift stores is that in most states the stores are required to clean and disinfect all clothing and shoes before displaying the items for sale. In addition, buying from a thrift store run by a charitable organization helps fund the organization.

Almost New Clothing Stores

In many cities Almost New or Nearly New clothing stores are on the increase. They bring a new dimension to the clothing market. No longer does the individual have to pay $350 to $500 for a new suit or dress that may only be worn on one special occasion. He or she can buy the same item for less than half of that amount and, after wearing it, can consign it back to the store to be resold. The concept is identical to the consignment type of Used Furniture store discussed in Chapter 23.

The store does not own the item being sold but is working as an agent for the owner of the item. Very expensive items of the latest style can be found in these stores at prices as low as 10 percent of the original cost. In 1983, my daughter, Cindy, bought a complete wedding outfit, including the veil, for $75.00. It had never been worn and when originally purchased cost $750.00. She decided to keep the outfit as a treasured memento, but she could have brought it back to the store, put it on consignment, and resold it for the same amount she paid for it. Her expense would have been limited to the cleaning -- about $12 -- and the fee -- about $7.50 -- charged by the store owner to resell the outfit. She could have had a total outlay for her wedding dress of under $20. Had she decided to resell the outfit, her expense of $20 would have been a fraction of what she would have paid just to rent the same outfit.

This is not an unusual example. It is repeated daily throughout the country and provides you the opportunity to wear and/or own expensive clothing at a fraction of the original item's cost. As long as the cost of clothing continues to increase and individuals continue to wear items only once or twice, this form of clothing outlet will expand. This is definitely an option that the person on a tight budget should consider.

The operator of the store will help you price the item and, if you want to, you can even make the price negotiable. Usually you leave the items at the store and the operator tags the item with a number assigned to you and the agreed upon price. You leave the store and may even forget about the item.

One afternoon while you are fixing dinner you get a phone call and a surprise, the store has a check for the sale of one or more of your discarded items. Your clothes budget has just been increased and you can now afford the items you have been waiting to buy.

Items that do not sell as priced in the store can be reduced in price or withdrawn from sale. These items can either be swapped, kept for a garage sale, or donated to a charitable organization. You lose nothing by placing the item on consignment.

FREE OR NEARLY FREE

Depending on your taste in clothing, the degree of adventure in your personality, and your resourcefulness, you can wear or acquire clothing free or nearly free.

Borrow

The most common way is to borrow clothes from your friends or family. You have probably already used this option at some time in the past. Most individuals, as they grow up, borrow an item of jewelry, a sweater, shirt, tie, or maybe shoes from a brother, sister, mother or father. I can remember a favorite item my daughters borrowed from me were my ties. They insisted that they looked much better on them than on me. At one time or another they borrowed just about every article of clothing and jewelry from each other and their mother.

My sons, having a different physique than mine, only borrowed ties, socks, and an overcoat from me, but, from their friends, they would borrow almost anything. My wife, Jean, would frequently think she was running a neighborhood laundry when she found that she had more clothes in the wash belonging to our sons' friends than belonging to them. They also loaned a lot of their clothes to others and must be mental giants to have kept track of what belonged to whom.

Remembering whom something was borrowed from is very important. Anything borrowed must be promptly returned if you want the friendship to last. Though this is an excellent way of expanding your wardrobe it must be played by the primary rule which is: Anything borrowed is cleaned and returned in a timely manner.

There are three other ways to acquire clothes with no, or a minimun, outlay of cash. Remember in Chapter 28 when I recommended that you set aside the clothes that you no longer would wear? The reason I made this recommendation is because these clothes have value.

Clothes Swapping Party

Even if your discarded clothes are not worth money in the true sense, they may have value at a "clothes swapping" party. This is a party you organize where you invite your friends to meet and swap clothing. The parties can take many formats, but a popular one is where all the items are thrown together in a pile and everyone takes turns selecting from the pile. At the end of the party the clothes that are not selected are returned to the person contributing them.

Another format of the party is to run it like a swap meet. You actually swap an item you have for one or more of someone else's. I will swap you two sweaters for the sports coat or two silk ties, the blue jacket, and the ski goggles. In addition to expanding your wardrobe by using your discarded clothing, the party can make for a really entertaining time, especially if you get into cross swapping.

Cross swapping is when person A wants an item that person C has but doesn't have something person C wants. Person B wants an item person A has but doesn't have anything A wants. It is now a challenge for person B to make a trade with person C for the item person A wants so that person B can then make a swap for the item desired from person A. It sounds confusing, but among friends it can be a lot of fun, especially since most of us like to barter. The items left over after the swap party still have value. Your challenge now is to turn them into money.

Garage Sale

Some of the hottest and fastest moving items at garage sales are jewelry, accessories and clothing. Any kind of clothing, men's, women's, dress, or work, it doesn't make any difference. Even items we would no longer think of as being in style will sell at a garage sale if the price is right. The hardest part of setting up a garage sale is putting the sales prices on items when you can still remember the original cost. It is very hard to put a 50 cent tag on a blouse that cost $10 or $12 new. For items still in style that are in excellent condition, set the price at no more than 20% of the original cost. Shoes, even in good condition, will seldom bring in more than a couple of dollars, and most accessories and accent items sell for under a dollar.

Be very careful not to overprice an item. Even if you let everyone know that the prices are negotiable, some people are too shy to make an offer, and you may lose a potential sale.

Get together with friends and neighbors to increase the size of the sale and make it more attractive, but be sure to set up in advance a means for accounting for the proceeds of the sale. It is amazing what people will buy and how quickly the nickels, quarters, and dollars add up to sizeable amounts. The proceeds from your garage sale can then be used to supplement your clothing budget, providing you with new clothes at no expense.

After the garage sale, the items left still have value to someone. You can either keep them for a later sale or donate them to a thrift store or other charitable organization. When you donate clothing, you get the satisfaction of knowing someone will get further use from your discards.

HOW TO SHOP

The rules on "How to shop" are included in the preceding text under the headings of "When" and "Where," however, they are worth identifying separately and make a good summary for this chapter.

(1) Only go clothes shopping after you have made your list of needs.
(2) Shop the sales.
(3) Look for original and unique places to shop.
(4) Shop for clothing when you have ample time to really shop.
(5) You can be "style conscious" while being "expense conscious."
(6) Don't rule out buys in "used" clothing.
(7) Shop for "free" or "nearly free" clothing (swaps, sharing, etc.).
(8) Look for easy care fabrics. Remember who does the wash.
(9) Shop for clothes with your mind as much as your eyes.

NOTES

_____

_____

_____

_____

_____

_____

_____

_____

_____

_____

_____

_____

HEALTH & RECREATION

"Don't Worry, Be Happy"

VIII

You have a job and are now earning your own money. You are able to provide for your own shelter, transportation, food and clothing. Now, if you haven't already done so, it's time to consider enjoying yourself. Enjoying yourself is as much an essential part of living as everything discussed so far. In fact, relaxation, enjoyment, pleasure, and fun, achieved through recreation, are necessary to reduce stress, combat boredom, and maintain your good physical and mental health.

Websters defines recreation as: "1) refreshment by means of some pastime, agreeable exercise, or the like. 2) a pastime, diversion, exercise, or other resource affording relaxation and enjoyment. 3) the act of recreating. 4) the state of being recreated." Unlike some of the other definitions, this definition really fits. Recreation is some form of activity that results in a recreation of the mind and body. All of us need a frequent, strong dose of recreation to aid us in overcoming the hurdles faced in day-to-day living.

However, to get the most out of your recreation you must be in good mental and physical health. And it would be a serious omission, when discussing health, not to include sex and sexually transmitted diseases. Nearly all of the reference materials used for this section indicate that sexually transmitted diseases, including AIDS, are rapidly approaching epidemic levels.

Chapter 30 is an open "no holds barred" presentation of the facts about SEX, VENEREAL DISEASE and other SEXUALLY TRANSMITTED DISEASES. A table showing symptoms, treatments, and consequences of the most common forms of sexually transmitted diseases is included.

Chapter 31 discusses methods for monitoring and maintaining your mental and physical health. The chapter includes a look at various forms of exercise, as well as an analysis of various forms of health clubs.

Chapter 32 discusses the use and abuse of time. The reader is encouraged to examine how their time is used, and some ideas for improving time management are presented.

Chapter 33 discusses recreation that may pay cash dividends (education). The many and varied forms of education, including their cost, are discussed with the emphasis on education as recreation.

Chapter 34 reveals some of the many sources of inexpensive and free recreation. The chapter discusses the "swapping" of the reader's resources -- time -- for free or expense paid recreation.

SEX

WARNING: Sex may be dangerous to your health!

30

THE MOVIES

You and your favorite date are at the movies. The scene before you is one that is shown over and over again. Girl and boy have just looked at each other across a room, and the sparks that flashed were so obvious the audience feels the electricity. The scene progresses through the introductions, the conversation, the casual holding and stroking of hands and the final question: "Your place or mine?"

The movie continues, and later the scene switches to the bedroom of a stylish apartment, the center of focus is the large round water bed where our stars are obviously engrossed in some serious and passionate sex. The picture is slightly out of focus so that the producer is not guilty of anything that would earn the dreaded "X" rating, but explicit enough to warrant the award of the coveted "R." If this movie is like most, exactly five and one half minutes later the sex scene is over, and, with passion spent, the couple either talk and smoke or fall blissfully asleep. The movie continues with the next scene.

This "Love" scene represents many like it which are designed to show the current concept of the "good life." Girl meets boy, girl likes boy, boy likes girl, and, in the movie writer's interpretation of life, they drift into immediate sexual coupling. The problem with the movie's representation is the failure to portray reality.

EDUCATION

Prominently displayed in my office, where it can be seen by all who enter, is a needlepoint that my daughter, Cindy, made of one of my favorite sayings. The saying is, **"Ignorance can be fixed but STUPID is forever."** Never before in the history of male/female interactions has this saying had more meaning. Nor have such vast amounts of money been spent in an effort to inform men and women of all ages about the dangers and possible outcome of unsafe sexual practices.

REALITY

(1)   If the actors in the movie really had sexual intercourse, there is a 10 percent chance that one was infected with a venereal or other sexually transmitted disease and, if so, a 95 percent chance that it was passed to the partner.

(2)   Over 10 million Americans are infected with venereal or other sexually transmitted diseases each year, and most are between the ages of 15 and 30.

(3)   The large majority of persons infected with these diseases are not aware that they are carriers and continue passing on the infection.

(4)   Condoms, of which no mention was made in the movie, offer some protection against the spread of most venereal and other sexually transmitted diseases but do not provide 100% safe sex.

(5)   In the past five years over 6 billion dollars have been spent in treating these diseases, and the figure is on the increase.

(6)   Some venereal and other sexually transmitted diseases either cannot be treated or, when treated, may reoccur meaning that once infected with these diseases, they are yours forever.

(7)   Depending on the reference you use, there are between 15 and 21 different venereal or other sexually transmitted diseases including Acquired Immune Deficiency Syndrome (AIDS).

(8)   Some venereal diseases have been directly linked to cancer.

(9)   There is a high probability that because of venereal disease infection this year, over 100,000 women will be rendered sterile.

(10)   It is never too late for you and your partner to get treatment for a venereal disease infection.

(11)   People do not build up immunities to venereal diseases. Reinfection, especially if the partner is not treated, is almost a certainty.

(12)   Most of the venereal and other sexually transmitted diseases react very favorably to treatment. Unfortunately, AIDS and Herpes Genitalis do not.

(13)   According to the U.S. Department of Education booklet, "AIDS and the Education of Our Children, A Guide for Parents and Teachers," dated May 1988, AIDS has been responsible for over 28,000 deaths in the United States, and the estimate is that over 1.5 million Americans are already infected with the virus and most of them do not know it.

(14)   Having one type of these diseases does not prevent infection by another type.

(15)   In almost all instances, the treatment, for those forms of these diseases that react to treatment, is inexpensive, painless, and quick.

(16)   Most individuals fearing infection do not seek treatment because of embarrassment or the pressure for the partner's name.

(17)   For treatment to be complete and long lasting, all sex partners must be treated. Otherwise the "ping pong" rule of reinfection will occur.

(18)   All studies, to date, indicate that it is difficult to be infected with any of these diseases from toilet seats or through casual social contact. However, when using a public restroom, common sense dictates care in using the facilities.

(19)   You can be infected and transmit many of the most prevalent forms of venereal and other sexually transmitted diseases, including AIDS, through heavy "petting" and foreplay without actual intercourse.

(20)   The only "*SAFE* SEX" is "*NO* SEX"! However, if you are going to have sex, make sure it is "*Intelligent* Sex."

INTELLIGENT SEX

The three rules for having intelligent sex are:

(1)   Determine if you are already infected.
(2)   Get immediate treatment if you are infected.
(3)   Protect yourself from infection.

Are You Already Infected?

Intelligent sex dictates that the first thing you do is ensure that you have not already been infected. This means taking another inventory. This inventory is personal and extremely important to your health and well-being.

Each of the following questions must be answered with the greatest of care and honesty. This is not the time to rationalize past actions, set blame, or feel guilty. This is the time for total honesty.

Are you sexually active?
Have you had any one-night romances?
Have you had sex with someone whose name you do not know?
Have you had sex with more than one partner?
Do you know or suspect that your sex partner has had sex with others?
Have you had sex without using a condom?
Do you use injected drugs and have used someone else's needle?
Does your sex partner use injected drugs?
Have you noticed any sores or rashes around your genitals or mouth, however minor, that have not been explained?
Do you have any burning or other unpleasant sensation during intercourse?
Do you have any form of genital discharge?
Have you had any unexplained fever recently?
Have you suffered from any unexplained sore or swollen glands?

An answer of yes to any of the above questions is sufficient grounds for concern. At the very least you should read the rest of this chapter, review the table provided, and closely monitor your body signs. An answer of yes to two or more of the questions is an indication that you need to:

(1)   stop having sex,
(2)   carefully read the rest of this chapter, and
(3)   see your family doctor or visit your local health clinic immediately.

Seeking Treatment

This is the 1990s. Even though we have venereal diseases in nearly epidemic proportions, we also have readily available treatment. If you don't want to call your doctor, free or very inexpensive treatment is still as close as your phone. Finish reading this chapter and review the table on the symptoms and consequences of the most prevalent venereal diseases. If, after reading this data, you feel that you may be infected with a venereal or other sexually transmitted disease, call your social services or county health center and arrange an immediate appointment.

Admit It!

When you arrive for your appointment, and in many cases you do not need an appointment, don't "hem and haw," come right out with the problem. The doctors, who receive their salary from the government, are there to help, not judge you or your actions. If, when you get to your appointment, you can't seem to put it into words, try these, "I think I may have a venereal disease because ..." Once you get started, the words will flow by themselves. The doctor can then focus on the problem and not waste time trying to diagnose a vague complaint of cramps, itching, soreness, rash, or other general complaints.

Relax, you will be treated professionally, not irresponsibly. You will be asked to undress and will be given a careful examination including the taking of genital, throat, and possibly anal smears. A sample of your blood will be taken for analysis.

While being examined you will be asked a number of questions, some of which you may find offensive. As a minimum, you can expect the following:

Have you had oral or anal sex?
How often do you have sex and with how many different partners?
Do you always use condoms?

Positive Results

And, if the tests show you are infected, you will be asked the one question no one wants to answer, "What are your sex partners' names, addresses, and phone numbers?"

Does answering these questions bother you? Do you feel that giving names is ratting on your partners, or are you embarrassed? You must fight these feelings. Some of these diseases, such as AIDS and herpes genitalis, cannot be cured. Others reoccur even after treatment. With this in mind, think of the consequences of not having yourself and your sex partner treated. Refusing to provide your partner's name is not only childish but irresponsible. It takes two people to transmit these diseases, and it takes at least that

many to cure them. If you still cannot bring yourself to give the doctor your partner's name, at least show him or her this chapter and suggest you go to the clinic together.

Curing yourself is only the first step. Your goal is not to protect the infected carriers but to eliminate these diseases.

Treatment

HOME REMEDIES FORBIDDEN!

Do not try any home remedies or self cures. You will only delay proper treatment and allow the infection to advance. The self administered treatment could even cause you additional harm.

If you think you may have AIDS, do not try any advertised products that promise "the wonder cure" or "spectacular results." In our society, there are people who want to make money out of others' pain. If you are already infected, don't compound your situation by also becoming a victim of unscrupulous practices. Seek qualified medical help immediately!

In most localities, public health facilities are available, where not only is the doctor's visit free, but so are the medications and drugs prescribed to treat the diseases. In all cases, treatment starts with the rule of no sex and, because of the drugs used, usually no alcohol until cured. This is not a severe hardship because most of the common venereal diseases that are treatable can be cured in a couple of weeks or less. The treatment will usually consist of either a shot, oral medication, or the application of a salve or cream. Whatever the treatment, the medication must be used for the complete prescribed period of time. Don't stop treatment just because the symptoms or visual signs of the disease go away.

Remember, during the period of treatment, the infected individual can transmit the disease to others. This means that an infected person who has sex while undergoing treatment can infect a new partner. The newly infected partner can, in turn, reinfect the cured original carrier at a later date. It can go back and forth, back and forth, over and over again, hence the term "ping pong" rule. During treatment there can be no sex if you really want to be cured.

Prevention

In doing the research for this chapter, it quickly became obvious that in spite of what the government puts out on TV and in other advertisements, the only true, 100% sure, prevention of infection when dealing with venereal and other sexually transmitted diseases is to not participate in any form of sex. When I say "any form of sex," I mean no heavy petting, stroking, deep kissing or foundling of nude genitals. This may seem drastic and even contrary to what you hear from other sources, but let me make my case.

Intercourse Not Required

Most venereal diseases are transmitted from one partner to another through body fluids. These body fluids, with some exceptions, include blood, saliva, semen, and anal and genital secretions This means that the diseases can be transmitted without full sexual intercourse. It is possible to unintentionally pass these secretions from one partner to another even during mild forms of sexual foreplay. This can happen when any part of one partner's body comes into contact with the contaminated bodily fluids of the other. If the uninfected person has any cuts, abrasions or other breaks in the skin, this contact is sufficient to transmit the disease.

Since bodily contact happens often during foreplay, even before the couple gets to the point of intercourse, it is possible to become infected without participating in actual intercourse. This is especially true of herpes, scabies, crabs and AIDS.

Add to the above the fact that scabies (mites) and crabs (lice) do not even need bodily fluids present to be transmitted, and the truth becomes obvious.

Horror Story

Everyone does not play fair. This story was passed on to me by a doctor friend. He heard it on a national radio talk show where the caller and the host both agreed that the behavior of the story's villain was unbelievable.

A young woman finding herself bored while attending an out-of-town convention was looking for some fun. During the course of the welcoming reception, she met a very attractive man. As the evening progressed, they found that they enjoyed the same sports and hobbies, and the attraction deepened. The reception was followed by a very pleasant dinner and a movie. When the couple returned to the hotel, she invited him up to her room for a nightcap.

He suggested ordering champagne from room service, and it wasn't long until, by mutual consent, they were having sex. The experience was very satisfying to both of them, and, relaxed, they quickly fell asleep. When the young woman awoke in the morning, the man was gone. Thinking he had an early engagement, she dismissed his absence. It wasn't until she went into the bathroom, where she saw the following message written in red lipstick on the large mirror: "Welcome to the wonderful world of AIDS!", that she understood the cost of casual sex.

The person recounting this story to the talk show host did not want to believe this could really happen. What do you think? Do you find this behavior understandable, or do you think it is "sick"? Whatever your evaluation of the story, you need to be aware that this behavior should be expected. When people are hurt, as the man in the story was by being infected, some will react exactly as he did -- by hurting others.

Some Rules For Having Sex

No one-night stands.

Know your partner well before even considering sex. You should know your partner well enough to take him or her to the clinic if that becomes necessary.

Carry your own condoms and insist on using them properly. Read the next topic in this chapter "The truth about contraceptives." As unfortunate as it is, in today's society, even your partner's word isn't good enough.

Practice good personal hygiene.

Stick with one partner at a time. Short flings or "revenge" affairs are dangerous and may even be deadly.

Know the symptoms of the diseases and seek help immediately if you suspect infection.

THE TRUTH ABOUT CONTRACEPTIVES

Contraceptives, with the exception of condoms, offer no protection against venereal diseases. When properly used, contraceptives will reduce the probability of pregnancy. That is all they do. Only condoms offer any degree of protection against infection by some venereal diseases.

Condoms

As stated earlier, there are no drugs or devices, including condoms, that will totally -- 100% -- prevent infection of venereal and other sexually transmitted diseases. In an attempt to educate everyone to protect themselves from contracting AIDS, the government and the media have placed too much emphasis on the protective properties of condoms. The objective of this education and even the distributing of free condoms is well meaning. However, to rely on the use of condoms without understanding the facts is a serious mistake. You may actually raise the possibility of having an undetected infection by ignoring your body's warning signs if infection does take place. It is easy for the uninformed to dismiss a rash, slight fever, sores, etc. as something other than venereal disease because "We always use condoms!" What an unfortunate, health wrecking, and possibly deadly statement to make.

The Right Way

Do you know how to use condoms? Do you know that they should be put on as soon as possible, but always before any heavy petting or serious foreplay? Do you know that they should be very carefully removed immediately after sex, and the genitals and hands washed in warm soapy water? Do you know that as an extra precaution, females should immediately douche and wash the pubic area?

Using a condom does provide some protection, which is certainly better than not doing anything to protect yourself. Properly used, they will prevent unwanted pregnancies and provide a high level of -- but not total -- protection against infection. If you are going to have sex, have intelligent sex and use condoms, but don't lose sight of the continuing and real problem. If you have sex, no matter how careful you are, you can get infected with a venereal disease. Remember, once infected with some of these diseases, the infection is not just for today or next week, but for the rest of your life!

THE TABLE

The table on the next page is provided to help you identify the symptoms and long lasting effects of the most common or prevalent venereal and other sexually transmitted diseases. This table is only the tip of the iceberg. For more information call your closest health service, visit your library, and read the books recom-mended in the Appendix, or call the AIDS Hotline. The Hotline number is 1-800-342-AIDS.

ACQUIRED IMMUNE DEFICIENCY SYNDROME (AIDS)

Unlike many other viruses, AIDS does not kill. What kills the infected person is the inability of the infected body to combat what would otherwise be minor or correctable illnesses. In plain language AIDS destroys your body's ability to heal itself. Once this happens, the most minor infection or illness can, and ultimately will, kill you.

According to the Department of Health and Human Services Publication No. (FDA) 88-1145, revised October 1988, AIDS can be traced back to the year 1977 and initially was transmitted by homosexual activity among men. The following is a quote from this publication on the present methods of spreading the disease:

"AIDS is a sexually transmitted, blood-borne disease that spreads from one person to another in the following ways:

- By sexual intercourse between a man and woman or between two men. The virus can be spread through vaginal, anal, or oral sex.
- By sharing contaminated needles or "works" used to inject drugs.
- By an infected woman to her baby during pregnancy or delivery and possibly through breast feeding.
- By transfusing of contaminated blood or blood components, although this risk has been sharply reduced by screening blood and blood donors and by new ways to process blood used to treat disorders such as hemophilia."

VENEREAL AND OTHER SEXUALLY TRANSMITTED DISEASES

NAME	SYMPTOM Male	SYMPTOM Female	*PREVENTION	TREATABLE	CURABLE	AFFECT IF UNTREATED Male	AFFECT IF UNTREATED Female
AIDS	Increased susceptibility to all diseases.		Condoms	NO	NO	No known cure, results in ultimate DEATH!	
Candidiasis	Itching and burning with irritating sweet smelling discharge.		Condoms	YES	YES, but may reoccur.	Because of the constant itching, burning, and sweet odor, this is a very distressing disorder.	
Crabs (Lice)	Maddening itch in public area.		No Sex	YES	YES	Embarrassing, intense itching, dirty feeling.	
Genital Warts	Growths on penis.	Growths at entrance of, and in the vagina.	Condoms	YES	YES, but may require surgery.	Painful Intercourse.	Painful intercourse and can be spread to infant during birth.
Gonorrhea	Burning when urinating, thick discharge.	No noticeable symptoms.	Condoms	YES	YES 1 week	Urine blockage and infection of the prostate gland.	Pelvic Inflammatory Disease - Sterility
Herpes genitalis	Blisters on penis and pubic region.	Blisters hidden in the vagina.	Condoms	YES	NO	Swollen glands, blisters, painful intercourse leading to possible meningitis. The virus can infect infants as they pass through the birth canal.	
Nongonococcal or Chlamydia-Nonspecific Urethritis (NSU), (NGU)	Same as for gonorrhea, except thin discharge.	No noticeable symptoms.	Condoms	YES	YES	Urine blockage and infection of the prostate gland.	Sterility. Passed to infant as eye inflammation and severe pneumonia.
Pelvic Inflammatory Disease (PID)	None	Recurring pain in lower abdomen and backaches.	Condoms	YES	YES	None, but is a carrier and transmitter of the disease.	Blockage of fallopian tubes preventing conception.
Scabies	Severe itching of finger webs and genitals.		No Sex	YES	YES	Severe irritation of genitals from scratching and burrowing of mites.	
Syphilis	Sore or chancre develops where disease enters body (genitals, anus, mouth).		Condoms	YES	YES, if treated early.	Blindness, damage to brain, nervous system, heart, and blood vessels.	
Trichomoniasis	Very minor itching of the penis.	Burning, itching, yellowish discharge, unpleasant odor.	Condoms	YES	YES 10 days	None, but is a carrier and transmitter of the disease	Chronic itching, burning and foul smelling discharge after menstruation.
Viral Hepatitis	Weakness, loss of appetite, nausea, abdominal discomfort, whitish bowel movement.		No Sex	YES	Yes, if treated early.	10% of infected people end up with some form of liver disease and damage.	

* When used properly condoms do provide some (not 100%) measure of prevention.

The publication then goes on to stress that infected individuals may feel no symptoms of the disease but are still carriers and spreaders of the virus, and *a person can become infected after just a single exposure to the virus.*

From the above, it is obvious that as far as contracting AIDS is concerned, whenever you have sexual intercourse with someone, you are really having sexual intercourse with everyone else the person has had intercourse with since 1977. However, according to the bulletin, "the AIDS virus is not spread by sexual intercourse between two people who maintain a sexual relationship exclusively with each other and who have not been previously infected."

The bulletin then recommends the following precautions to *reduce the risk* of exposing yourself or others to the AIDS virus:

- **"The best protection against sexually transmitted infection by the virus is, of course, to abstain from sex or to have a mutually monogamous relationship with an uninfected person. Avoiding sex with people who have AIDS, people who have tested positive for the AIDS virus antibody, or people at risk of infection, would also eliminate the risk of sexually transmitted infection.**

- **Unless you're absolutely sure that your sex partner is not infected, avoid contact with his or her blood, semen, urine, feces, saliva, and vaginal secretions:**
    Use condoms, which will reduce (but not eliminate) the possibility of transmitting the virus.
    Avoid sexual practices that may cause tears in the vagina, rectum or penis.
    Avoid oral-genital contact without a condom.
    Avoid open mouthed, intimate kissing.

- **Do not have sex with multiple partners. The more partners you have, the greater your risk of infection.**

- **Do not use illegal intravenous drugs. If you do, never share needles or syringes."**

The bulletin continues by advising anyone who feels that he or she has been in intimate contact with an infected individual to immediately seek counseling and medical evaluation. For more information about AIDS, call the National AIDS Hotline, 1-800-342-AIDS, or use the list of resources under this section number in the appendix of the book.

The good news, if there is good news when discussing AIDS, is that according to the U.S. Public Health Service: "The AIDS virus does not spread through casual social contact. In more than seven years of tracking and studying AIDS, scientists have found no evidence that the virus is spread casually through contact at school or on the job, by sharing meals or office equipment, or by handshakes or hugs with an infected person. There is no reason to avoid ordinary social contact with a person infected with the virus."

For your safety and good health it is important to stress that the quoted article strongly recommends the use of condoms and not other methods of contraception. Remember, other contraceptives -- oral, IUDs, diaphragms, and spermacides -- though possibly preventing pregnancy, do absolutely nothing to protect you or your partner from the spread of the AIDS virus or other venereal diseases.

Some of you may have found this presentation of the quoted text crude, explicit and even offensive. I understand and respect your feelings, but accept some hurt feelings as a small price to pay in trying to fix the "ignorance" that interferes with the combating and eradication of this most deadly and preventable disease.

SUMMARY

Most older adults, including your parents, are still able to remember their teenage and subsequent years quite clearly. Clearly enough to remember that when the situation presents itself and emotions are high between two consenting members, they will probably have sex. Sex takes place regardless of age or the religious, or family background and upbringing. It takes place without regard to the income structure or area of residence, and, as has been proven over and over again by the statistics, it takes place in spite of the intelligence or educational level of the participants.

This chapter is not intended to promote premarital or extramarital sex. If you are past your sophomore year in high school and, for whatever reason, -- moral, religious or personal preference -- you have not participated in sexual intercourse, I applaud you. Not because of your reasons but because deciding not to have sex before making a long and lasting commitment is a very important step towards surviving.

Today, because of the threat of AIDS and other sexually transmitted diseases, you face added stress in trying to cope with your natural sexual drives. Not only do you have to reconcile the moral issues of right and wrong but the added issue of AIDS and the other sexually transmitted venereal diseases. If you are smart enough to read and understand this book, you are smart enough not to contract sexually transmitted infections. You are also smart enough not to be responsible for an unplanned or unwanted pregnancy.

Sexual intercourse is only one of the many ways adults have for expressing and demonstrating strong affection for each other. The problem we humans have is, that in the heat of passion, it is difficult to think of the other ways. At the beginning of this discussion, I made a point of reminding you that you alone have the right to decide to have or not have sexual intercourse. Along with that right comes a very serious responsibility, the responsibility of protecting yourself and your partner from being infected with AIDS or any other sexually transmitted disease.

If you are intimate enough with your partner to consider sex than be considerate enough to insist it be *"intelligent sex."* Anything less is not only irresponsible **it may be deadly**.

NOTES

_____
_____
_____
_____
_____
_____
_____
_____
_____
_____
_____
_____
_____

HEALTH
A healthy body is a happy body!

31

To enjoy yourself and get the maximum benefit from recreation, you must be mentally and physically healthy. If you turn to the health section of any large city's newspaper or pick up a health or family oriented magazine, you are sure to see one or more articles on "stress" and the impact of daily "stress" on your mental and physical health. You will also have great difficulty finding a doctor who will not agree that mental and physical health are closely intertwined and very difficult to separate. This chapter is a practical, nonmedical discussion based on personal experience and observations. Under no circumstances is it intended to contain medical diagnosis or advice. The Appendix contains a list of some excellent, easy to understand books dealing with both mental and physical health.

MENTAL HEALTH

This is not a discussion of mental illness, nor is it a discussion of "sanity" or "insanity." It is a discussion of some of the mental processes that we experience continuously that affect our health and feeling of "well-being." A more simple way of identifying this subject might be those things that together form our individual awareness of ourselves and the world we live in. This awareness will provide the motivation or lack of motivation for just about everything we will do as adults and can be categorized as:
(1) Awareness of "self,"
(2) Awareness of surroundings,
(3) Awareness of how we fit into the surroundings.
Into these three categories fall all our personality traits, our values, our morals, and our understanding and acceptance of the rules of our society. The degree to which we understand and accept our place in our environment and society will have a strong influence on the amount of, and our ability to cope with, daily stress.

Awareness of Self

Do you really know and understand who you are? If asked to describe yourself, can you put into words who and what you are? If the answer is yes, can you accept the answer and feel good about the person described. This is what I mean about awareness of self.

Most of us, if asked to describe ourselves, would answer with a description just like the one written on our driver's license. It would state our height, weight, color of eyes, etc. Though this is a physical description of our body, it is definitely not a description of what makes us original and unique. By the time we reach adulthood, most of us have accepted our physical makeup. We know and are aware of the fact that we are short or tall, thin or fat, light or dark, strong or weak, have straight or crooked teeth, or need to wear glasses.

This awareness and acceptance does not mean that we will never try to change our physical appearance. The opposite is true. Most of us have one or more physical traits that we will always be working to change or correct. My personal trait is that I tend to be overweight. No matter what diet I try or how much I exercise, if I eat I gain weight. My real problem is that I really do like to eat.

I am not alone. Very large sums of money are spent each year by people trying to improve or change their physical appearance. Dieting and other weight loss fads, braces for teeth, health clubs, eye glasses, contact lenses, and cosmetic surgery of all kinds make up large portions of some people's budgets and result in significant contributions to our economy.

Knowing what we look like and knowing

who we are, are not the same. Every time we look in a mirror or other reflective surface, we are reminded of what we look like, but how do we know who we are? This can only be done by what used to be called "Deep Soul Searching," not from the purely religious aspect but from the total self aspect.

Just as you needed to take a clothes inventory to find out what you had so you could identify your clothing needs, you need to do a self or "me" inventory to become aware of what or who you are. The books listed under resources in the appendix will provide you with a more professional and detailed approach to this self inventory, but here are a few questions to get you thinking in the right direction.

What do I believe in?
What are my values?
What are my goals?
What things are important to me?
What things anger me the most?
What things frustrate me the most?
What do I like most about myself?
What would I most like to change about myself?

Even though you are probably tired of writing by now, I strongly suggest that after serious consideration you write down the answers to the above questions. We will get back to the answers at the end of this topic.

Awareness of Surroundings

When discussing the awareness of surroundings, we must not limit ourselves to our home, office, or close group of friends. We must consider each of our environments, starting with home and family and moving out to include the society we live in and even the whole earth. We do not live or function in a vacuum. Everything we do affects others, and our interaction with others is what makes our daily living either very pleasant or very unpleasant.

Before we can determine how we fit into our society and even into life on this planet, Earth, we must know the ground rules for acceptance by both our society and the environment.

Even wild animals living in jungles have rules for acceptance. These rules are stronger for those animals that live in packs or herds than for those that are considered loners, but for all there

are still rules. The difference between wild animals and civilized society is that, because of our ability to think and rationalize, our rules are more complex. But it doesn't make any difference if the rules are simple or complex, the objective or goal is the same: survival of the species.

If society, as we know it today, is to survive, there are rules that must be adhered to. In our society, rules can always be questioned, but even while the questioning is taking place the existing rules must be obeyed. If no one complied with the rules of society the result would be chaos, mayhem, and eventually the total destruction of the society.

You will be dealing with society at three basic levels or environments:
(1) Home environment
(2) Work environment
(3) Social environment

For each of these, you need to do an inventory similar to the one you did for "self," so that a comparison can be made that will indicate how well you fit into your environment.

Home Environment

You will have to restructure the questions used for the "self" inventory somewhat so the questions and answers make sense and provide you with meaningful information. For example, the first and second questions may not be applicable to home environment, but, if you are leasing a place to live, changing the third question to "What are the owner's or management's goals?" is definitely important. Understanding the answer to this question helps in understanding and accepting the rules contained in your lease.

If the owner of the complex wants to provide a fun atmosphere, for singles and couples, a "no children allowed" rule makes sense. This is especially true if the complex has a pool, sauna, and weight room. The insurance on these facilities could be unbearable if children lived on the premises or were allowed to use the facilities. However, if the apartment complex you are living in is oriented towards families with children, you can understand tighter rules pertaining to late, noisy music or parties.

These questions are even more important if you are planning to share your apartment or house with someone. They will provide you with an insight on the probability of you and your roommate(s) being able to live together with a minimum of friction. You can modify the other questions or add questions of your own that will provide the information you need to better understand your home environment.

Work Environment

The very same questions, slightly modified, can be applied to the company you work for. Companies do have goals, values, and rules. You, like everyone else, will find things you like and dislike about your employer and job even though you may be very happy at work. To see how these questions could be applied to your work environment, let's take Jo Ann and her job at Green Toe Nursery as an example. She could actually have started this list as part of her list of pros and cons when she went for her job interview back in Chapter 3. However, it takes some time on the job to answer most of the questions about your job and employer. Her findings about her employer and job are:

The nursery owners believe in high quality service and workmanship.

The values of the company, and most of the employees, include fairness and honesty.

The company's goal is to maintain a good profit but not at the expense of quality of work or employees.

The company's reputation and the safety of the employees appear to be equally important.

The owners get most angry at poor workmanship and unreliability of employees.

The owners get frustrated by the weather and their suppliers' unreliability.

Jo Ann most likes the fair way she is treated by her fellow workers.

She would like to change her supervisor and get more time for lunch.

She likes the overtime pay but sometimes wishes she did not have to work on weekends.

This example is to show that the same questions you asked about "self" can be applied to your work environment. You can expect your answers and list to be very different from the example. In fact, two people holding the same job for the same employer would be expected to have different lists. We all perceive our environments differently because even as we ask ourselves the questions and list the answers, we are judging the environment against our own values and beliefs.

Social Environment

Determining how we fit into our social environment is possibly the most difficult, even though, except for self, we have all lived with this environment the longest. The reason this is most difficult is because, until now, you probably had someone working as a buffer between you and society -- your parents or guardians. This buffer has provided you with protection and, at the same time, possibly shielded you from some of the harsh realities of living and functioning in our society. This buffer can work so well in some families that as we are growing up we do not even consider the true expectations of our society.

Try to grasp the concept that what you do can possibly have an impact on every living thing on the planet. If you have a broad enough imagination, it is even possible to broaden this concept to include the universe.

The Water Test

To help you relate to this concept, think of society as a bowl or bucket of water. Put your finger into the water directly in the center. You are born. Now try to move your finger without creating ripples that spread to the outer confines of the container. You cannot. You are an integral part of society. If you quickly remove your finger, the water remaining rapidly moves to fill the space vacated lowering the total level a very small amount. Some scholars have used this shortness of time the water takes to fill the void as a representation of how little we are each missed when we die.

I prefer to point out, that no matter how little time it takes, or how small the drop, the entire level of the water falls, demonstrating that the individual is no longer there. This drop in the level of the water reinforces the premise that, no matter how small, each of us does have a lasting effect on our surroundings.

You can modify the same questions used for "self," "home" and "work" and apply them to your city, state, and society as a whole to increase your understanding of the codes, rules and expectations society has for each of its members. Your objective at this time is not to challenge or change any of society's expectations but to gain a fuller understanding of them.

To help you get started, the question you asked of "self," "What do I believe in?", becomes "What does our society believe in?". The answer, at least for the United States, is "freedom." However, freedom by itself is not enough. Freedom in our society has restrictions and limitations, as well as expected behavior patterns. You are not free to take anything you want, nor are you free not to follow the rules established. Our entire form of government is designed to provide the checks and balances necessary to maintain this belief.

The same rephrasing should be done for the values, goals, and other questions.

Fitting in

Now that you have taken the four inventories -- self, home, work, and society -- sit down and match your answers for self against those you have for your three environments. If you are like the rest of the individuals that collectively make up society, you will have anything but a perfect fit. This should not be thought of as a problem. Remember, you have taken on this exercise to get a better understanding of yourself and your environment in order to help you understand and cope with stress. To do this, you must have an understanding of what causes stress. Stress is usually caused by the difference between self and environment. With this understanding comes the ability to cope.

A long time ago, in 1934, the *Serenity Prayer* was written by Reinhold Niebuhr. If we could incorporate this prayer into our lives, we would be well on our way to removing stress. The prayer reads:

"God, give us grace to accept with serenity the things that cannot be changed, courage to change the things which should be changed and the wisdom to distinguish one from the other."

Alcohol, Drugs, and Tobacco

Let's call these the "big three." All of them have the potential of eventually killing you. I know that the "realist" will quickly point out that we are all going to die sometime. To use this as an argument or excuse for excessive drinking, continuing to smoke one or more packs of cigarettes each day, or for using drugs is a cop out. It is like stopping your car on the railroad tracks in front of a fast moving train and explaining the action away with the statement, "If it's not my time, I won't die." I hope the attendees at your funeral or memorial service understand your logic.

These are controversial issues. Issues on which you are constantly receiving conflicting messages. On the one hand, the Surgeon General and almost all doctors and health officials tell you that the "big three" will kill you, while at the same time tobacco and alcohol are legal, if you are of legal age. In addition, each day newspapers carry one or more articles about popular and respected individuals undergoing drug and alcohol treatment or dying from a drug overdose or related illness.

To use or not use the "big three" is your decision. How you make it could affect the rest of your life.

Do you pay attention to the warnings on tobacco and the statistics compiled by the cancer treatment agencies, or do you smoke because everyone else in your group does? Do you think that, because Uncle Joe drinks a fifth of scotch and smokes two packs of cigarettes a day and is 83 years old, he and, therefore, you are immune to the risks and consequences? Have you ever lived with an alcoholic or watched a close friend or loved one die of liver failure or cancer?

I am not going to discuss the dangers of using or abusing drugs. The use of these substances in any nonmedical situation is against the law. A discussion of this topic would fall in the same category as discussing theft as an option for obtaining appliances, furniture, and clothing. I did not write this book to teach honesty or any other value system. The use of drugs in our society is illegal. Knowing this, if you still choose to use them, you must expect to pay the consequences. If you don't agree with these or any other laws, you have the freedom, as discussed earlier, to work within the law to bring about changes.

I have included recommended readings and

sources of help in the Appendix on all three of these topics. As with the AIDs threat, you owe yourself the time it takes to become fully informed on these subjects.

PHYSICAL HEALTH

Without a doubt, our physical health is just as important as our mental health is to our ability to satisfactorily function in the real world. Chapter 4 discussed your need for health insurance, Chapter 14 discussed walking and riding a bicycle for exercise, and Chapters 24 and 25 discussed vitamins, minerals, and the selection of food items to promote good health. However, there is more to physical health than was contained in these discussions. In this chapter, I am going to discuss other ways to enjoy recreation while at the same time maintain and/or develop good health.

It is impossible to maximize the returns of recreation if you do not "feel" good. Even watching TV or reading a book are no fun if you are physically hurting in some way. The first step in maintaining your physical health is to learn to recognize the difference between "static" pain and pain that indicates you need professional help.

Pain

Pain is the primary way in which our bodies let us know that something is not right. "Static" pain is the physical pain that occurs in our day-today living, even when we may otherwise feel great. It is the sore muscle from too much tennis or yesterday's football game. It may be the stomach pain caused by overeating or eating food rich in seasonings. It can also be the headache resulting from too much partying or from being out in the sun too long. Pain associated with the common cold, flu, or hay fever can also be classified as "static" pain.

Most people combat "static" pain with non-prescription drugs and a promise to themselves not to participate in the activity that caused the pain again. Since these promises are usually not kept, most people have the contents of a small drug store in their bathroom cabinets.

We do not need, nor can we afford, to run to the doctor's office with each ache or pain that we get, but we do need to know the difference between this "static" pain and something more serious. For instance, the feeling that what you are experiencing is sore muscles can easily hide a

fractured bone, torn ligament, or severe bruise requiring medical help.

Unfortunately, there is no given formula for making this distinction, though a good rule of thumb is to monitor the severity and/or duration of the pain. A simple headache should go away when treated with non-prescription pain medication and a little rest. Unless it is acute, hay fever discomfort should be relieved by over-the-counter medications in a short period of time. Sore muscles are normally relieved by a non-prescription medication after a couple of days, and a plain upset stomach also reacts to medication rather quickly. If any of these symptoms or any other pain is acute or persists for more than a short period of time, you should seek medical attention.

The pain you are experiencing may not indicate a serious problem at all, but as long as it persists recreation of any kind will be difficult if not impossible to enjoy. Think about doing toe touches with a sinus headache. Just thinking about this situation hurts.

A visit to the doctor or dentist will be well worth the expense when a pain that you have, even if not a serious problem, is relieved. You benefit two ways: first, is the relief of the pain itself, and second, is the peace-of-mind that results in having identified the cause, so you can begin to take corrective action.

In addition to pain, there are a number of other signs that indicate you may have a problem that requires professional treatment. Rashes or other unexplained skin irritations on any part of the body, swelling or discoloration of the skin, lumps or bumps that appear for no obvious reason, blurred vision, dizziness or weakness, and difficulty in hearing are all ways that your body lets you know that there is a potential problem. Know your body as well as, if not better than, you know your "self" so that you can recognize these indications and take appropriate mea-sures to correct them.

Keeping Physically Fit

There is much you can do to prevent some of the "static" as well as the more serious pain that afflicts people. You should be as concerned about your physical fitness as you are about your mental health.

Cooking safely and eating the proper balance of foods are steps in the right direction. Everyone should be concerned about these things, but, in addition, you should also participate in some form of planned exercise program. Your program does not have to be formal and cost a lot of money, but it should be planned and, at the very least, be one that results in good lung and heart action.

We all need physical exercise. That's right, even Jo Ann who works physically hard at her job with the Green Toe Nursery needs an exercise program. In fact, she may need more exercise than some of us, because she may wish to increase her strength as well as improve her heart and lung condition. Just because you have a job that involves manual labor, do not get the wrong impression that you are providing the necessary workout that your body needs. Heavy daily labor may only work some of your muscles hard and others not at all. Because of the stop and go nature of the work, it may not provide the heart and lung exercise that one half hour of brisk walking does.

The same is true of playing weekend sports. Playing tennis, baseball, football, soccer, or even swimming on the weekend, with no other physical exercise program during the week, will not only not provide the exercise your body needs, but may cause harm. Without proper exercise during the week, your muscles tend to tighten up. Then, on the weekend, if you go right into your favorite sporting recreation, without proper stretching or limbering exercises, you may actually apply harmful stress to both muscles and joints. Instead of the recreation helping to reduce stress, it may cause damage to your body.

What Does It Take?

Most doctors agree that one half hour of brisk walking or other general aerobic type exercise -- running, jogging, swimming, cycling, or cross country skiing -- three to four times a week, is all that is necessary to keep the body's heart and lungs in good shape. In addition, you need to eat smart, not smoke, and get sufficient rest nightly. You definitely do not need to work out with weights or on the latest exercise equipment for an hour every day to stay fit.

If you are interested in body building or developing additional strength, you can participate in a more strenuous exercise program. Programs of this nature should be approved by your doctor or other qualified professional. In Chapter 34, we will explore the various ways of exercising and the associated costs.

SUMMARY

Stress in our lives is not all bad. Stress provides motivation for most of us, and, without it, many great accomplishments may never occur. It is our understanding of stress and how we deal with it that is either healthy or unhealthy.

To understand stress, it is important that we understand ourselves and how we fit into our environment. It is equally important that we understand our body and how it works and continuously strive to keep it fit, both mentally and physically. Participating in recreational activities, be they, reading, sports, volunteer work, crafts, or watching TV are all ways to improve our health and assist us in coping with everyday stress. Devoting just 20 minutes a day to quiet time will produce extraordinary results.

If you have not started using drugs, alcohol or tobacco, don't! If you use any of these substances, get help to stop even if you do not believe you are addicted. Nicotine is one of the deadliest forms of poison known to man; it takes a very, very small amount of it, in a distilled form, to quickly and painfully kill. Alcohol is a depressant. Many alcoholics will die either from liver failure or by committing suicide, if they don't first kill themselves or others by driving under the influence. Just because you are smart enough not to drive after you drink does not mean you don't have a drinking problem.

If you do not use or abuse the "big three," exercise is one of the keys to maintaining good mental and physical health. If you do use the "big three," exercise may not help either your mental or physical health. No matter what age you are, you are never too young to start a planned, structured exercise program. Not only will you feel better now, you will continue to benefit through the years.

TIME MANAGEMENT

**You can always find time
for what you want to do.**

32

Recreation may add stress to your life! In order to prevent this, recreation must not be approached with the same attitude as you tackle your job. Many of us try to put recreation into an already busy schedule and get disappointed when we do not reap the expected benefits. Not only are we not refreshed and don't feel better, we are actually under more stress, because the whole time we were supposedly enjoying our recreation we were thinking, planning, or even chastising ourselves for wasting the time.

Remember, the definition of recreation is "a pastime or activity designed to provide diversion, relaxation, and enjoyment so we will be re-created." The objective of recreation cannot be achieved if we do not give ourselves adequate time to enjoy it. We must forget, or at the very least temporarily suspend, our concentration on the everyday situations that are providing the stress.

The time devoted to recreation must be free time we can feel comfortable in devoting to getting exercise or just having fun. One of the great joys of fishing is not catching fish but getting away from everything, even the phone. You can sit, just watching the water, sky, clouds, and your fishing pole, and let your mind drift. No worries, no concerns, just peace and quiet, possibly enjoying some good company and nature. Catching fish is an extra benefit, not a requirement, to the person who enjoys fishing for recreation. As soon as an individual takes a mobile phone on a fishing outing so contact can be maintained with the office, fishing is no longer recreation, it is simply another activity.

TIME

Time is an asset that is always there. People do not make time to do things. Rather, they find time to do them. However, no matter which term you use, "make" or "find," the process is the same, but the menal attitude can be quite different. Making time implies a reluctance to use it, which, if true, will defeat the objective of recreation. Finding time implies a willingness to manage your time and to spend it, without regret, supporting the objective of recreation.

Since time is always there (24 hours, 1440 minutes, or 86,400 seconds elapse between each sunrise), your assignment is to make the most of it. This is not to imply that you should be working every hour, minute and second of the day. Instead, what I am suggesting is that with awareness, planning, and management, you have more than enough time each day to feel good about investing some of it in recreation. How do you gain this awareness? The very first step is to do another of our famous (Are you ready for this?) inventories.

This inventory is not to determine how you waste time, but how you presently use your time. Once you know how you use your time, you can explore ways to do things concurrently, simultaneously, or in a different sequence, thereby saving or finding time you never realized you had.

Concurrently means "to happen together or side by side." When discussing time it means "two or more things happening during the same time frame."

Simultaneously means "two or more things happening at exactly the same time." There are very few tasks that we can actually do simultaneously.

For example, it would be difficult for us to take a shower, brew a pot of coffee, and bake biscuits simultaneously. But, by starting the coffee, putting the biscuits in the oven and then taking a shower, we can easily accomplish all three functions concurrently, in just the same time it takes to brew the pot of coffee. This demonstrates not only efficiency, but also time management. Even if you already have adequate amounts of spare time to enjoy your recreation without concern for the time used, you may still want to perform the following exercise for what it will reveal about yourself and your habits.

Time Inventory

The reason for doing a time inventory is to document those things we presently do and the time it usually takes to do them, even the ones we do by habit. We are all creatures of habit. Often we do not know why we do things a certain way, we just do them. Getting dressed is a good example. Some people dress from the bottom up, others from the top down, and still others seem all mixed up. Some people dress before eating breakfast, others after breakfast, and some even during breakfast -- look out for ulcers! And, as we all know, some people do not eat break-fast.

Get yourself a long sheet of paper, sit down, and make a list of everything you do from the time you wake up on a typical Monday morning, until you go to bed on Sunday evening. If this sounds like too large a task to do at one time, then start with a typical workday. List everything you do from the time you wake up on one day until you wake up the next morning. Once you are satisfied that the list is complete, put down your best estimate of the time it takes you to perform each item. When you total up the times don't be surprised if the total doesn't come close to 24 hours or 1440 minutes. On our first attempt, since we usually don't think of how much time each little function takes, we tend to over or under estimate. In some cases, we even forget things we do, for instance, the time it takes to: travel to and from work, put out the garbage, clear the table, or talk on the phone.

Now comes the hardest but most important part. Use your watch. Become aware of time. Try to convert your estimates into valid averages. Let's face it, if you never have extra time but your estimate of a workday only accounts for 22 hours, your estimates are wrong or you missed something. If you are really going to learn to manage time, you have to be honest and complete in your data collection. You are not trying to see how fast you can do something, just how long it really takes.

For a couple of days do your own "time and motion study." Place little pieces of paper all around the house, in your bedroom, bathroom, kitchen, dining room, and living room. Also, keep paper in your car and carry some with you when you are out. You should write down specific items and the time required to do them.

Do not lump a whole Saturday into "house-work, laundry, shopping, movies, etc. -- 10 hours." This will not help you at all. What you need are the individual times. How much time did you spend doing housework? Pay special attention to the "etc." Was it lunch with friends, time at the library, or getting the car fixed? You need the details, including the time spent.

Once you have a good inventory of a work-day, expand the list to include after work and a typical weekend. If each weekend is different, use three or four weekends to develop an average. When you are finished, you will be surprised at what you will have learned about yourself and your habits. In addition to helping you manage your time, this inventory will help you better understand the "self" discussed in the last chapter.

An Investment

By now you are asking where you are going to get the time to do this time consuming inventory. You are already busy and don't even have time for recreation, and I am asking you to use more time for this inventory. Make the time; force yourself to do the inventory. It is the first and most important step to time management. If you must think of the time used to take the inventory as time spent, than I can assure you it will be *well spent*.

Time Analysis

Everyone's inventory of time usage is different. We not only do different things but, those that we all do, we do at various speeds. This analysis can only be done by you. I can offer things to consider as you do your analysis, but only you can honestly decide if you can better manage your time.

As you look at your time use inventory, ask yourself the following questions:

Is this the best sequence of events?
Do I have some reason for following this schedule?
Are there things that can be done concurrently?
Am I misusing time?
Is there a faster way of doing some of the things I do without sacrificing safety?
Do I have other things I would rather be doing?

Am I willing to change some habits to gain more free time?

If you are serious about organizing yourself a little more or having more time to do the things you want, read on.

Manage, Manage, Manage

Some people think that time management means that you start by putting a time limit on everything you do. Ten minutes for a shower, three and a half minutes to get dressed, eight minutes for breakfast, and so on. This is not my interpretation of time management. Time management is the study of your own behavior, and the reorganization of that behavior to minimize the overall time it takes to do the things that must be done. This should leave adequate time for doing the things you want to do, including recreation or just relaxing.

Thus far I have presented a number of suggestions that lead directly to this end. Starting in Chapter 19, under selecting a place to live, one of the conside-ations was convenience to work, while another was considering laundry facilities in or near your new home. When discussing cooking and menu planning in Chapters 24 and 25, I discussed planning ahead to reduce time needed to prepare meals. The discussion of grocery shopping in Chapter 29 included organizing your grocery list so you only had to make one pass through your favorite grocery and knowing the slack times at the grocery store so you could arrange your schedule to take advantage of them. All of these considerations are time management techniques.

Change Habits

The items presented so far by no means form a complete list. Consider the following: Do you take a shower or bath in the morning? If so, why? Before air conditioning, people took showers and baths in the morning so they could go to work fresh and clean. But, today, if you have air conditioning, do you really need to shower in the morning? If you do, can you be fixing breakfast at the same time? Preparing lunch takes time. Can you do it the night before?

What about going to work? There are many parts of our country, especially in large metropolitan areas, where leaving for work 15 minutes earlier would cut 30 to 45 minutes off the travel time. Can you change your work hours to take advantage of this savings in time? If you can't change you work hours, can you get to work early and use the time saved to read, write letters, make up your grocery list, or just relax? Be careful, it is easy to start out relaxing when you get to work early and then gradually progress to adding more time to your work day.

Do you use your whole lunch time eating? Do you have time to relax after eating your lunch? I have a friend who could nap for 15 minutes at lunch and wake up as refreshed as I do after a full eight hours of sleep.

After work, can you run errands on your way home or while you are still out? It is definitely less time consuming to stop at a store you pass going home than it is to go home and then return to the store you passed. If you go out to do your laundry, can you do it once a week instead of two or three times? Remember, with three machines you can do three loads in the time it takes to do one. Can you use the time it takes to do the laundry for recreation or relaxation?

If you do laundry at home, can you adjust your schedule so that you put the laundry in before you start dinner? If you can, by the time you are finished the dishes, the laundry should also be finished.

In the Kitchen

What about cooking dinner? It takes almost as long to cook enough food for one meal as it does for two meals. If your refrigerator has any freezer room at all, consider cooking enough for two meals and freezing the leftovers. Then, when you want to go to a ball game or bowling but still want a hot meal, take the food out of the freezer in the morning, let it thaw in the refrigerator all day and just heat it up for dinner. Or you may want to make this type of outing one of those when you eat "fast foods."

As you are cooking, think of ways to nest the preparation of the meal so that you can do it concurrently instead of one step after the other. Prepare the item that requires the longest cooking time first. As it cooks, go to the next longest item and so on, which should leave the salad for last. By the time the salad is prepared, the rest of the meal should be ready to eat. It takes the same amount of time to brew one tea bag as it does to brew three or more bags. If you are going to make it for iced tea, brew three bags at a time and put the extra brewed tea in the refrigerator. By not mixing the lemon and sugar in it before refrigerating, it will stay clear and fresh for a couple of days. Or better yet, save a quart or larger clear glass jar and brew sun tea in your brightest window while you are at work, eliminating all preparation time.

Example

I have a routine that really saves me time in the mornings. I shower in the evening and lay out the clothes I am going to wear the next day. In the morning when I get up, I turn on the coffee maker, set up the night before, then I shave. Next, I do about ten minutes of exercise: toe touches, side bends and running in place. I have fixed a mirror in the utility room, which is where I shave because it is closest to the hot water heater -- instant hot water, and the kitchen. This saves time and steps. I then get dressed, make breakfast -- the coffee is ready, eat, and am easily ready to go to work within 30 to 40 minutes of getting up.

For breakfast I either have coffee, juice, fruit, and cereal or coffee, juice, fruit, and toast with jelly. When I take lunch, I try to make it the night before and leave it in the refrigerator. On those days I am running early, I may empty the dishwasher from the night before or, in the spring and summer, bring in some fresh cut flowers to brighten up our kitchen.

I mention my schedule for two reasons. One reason is to demonstrate that time management works, and the other is to demonstrate that, if you manage your time, you do not have to be rushed.

SUMMARY

Nowhere in this chapter have I discussed wasted time. I do not believe that people really waste time. I believe that, at times, we are all guilty of misusing time by not thinking about what we could be doing if we better managed our time.

Time management can be learned, but it is more by practice than by teaching. Sure, I could look at your personal schedule and say, "If you change the sequence of these items, or if you nested these items, or reduced the time you spend on these items, you will have more time." Doing this has no meaning unless the person is willing to make the changes to optimize the time.

Please do not forget your objective. The reason to manage time is to have more time to spend on those items you want to do for relaxation and recreation. Time management does not mean that you do everything faster and possibly less safe. Never sacrifice safety to gain a little time. To do so violates everything discussed in the previous chapter.

Be reasonable in what you try to do concurrently. Recently, I was on the freeway traveling at about 55 to 60 miles an hour when a station wagon passed me on my left. The vehicle was moving from side to side, and I thought the driver was either ill or intoxicated. I added a little gas and tried to see if the driver was ill. As I got a little closer, I realized that the gentleman, driving in excess of 70 miles per hour, had a mobile phone, in his right hand and a biscuit or some other sandwich in the other. As he tried to eat and talk on the phone, he had to keep juggling with his two hands to steer his automobile causing the erratic and unsafe behavior. This is not what is meant by time management.

This chapter presented some suggestions and examples for time management; now, it's your turn to take your inventory and try to increase the amount of time you have for fun.

EDUCATION
Learning can be fun and profitable!   33

You are probably asking yourself, what is a chapter on education doing in the section on recreation? The answer is simple. Recreation is some activity or pastime that you do for pleasure, enjoyment, or fun. Education, in the context presented in this chapter, definitely fits this definition. Not only that, some of the courses and classes I am going to discuss may even add money to your budget.

You may think now that you are out of high school, you do not have to have any more education. No one can make you go to school. Both of these sentences are only partially true, as Jo Ann found out.

NON-RECREATIONAL EDUCATION

Job Related

Jo Ann was at her new job with the Green Toe Nursery for only six weeks when her supervisor notified her and a couple of other new employees that they had been enrolled in a course on environmentally safe pest control for plants and flowers. The course would run for three days starting the following Tuesday and would be held during their normal work hours. They would receive full pay while attending the course. The supervisor further explained that the demand was high for the course and taking the course now would provide them training and understanding in a new and very popular aspect of the nursery business. In other words, those that successfully passed the course and practiced what they learned would have an edge over those individuals not having the course.

This example, using Jo Ann, is presented to dispel the idea that because you have a job and are out on your own, no one can make you go to school. You may be technically correct, however, your employer can take into consideration your refusal to attend school when evaluating your performance, assigning tasks, and definitely when making selections for promotions. This is reality. This is life in the work force.

Basic Education

There is another type of non-recreational education. This is education you decide to participate in with a fixed goal or objective in mind. Even though you may enjoy some or all of the courses, you have not enrolled in the courses simply for pleasure or enjoyment.

For example, if you do not have a high school diploma and decide to take evening courses to prepare for the High School Equivalency Exam, you are not doing so for recreation. Passing the High School Equivalency Exam is very important and something you should do at your earliest opportunity, but it is not done for pleasure or enjoyment. It is done to make yourself more marketable and to provide the foundation you must have before pursuing any form of formal higher education. When you complete the training and pass the exam, you will feel a strong sense of accomplishment which may allow you to look back on the training with a feeling of enjoyment. But, while you are taking the course, do not treat it with the same casual attitude you may treat a course taken for pleasure.

Advanced Credit

Other education of the non-recreational type would be evening classes taken for credit at a formal college, university, business or trade school where your objective is obtaining a degree or a better paying job. Since your main objective is not pleasure or enjoyment, the activity cannot be classified as recreation.

RECREATIONAL EDUCATION

You will find that you can get pleasure and enjoyment from education, especially now that the pressures of going to high school have ended. All courses that you decide to take need not earn you credits towards a degree. In fact, some of the classes you decide to take may not even be formal. When participating in education as recreation, the only motivation you need for taking a course is the desire to learn something new. If you can also earn credits or turn the new skill into extra dollars, that is an extra benefit but not the objective. What you are looking for is relaxation, pleasure, and enjoyment. If this goal is met, you will know it. You will look forward to attending the classes and will have no trouble finding the time to do the assignments. If you really want to learn, you can usually find courses available in just about any subject. And with current technology making the use of audio/video media so inexpensive, you don't even have to live in or near a large city or college town.

Courses Available

Practically every newspaper, magazine, and bulletin board contains offers to provide you with courses or training in just about any topic you can imagine. I admit I haven't seen too many advertisements for courses in brain surgery or meteorology but that is where the scarcity stops. If you look in your library, newspapers, magazines, and watch public TV channels, you will be deluged with offers for training and education.

There are numerous courses available in sports, including tennis, golf, bowling, archery, duck calling, fishing, snorkeling, skin diving, skating, skiing, and many more. If the arts are your preference, try painting, dancing, comedy, acting, sculpture, model building, photography, singing, ceramics, and so on.

You say you're more into crafts. Fine, there are many courses offered in picture framing, needlepoint, tole painting, furniture refinishing, sewing, stenciling, upholstering, PVC pipe furniture design and building, and even bread varnishing.

To develop or improve your skills, one or more of the following may be of interest: auto mechanics, auto body refinishing, woodworking, drafting, auto painting, typing, sheet metal, electricity, welding, pipefitting, electronics, accounting, business law, secretarial skills, word processing, computer operations, TV repair, and small appliance repair. This is only a small part of the list of available courses that teach trades or skills.

Courses for general self-development include: self-defense, stress management, communications, cooking, sewing, interior decorating, financial planning, foreign languages, and gardening. You can even find a course in managing your boss.

In addition to the above short lists of courses, most colleges and universities offer both formal and informal curriculums. In many cases, the courses may be taken in the evenings and on weekends allowing students to work part or full time, while still working towards a degree.

Where?

The widest known and most obvious places offering courses are colleges, trade and vocational schools, private business schools, computer schools and adult education centers. But there are many other less known and more exotic places that offer courses. Bowling alleys teach bowling; music stores usually offer courses in playing instruments and singing; golf courses have pros who offer courses to improve an amateur's swing or putting; and swimming and recreation centers offer a variety of sports related courses. By knowing what you are interested in learning and being aware of your surroundings, you will be able to find courses offered at what may seem strange places. With the universal use of VCRs and the inexpensive cost of video tapes, you can find many correspondence or self paced type courses available by purchase or rent through the mail. The advertisements for these are usually run in newspapers and magazines. Most large libraries lend, and many video rental stores rent, both instructional and "how-to" tapes.

In towns and cities with colleges close by, the colleges will usually put an insert or circular in the local newspaper at the beginning of each school session. Look in your yellow pages, under public schools, for vocational and trade schools or local high schools offering special adult education programs. Call the schools and ask what courses are available, and request that your name be placed on their mailing list.

Sporting goods stores, recreation centers, and fitness centers are great places to find out about courses to assist you in learning or improving your athletic or self protection skills. Speciality counters in large stores or speciality shops are excellent sources of information on courses for crafts, cooking, interior design, sewing, clothing design, music lessons, and many others. Many stores even offer beginning courses in these subjects as a method of promoting sales. Since these beginning courses are a form of advertising and marketing, the cost for taking them is usually small. The stores make their profit from the materials you buy, not from the tuition for the course.

Don't forget about the wealth of informal courses and instruction that is available. The advertisements for these types of instruction are usually found on bulletin boards of stores, libraries, and at work. Advertisements for personal training and tutoring are often found in neighborhood papers, flyers, church bulletins, and through word of mouth. Before signing an agreement or paying any money, satisfy yourself that the person can really teach what is advertised. The best way to do this is to ask for names of references and past students.

If you ever want to know more about a topic but don't seem to be able to find a course offered, call your library for assistance. If your library personnel are not able to help, call or visit a business that specializes in the use and/or services related to the topic you are interested in learning and ask for information on schools and classes that are offered in your local area. If the businesses really know their products, they will know where you, the customer, can obtain training.

What's the Cost?

Free

A wide range of training and education is available to everyone free of charge. Since nothing is really free, the above sentence means that you are already paying for a number of sources of education. These sources are available for us to use, at our own pace, without additional charge. Part of your tax money goes to parks, recreation centers, and the local library. The rest of your tax money is used to provide streets, police and fire protection, schools, and the other services provided by your local and state governments.

So, in effect, you have already paid for at least three sources of education: libraries, parks, and recreation centers. To make use of these sources you need to pay only a token fee for parks and recreation facilities or no fee at all for using public library.

Traditionally, because they are funded with your taxes, public libraries do not charge for the use of their services. However, they do charge for the abuse of services, for instance, keeping a book, tape, or video longer than the specified checkout period, or losing or damaging a checked out product. Each and every nickel charged in library fines or received as payment for a lost item is put back into the library system. So, when you pay a fine, remember that the money is going towards improving your library and its services.

The first place I suggest you go if you are interested in learning a new subject is your public or school library. This is true for any of the subjects discussed in this chapter or any other fields or subjects you can imagine, even brain surgery! There are two reasons for this suggestion. The first is that by checking out a couple of books, you can get an introduction to the complexities of the field or subject you are interested in. Second, since the use of the library is free, you have not invested any money if you decide the field is not what you thought it was.

Libraries contain a wealth of information in many forms. At most libraries, not only can you check out books on a wide range of subjects, you can also check out cassettes and video tapes, both for information and for self-paced training. Many larger libraries have courses on both cassettes and video tapes covering topics ranging from "An Introduction to Basic English" to "Advanced Geometric Design." Included in the range are many "How-to" tapes and cassettes covering sports, crafts, arts, vacationing, self development, and other topics. All of these are available for checkout, "free of charge."

Inexpensive

Parks and Recreation Centers

Since your taxes pay for parks and recreation centers, these agencies offer inexpensive courses to the public. Initially, courses offered by the public parks and recreation centers were devoted to sports or fitness related topics. Tennis, golf, swimming, and first aid lessons were some of the more popular adult courses, while "little league" sports and track events were offered for the younger group. In many areas, you can now find courses offered in a wide variety of subjects including public speaking, financial planning, crafts, painting, music, ceramics, square dancing, ballroom dancing, and landscaping.

You can expect to pay a registration fee and buy your own supplies for each course. The registration fee is usually small, $5 to $25. The registration fee pays for the instructor's salary and also forces a commitment from the student. You are more likely to complete a course you have paid for than one that is totally free. Additional costs for books and supplies is dependent on the type of course you enroll in.

Businesses

Courses offered by businesses that sell the materials used in the courses can either be free or cost a small registration fee. The logic is the same as with the parks and recreation courses. Companies know that by charging a small fee you feel a commitment to complete the course. Frequently, a company will include the training cost in the price of the product purchased. For example, computer stores offer free classes in operation and use of software purchased with a computer. Stores that sell pianos include six months of free lessons in the price of the instrument, even though they may advertise it as "...and receive six months of free lessons."

Hardware and building supply stores all offer many forms of training, from the free brochure on how to build bookshelves, to formal courses on the use of special new products. Currently, one of the stores in my area is offering free classes on installing and maintaining underground watering systems. The course is free and there is no obligation to purchase any merchandise, but the store owners hope the students of the classes will buy the supplies from them if they decide to install a system. In fact, just having the class in the store brings in potential customers for their other products, even if they do not buy any sprinkler system supplies.

In 1977, my wife, Jean, and our oldest daughter, Kim, enrolled in an outstanding course offered by Chrysler Corporation called "Women on Wheels (W.O.W.)." The cost was about $10 per person and the course was approximately 12 hours in length. It covered, in detail, the basic mechanical workings of an automobile with concentration on safety and normal maintenance requirements. At the conclusion of the course, the students could check and add all fluids, change tires, check for worn brakes, and test for and replace burned out fuses. Most importantly,

the graduates were aware of how a well running automobile sounded as compared to one needing a tune-up or transmission work. Today the course would be considered by some to be sexist because of the targeted students, however, I believe it should be added to all driver trainee programs and presented to both sexes.

Trade and Vocational Schools

Since state administered trade and vocational schools are also partly paid for with your tax money, the tuition charged for the offered courses may be quite small. In the early 1960s, I taught keypunch operations and programming courses for a trade and vocational school in Louisiana. The cost of the courses were under $25 each, plus supplies and books. In the past 25 years, the costs have not even doubled. This source of excellent education, encompassing many fields of study, should not be overlooked. You already have an investment in the school in the form of taxes paid. Additionally, the facilities are usually modern and well maintained, the curriculum is current, and the quality of instructors is excellent.

The cost of adult education courses offered by your local public school system should be affordable and cover a range of subjects of interest to adults. As funds become scarcer and scarcer, many public school systems have had to limit the course offerings for adults to the basic survival skills of reading and writing and preparation for taking the High School Equivalency Exam.

As with other forms of public education, the cost of this type of training is usually a token registration fee since the facility and instructors are provided by the taxpayers. Some schools will also have courses that have a wide application to the public, such as, preparing your own income tax return, health and hygiene, and living on a budget. A quick call to the local school board will bring you a schedule of all offered courses including times, costs, and an estimate of needed supplies.

More Expensive

Correspondence courses, courses taken through the mail or other self-paced courses, can be more expensive. Before signing up for one, consider whether the subject is one that can be learned from a text or through videos. If not, ask yourself and the company offering the course how and where you get the practical training. Some examples of the subjects that require physical skill development training are large (18 wheel) truck driving, house construction, ceramics, auto mechanics, TV/VCR repair, and com-puter operations/repair. I have recently seen newspaper or magazine advertisements offering to teach all of these topics in the convenience of the student's home. I will not say this is impossible, just that I would want more information. Since these courses can be very expensive, in some cases costing well over $1,000, you should request a copy of the contract in advance and be sure you understand it or check with your local Better Business Bureau before signing anything.

Expensive

College courses are generally the most expensive, especially if they are taken for credit towards a degree. If you are a part time student, most public colleges charge between $75 and $150 per credit hour. A part time student is one who is not enrolled in more than 11 hours of classes in any given semester. If your local college is on the quarter system and you are taking less than 15 quarter hours at one time, the costs will run between $45 and $70 per quarter hour. A quick method of converting semester hours to quarter hours is three semester hours equates to five quarter hours which usually makes up a course of instruction. Those courses requiring laboratory periods will have hours added in both the semester and quarter hour systems.

Most undergraduate degrees require about 123 semester or 215 quarter hours of instruction. If you multiply this requirement in hours by the cost per hour, you will find the tuition for a bachelor's degree at a public college in 1990 will cost between $9,000 and $18,000. Private -- non-tax-supported -- schools may cost as much as twice this range.

In addition to tuition, you will need books. You can expect to pay between $30 and $75, or even more, for new books for each course. My son, Chris, a full time student at the University of Arizona, is paying between $150 and $200 per semester for his primary books. He also has periodic requirements for supplemental texts and other supplies.

You can see that college is not cheap, in fact, going to college is very expensive. However, the pay back is tremendous, not only in earning potential but also in knowledge. If you are thinking seriously about getting a degree, do not let the cost bother you. There are still many ways for the serious student to get grants and loans, even if enrolled part time. The difference between grants and loans is that grants are gifts, usually based on need, and are for students who are carrying a full course load -- 12 or more semester hours -- and do not require repayment. Loans, on the other hand, are borrowed under a government-backed guarantee and must be repaid with interest. Between the two programs, and with all the variations, the serious student with a steady job usually need only worry about the immediate expenses of room and board. The cost for tuition, books, and fees can be deferred until after graduation when the student's earnings increase.

* * * N O T E * * *

If you are seriously thinking about enrolling in college to work towards a degree, do it now. With each year, as federal budget cuts are necessary, the Student Financial Aid Program is one of the first programs reduced. Make use of these programs while they still exist. Next year or the year after may be too late.

* * * * * *

If you are not interested in getting credit for the course, there is a less expensive way of taking college courses. Most colleges allow individuals to take selected courses without credit. This is usually called auditing the course. You still need your books, still pay for the course at about 50% reduced cost, still go to classes and learn the material, but, you do not take the exams and do not receive credit at the end of the course. For courses you wish to take for recreation purposes or basic knowledge, for instance, business math or introductory Spanish, this may be a very satisfactory option. By adding an additional savings of about 35%, by buying used books, to the savings in enrollment fees, you can take courses that cost between $255 and $500 for between $130 and $250. As an extra benefit, you have none of the pressure of preparing for exams. To get the most from this kind of arrangement, you must be committed to doing all of the assigned work, just as if you were taking the course for credit.

IN CONCLUSION

I know it is hard for the recent high school graduate to believe that education can be recreation. But education can be an activity that gives fun and enjoyment, relieves the stress and routine of working at a new job, and one that you can look forward to with pleasure.

Remember, we are discussing all forms of education, formal and informal, credit and non-credit, free and very expensive. It doesn't make any difference, if there is something you really want to know more about, then enroll in a course. Use your library first and then, when you are sure you are committed to learning a new topic, look for the best, least expensive, convenient way to obtain this new knowledge.

If you learn a new skill and using it adds to your income, so much the better. There are no rules that say you can't have fun while you earn money. In fact, this is the ideal situation. There are very few people who can say they really have fun doing what they do to earn a living.

There is a wealth of knowledge and learning opportunities available to just about everyone in this country. The pressure is off, all you need is a desire and commitment to learn.

There is another needlepoint hanging in my office also made by my daughter, Cindy, and it reads: "If you think education is expensive, try ignorance." This is the bottom line.

Have fun learning.

NOTES

SOURCES OF RECREATION
It's out there if you know where to look. 34

FUN ON A BUDGET

Do you want to have fun? Do you have a lot of money? If you are like most wage earners you answered "yes" to the first question and "no" to the second. So our task now is to identify the types and sources of inexpensive "fun."

For the last three chapters, we have been discussing some of the many things that people do for recreation or fun. In Chapter 31 we discussed mental and physical health and in Chapter 32 we looked at ways to manage our time so we have more time to devote to recreation. The last chapter introduced the concept of education as recreation, and, in this chapter, we are going to examine what other types and sources of recreation are available for the individual, on a budget, who wants and needs to have fun.

It doesn't make any difference if you call it fun, recreation, relaxation, pleasure, or enjoyment. You are talking about the same thing. Some activity that provides a change of pace, a way to help you cope with the drudgery and stress of being on your own and having a full time job. For this discussion, being enrolled in college is equal to having a full time job and being on your own.

Since you, like everyone else, are an individual, you already have a group of activities that provide your idea of "having fun." So far, these activities are based on background, including your environment, friends, and family. Now that you are on your own, you can be adventurous and try new and different activities. Many of these activities, though free or almost free, will provide many hours of fun and relaxation.

EXERCISE

As discussed in Chapter 31 under Physical Health, exercise is possibly the most important recreation you can do for yourself. By main-taining your physical health, you feel better and are able to reap the rewards of other recreation.

Where

Where you exercise depends mostly on what you have chosen as your exercise program and your personality. If you like to work alone and have a program consisting of floor exercise (i.e. toe touches, stretching, sit ups, leg ups, side straddle hops, and running in place) or you are using one of the video aerobic tapes, you will be able to exercise without leaving your home.

Programs that consist of walking briskly for one half to one hour, three times a week, can be completed in conjunction with going to or from work, going to the cleaners, or even doing light shopping. In this case, you will probably do your exercise right in your neighborhood. The same is true for jogging or riding your bicycle. In addition to convenience, this type of exercise program is very inexpensive.

Health Clubs (Gyms)

If you desire the companionship of others or want to use special exercise equipment or a swimming pool, you may have to join some form of "health" or "exercise" club. These clubs used to be called "Gyms." Before we get into this discussion too deep, there is one point I would like to make. In most cities it is not necessary to join a club so that you can walk or jog around a track 10 to 15 times a day. As discussed in the previous paragraph, you can participate in this kind of exercise, free of charge, right around your neighborhood or work .

Health or exercise clubs generally fall into four categories:

(1)   company sponsored,
(2)   contribution sponsored,

(3)   taxpayer sponsored, and
(4)   privately owned.

Company Sponsored

The most desirable, because of the benefits to you, is the company sponsored health club. Your company outfits an exercise room, provides for intramural sports, and may even have a pool for your use either during or after working hours. You have free access or pay a small monthly upkeep charge for the use of the facilities. The company benefits by having healthier employees, and you gain by having a convenient, inexpensive place to get some recreation. However, since this concept is not very widespread, let's look at the other options.

Contribution Sponsored

The "Ys," Young Men/Women Christian Associations -- YMCA and YWCA -- which were originally for just men or just women now cater to both sexes. They are called Christian Associations, however no religious affiliation is required of members -- anyone in the community may join. They are sponsored by charitable contributions which help defray the costs and keep the charge for membership at a less expensive rate than you will pay to belong to a private gym or health club. Most "Ys" provide complete indoor sports facilities including weights, supervised exercise and aerobic programs, swimming, racquetball, basketball, volleyball, tennis, and handball. Many of them even have quiet rooms for playing board and card games and reading.

The only complaints I have heard are that some of the facilities were built a number of years ago and the equipment is not always the most modern. Another factor that must be considered is that, because of their locations, they are not always easily accessible to people living in rural or suburban areas.

Taxpayer Sponsored

City, county, and state parks and gyms are facilities, funded by the taxpayers of the community where they are located, that provide a place for everyone to participate in a wide variety of recreation activities. Community pools, exercise areas, parks, and sports fields, as well as inner-city recreation houses and centers, are available in most medium to large size cities.

Not only do these facilities offer the same kinds of atmosphere as the "Ys," they cater to all ages and frequently offer more than exercise and sports activities. Most taxpayer sponsored recreation centers sponsor dances, parties, arts and crafts events, and field outings in addition to team and individual sporting events.

The major drawback is the popularity of the facilities which results in large numbers of members. If you find that you have difficulty using the equipment or facilities you desire, you will have to schedule your use of the facilities during the slack times.

The well run, well maintained, taxpayer sponsored recreation facility offers something for everyone at a very small cost. Depending on where you live, the cost of membership in the local recreation center can be as little as $10 to $25 per year, and the use of state and local parks and playgrounds is free.

Privately Owned

These operations are popping up all over, offering the latest in exercise facilities and programs. They are usually housed in modern, air conditioned buildings with trained professional staffs to assist in anything from setting up a personal diet or exercise program to organizing group sports and other activities. I have never been in one that was not visually impressive. The mirrors, the chrome, the latest equipment, and the large indoor swimming pools and tracks are all spectacular to see. You take one look at all this new, well maintained, and spotless equipment and you can feel the adrenalin building and see yourself achieving extraordinary physical feats. This is called visual marketing. The whole setup is designed not just for functionality but to visually stimulate. The more impressed you are, the easier it is to sell you a membership.

You need to be aware that private health or fitness centers may be dangerous to the health of your budget. Initially, you will be signed up under some form of special introductory membership. It may be a special six months membership for just $10 a month, maybe a two-for-one special, a new opening special, or some other form of high interest offer.

Once you have joined, each time you visit the facility you will be asked to buy either a one year or a "lifetime" membership. The goal is to sell you the "lifetime" membership, and though it is hard to understand from an economics point of view, the longer you hold out, the more appealing the management will make the lifetime membership. The cost of the membership will either be reduced in price, the monthly maintenance fee will be lowered, or you will be offered other incentives like a free massage every month for the first 12 months.

During this time, the management will be reminding you that your special membership is temporary and will expire shortly. They will also point out that the regular monthly dues is two to three times what you are now paying, and a "lifetime" membership only costs the total of one and a half or two years full dues.

All of the above statements are true, the catch is in the term "lifetime." In most states a "lifetime" warranty or guarantee is good only for the life of the company not for the "lifetime" of the buyer. If the company goes bankrupt or sells out to another buyer or simply closes its doors, the "lifetime" membership is terminated. This is true even if the business opens up the next day under new owners.

I am not implying that all "lifetime" memberships are traps or frauds, simply that as a smart, expense conscious shopper be sure you understand and accept the terms and conditions of any contract before you sign. Be aware of reality, look around the fitness center, ask some questions, and do some calculations. How many members does the center have? What is the monthly maintenance fee? How long has the center been in business under the same owners?

Example

Suppose Jo Ann is considering buying a "lifetime" membership in the Muscle Tone Fitness Center which is a new large health center currently offering discounted introductory memberships at $15 a month for six months. The facility is housed in a two story, 20,000 square foot building outfitted with everything Jo Ann wants in a fitness center, including a large indoor swimming pool.

The Sales Pitch

On Jo Ann's sixth visit, she is stopped by the receptionist (salesperson) who explains that Jo Ann has been recommended for one of the very limited -- only 1,500 -- lifetime memberships. She also explains that the memberships usually cost $750 and after that there is just a maintenance fee of $5 per month. For Jo Ann, because she is young and does not have a lot of money, her "special" deal is a lifetime membership for just $550 and the first year's maintenance is free.

Because Jo Ann hesitates a little, the receptionist quickly adds that Jo Ann can even pay for her lifetime membership through easy payments. There is a down payment of $100 followed by 12 monthly payments of $40 each. At just 12% interest, she will pay $30 in interest charges. The offer is only for one week, and if she doesn't take the offered deal, she will have to pay dues of $30 each and every month of her membership after the introductory membership expires.

The Facts:

Jo Ann really likes the center and considers buying a "lifetime" membership. After listening to the management and doing some simple arithmetic she compiles the following list of facts:

(1) Management claims the center costs one million dollars.
(2) The club is open 24 hours a day and has a staff of 15 counselors, three office personnel, plus management.
(3) All 1,500 lifetime memberships can be bought for what she was offered -- $550, resulting in income of $870,000 -- 1,500 times $550.
(4) Fifteen hundred lifetime members paying $5 a month only adds up to a monthly income of $7,500.
(5) The contract states that the "initial lifetime membership drive is for 1,500 members," not that lifetime membership will be limited to 1,500 members.
(6) There is no limit on the number of non-lifetime members, and they each pay $30.00 a month.

Using the above information, Jo Ann arrives at the following conclusions:

If all lifetime membership fees are applied to the cost of the facility (one million dollars), the facility will not be paid for. The fees fall $230,000 short. If there are no non-lifetime members, $7,500 a month will not come close to paying for utilities, insurance, and upkeep, not to mention salaries for 18 employees, all of whom are supposed to be trained professionals.

The Decision:

Jo Ann decides not to become a lifetime member but still decides to join the center and pay the $30 a month from her personal and entertainment budget amounts. She likes the location, the facilities -- especially the pool -- and the counselors. She figures that if she uses the facilities just three times a week her cost is $2.50 a visit, which she feels is worth the expense.

You should go through the same process before signing a contract for a "lifetime" health club membership. In most cases, once the contract is signed, the membership is not transferable either by you or by the company. If you move, you do not get any money back, and if the company sells out, at the very best, you may have to go to court to collect even a small part of your expense.

Cheap Thrills

This title is appropriate because, for the person interested in exploring the many opportunities for having fun, there is an unlimited range of activities, in addition to exercise, that are free or very inexpensive. We have discussed a number of these in Chapter 31, now let's take a closer look.

Under this heading, we have activities that include sports, the arts, hobbies and crafts, and, as discussed in the last chapter, education.

There is very little cost in participating in most team sports except for the purchase of appropriate clothing and shoes. The same is true about walking, jogging, hiking, and camping. Being a spectator is even less costly. For many of the amateur sporting events held at recreation centers and parks, there isn't even an admission fee.

Many hours of free recreation and entertainment are available through your local library. Not just in the books that are waiting to be checked out, but also in the form of cassettes, compact discs, and video tapes. Larger libraries offer additional free entertainment in the form of lectures, music, and even art shows featuring local, national, and international artists. All of these forms of recreation are available at little or no admission fee.

Church groups, high schools, colleges, and amateur dance and theatre groups all sponsor entertainment that ranges from the classical to the contemporary. My family and I have attended many first rate presentations of plays, musicals, and concerts for minimal admission fees. In some cases, we were just asked to make a donation. Generally, these presentations are not crowded since there is not much money to spend on a big advertisement campaign. So, the individuals that seek out this type of entertainment not only obtain the enjoyment of excellent performances but, by arriving a little early, are guaranteed prime seating.

Obviously, listening to the radio, stereo, or watching TV, once the appliance is owned, does not cost very much. The only cost is in the use of electricity and the depreciation on the appliance. In the present economy, neither of these costs are worth considering. Radios, TVs, and stereos cost just pennies a day to operate, about as much as providing yourself with light to read.

Reducing Costs

Reading library books instead of buying your own, listening to cassettes and compact discs from the library, and attending sponsored shows and concerts are all ways to reduce the high cost of recreation and entertainment. The examples presented in the earlier chapters should not be considered a complete list of what's available. The individual looking for fun on a budget has to make use of all the options including renting expensive sports equipment instead of buying it. Skis, scuba diving equipment, skates, tools for hobbies, golf bags and clubs, and camping gear are just some of the costly recreation items that can be easily and inexpensively rented.

The cost of renting equipment must be balanced against the cost of buying the same items. If you are going to use the item only once or twice a season or the item is very expensive, renting instead of buying is a valid option. For instance, renting a pair of skis and poles as part of a ski package may cost as little as $10 per day compared with buying your personal set which could easily cost in excess of $250. If you go skiing only two or three times a year, renting the equipment is definitely a way to save money. People have been doing this for years. Every time someone rents a limousine or books a charter fishing trip, they are doing the same thing. Very few of us can afford to own a stretch limousine or a boat large enough to take us on a deep sea fishing trip, so, when we want to use these services, we rent them.

The item being rented does not have to be expensive. It can be of limited use as with movie videos. The renting of movie videos is a multi-million dollar a year industry based on the fact that movies and similar items that are used only once or infrequently are definitely cheaper to rent than to buy. If you own or can rent or borrow a video cassette player, you can watch three to five current movies for the cost of just one single admission to the movie theater. You can even reduce the cost more by either viewing the movies with a group of friends or sharing or swapping them. If you swap rented movies or items you borrow from the library, remember the person that signed the rental receipt or checked out the items is responsible for returning the items in good condition and on time.

Pay With Service

Your time is worth money. Using it provides another great way to reduce the cost of your recreation. You get paid by serving as a guide, chaperon, or assistant with a church, scout, or other charitable organization. Though you do not get paid in cash, you still get paid. Your pay is in the form of transportation, admission, and meals that are made available when you assist a needy group.

The groups may be made up of the elderly, the handicapped, the young or any mix of individuals that require a little assistance from a healthy and responsible individual.

Many forms of entertainment such as tours, concerts, entertainment parks, camping and nature trips, canoe and raft trips, sporting events, circus and ice skating shows can all be free of charge. All it costs is your willingness to give of your time and attention. Ninety five percent of the time you will be able to fully enjoy the entertainment. You should never be on your own. There are always one or two paid professionals with the group that you are assisting. You are there to assist by monitoring and helping the less demanding members of the group, allowing the professionals to handle emergencies and care for the individuals requiring special attention.

Just recently my wife, Jean, assisted one of the local elderly care centers on a trip to a botanical garden during azalea week. For her, it was a free half day trip including transportation, admission, and lunch. All she had to do was to assist some of the older members of the group on and off the train, help keep track of where everyone was, and see that their individual needs were met. There was no special training required and the professionals were always there if needed. She had a great day touring a really beautiful garden.

This is not a rare situation. Church groups, scout groups, social services, and centers for the elderly are always looking for energetic, fun loving, responsible individuals willing to serve as an assistant or chaperon for a sponsored needy group.

Do you ski? Can you assist a group of 12 and 13 year old students on a ski trip in return for free transportation, lift ticket, and equipment? Your cost will be to make sure no one gets lost, mend a few broken spirits and help a fallen skier or two. You will have plenty of time to hit the slopes while the kids are taking skiing classes or involved in other activities.

What about a free week long camping trip including transportation, meals, and equipment? Your cost may be guiding some of the members on hikes, overseeing the cleaning and cooking of some meals, and treating insect bites and minor scrapes and scratches. Or would you be interested in a free day of rafting down your favorite river? Your cost: making sure the kids have on their life jackets and follow the professional guides' instructions.

If you are interested in any of the above, you are a much needed resource. The opportunity is there. All you have to do is let the organizations that sponsor these types of activities in your community know of your interest and willingness to help. Once the word gets out that you want to volunteer your services, your assistance will be requested. You benefit by having some of your recreation provided without affecting your budget, and the people you help benefit by having the opportunity for recreation that would not be available without your help.

SUMMING IT UP

No matter what label you use, relaxation, fun, entertainment, pleasure, or enjoyment, recreation is available. Not only is it available but, contrary to popular belief, it does not have to cost a lot of money.

If you like the atmosphere of a gym or health club, use your yellow pages to locate those that are public and check out their facilities. If you decide to join a private health club, be sure to read and understand the contract before you sign and pay any money. Whenever the word "lifetime" is used in a contract, be sure you understand what or whose lifetime is being discussed.

There are many, many activities that you can do alone or with groups of friends that will result in recreating yourself and assist in coping with the stress of your daily routine. However, be careful. I know individuals that have managed to completely remove recreation from recreation. They have done this by treating their pleasure the same way they treat their job. It is scheduled, hurried, enjoyed(?), and forgotten so that every-thing else can get finished. No matter what the cost, this is not recreation. The most spectacular, expensive cruise or even trip-around-the-world will fail miserably in meeting the objective of recreation if experienced under these conditions. To maximize your pleasure, review your options, look for new, interesting and fun things to do, and then shop around for the lowest cost. Like the other expenses discussed in this book, recreation can be shopped for and you can and should optimize your return. This includes using what you have to offer, yourself and your time, in return for reduced or eliminated expense.

NOTES

_____

_____

_____

_____

_____

_____

_____

_____

_____

_____

_____

_____

_____

_____

_____

COMPLETING YOUR SURVIVAL KIT

Making it all work!

IX

Woven throughout the first eight sections of this book is a discussion of the four tools that your survival kit must contain. They are: setting objectives or goals, positive motivation, obtaining knowledge, and resourcefulness. The first three are the foundation of all problem solving and decision making and the fourth determines the method and effectiveness of implementing your decision or problem solution.

An example: You are lost. I know this is hard to believe, but it does happen. You are on your way to a party, and, even though you followed the instructions, you find yourself driving around in circles. There is no question that in this situation, the objective (locating the party), as well as the motivation (partying), are present Under the heading of knowledge, you have the name and address of the friend who is hosting the party, the fact that you can drive, and the fact that you can communicate.

Simply stated, the problem is that you want to be at the party, and you are not.

Resourcefulness enters the situation in how you decide to correct your problem. Do you:

(a)   continue to drive around all night hoping you will eventually find the party?

    (b)   stop and ask for directions?

    (c)   find a phone, look up the phone number of your host or hostess, and call for assistance?

    (d)   find another way of quickly finding the party's location?

Even for this simple problem your action depends on your level of resourcefulness. Unfortunately, there are a large number of people who will select and act on choice (a).

Chapter 35 will define, demonstrate the meaning of, and restate some examples of using resourcefulness previously covered in the first 34 chapters of this book.

This section and the book conclude with **Chapter 36** which contains some of my favorite reflections, phrases, and expressions which you may find interesting and thought provoking.

RESOURCEFULNESS
The McGuyver Syndrome.

35

Possibly the most important key to your ability in overcoming life's hurdles and surviving with a minimum amount of wear-and-tear on your pocketbook and person is resourcefulness. Resourcefulness is defined as: "the ability to deal skillfully and promptly with new situations and difficulties." Most dictionaries then list ,as synonyms, the words: "inventiveness," "adaptability," "ingenuity," and "cleverness."

SKILL

If everything that we do falls into either of two categories, art or skill, then resourcefulness falls into the skill category. A skill can be learned and generally does not require that an individual be born with abilities or talents that are not available in the general population. On the other hand, to be a great singer, musician, or artist requires that the individuals be born with unique abilities and talents.

As a skill, resourcefulness can be learned, which means that the majority of this earth's inhabitants can be taught or teach themselves to be more resourceful. Most individuals develop a degree of resourcefulness by the hit-and-miss method of gaining experience. However, I believe the skill should be taught in school through a structured program requiring the individual to cope with progressively more difficult problems. These problems can either be real or fictitious. In either case, the degree of the individual's resourcefulness would have to be measured and the individual would be given feedback on performance and recommendations for improvement.

Resourcefulness should not necessarily be taught as a separate subject, but, rather, every time a student is exposed to any form of problem solving, the exercise should emphasize resourcefulness.

Once the basics of being resourceful are taught, the skill is honed and developed by practice.

THE CONCEPT

To be resourceful you must develop the following faculties:

(1)   Awareness
(2)   Knowledge
(3)   Ability to relate knowledge and awareness to the situation
(4)   Ability to act once the relationship is completed

Though formal training would be helpful in developing these faculties, you can develop them on your own by following some of the methods presented in the first eight sections of this book. As a review, I will present each briefly.

Awareness

You should get into the habit of being aware of your surroundings at all times. In Chapter 31, under the heading of "Mental Health," I discussed awareness of self and surroundings. This was a formal exercise requiring you to actually ask specific questions and write down the answers. The awareness being presented now is very similar but less formal. It involves the constant collection of data, and, through discipline, the mentally stored data is recalled as needed.

One of the best techniques currently being taught to develop this awareness is the one used in defensive driving courses. To be a defensive driver, you must consider that the other drivers on the highway will make mistakes and that you will need to immediately react to these mistakes. To be prepared, you are taught to constantly let your senses feed back to your mind the status of your immediate surroundings.

The type of feedback might be: the car on the left is gaining speed and will be in front of you very shortly, the car behind you has just put on its right blinker, but there is no room for it to pull over at this time; you, the car on your right, and the car immediately in front of you are all driving at the same constant speed.

While your mind is collecting this data, your eyes are also looking ahead, and your mind records the fact that you will be approaching an on ramp to the highway, and there is a solid stream of cars entering the traffic pattern. Though the cars entering the highway from the on ramp are not entering your lane, some of the cars in the lane to your right are pulling over into your lane to allow this traffic to smoothly enter the highway. Using this data and your current status (car in front at constant speed, car on right at constant speed, car on left accelerating, and car behind looking to change to the right-hand lane), you mentally run through a number of "what if" questions and try to anticipate your required action if someone makes a mistake. The result is enhanced awareness.

Starting with the first chapter, when you were looking for available jobs, every time I discussed taking an inventory or the need to identify your options you were encouraged to increase your awareness. This was true even in the previous chapter when the recommendation was made to look for agencies and organizations needing assistance, so that by providing the needed assistance you could stretch your limited recreation dollars. Every chapter in this book contains these types of suggestions that, if followed, will expand your awareness.

Knowledge

Everything new that you do should result in an expansion of knowledge The wider your scope of knowledge and understanding of your environment, things, and how they work, the greater the degree of your resourcefulness.

Everything that the star does in the television program McGuyver, no matter how farfetched, is possible. Being in situations, week after week, that require that degree of resourcefulness is not realistic, but everything he does is technically accurate. Since the sum of an individual's understanding provides the individual's level of knowledge, a real life McGuyver would need a vast understanding of things, how they work, and how they interact.

To demonstrate the value of obtaining knowledge, let's look at a couple of stories.

Desert Island

This story is about the discovery of a small island in the middle of the ocean. The discoverers are drawn to the island because of a bright reflection which they at first believe to be some form of wreckage. As they draw nearer to the island, it appears inhabited because what they first thought was wreckage is, at a closer look, a small structure made of tin cans. Thinking they may be in time to rescue the inhabitants, they hail the island.

They receive no response. On landing, they realize they have arrived too late.

Inside the structure they find the remains of an adult male dressed in a type of native costume. The costume consists of a shell necklace, a loincloth made of palmetto leaves, and sandals made from tree bark. With the body, they find a half of coconut shell and a sharp stone knife. The question they ask themselves is: "How did this man die?"

Without question, the man was resourceful. Using plants to clothe himself, stone to provide a cutting implement and the cans to provide shelter demonstrates an awareness, knowledge, and the ability to not only relate but to act. Unfortunately, his knowledge level was lacking. The results of the autopsy were conclusive. He died of starvation.

He did not know that food is stored in cans, so he died of starvation, while using hundreds of cans of fruit for shelter.

Child-proof(?) Containers

This is a story that was passed to me as fact. I do not know if it is true, but I lean towards believing it. The story takes place a number of years ago when the public was concerned about children being poisoned by accidentally swallowing adult prescription drugs. The government sponsored an all out effort to develop child-proof medicine containers.

Engineers worked on developing twist caps that could not be twisted unless they were pushed down and turned at the same time and caps that had to have the arrows match up before they could be pried apart. Some screw-on caps required that an individual press down or pull up at the same time they were turned. All of the new designs were based on adult levels of dexterity and strength.

As the story goes, one of the engineers, very

pleased with the laboratory results that showed that no normal child under 10 years of age could have the strength to open the newest pill bottle, took one home. That evening, he filled the pill bottle with small candies and told his three-year-old daughter that if she could open the bottle she could have the candy.

The young girl tried once to twist off the cap and once to pry off the cap. Neither attempt to open the container worked. Without hesitation, the child picked up one of her larger wooden toys and, without expending much effort, crushed the plastic pill bottle and ate the candy. Her awareness and knowledge that plastic could be crushed resulted in a very high level of resourcefulness.

These containers are still among the ones used today because the engineers decided that her behavior was not representative of the normal three year old. What do you think?

Ability to Relate

Being fully aware of your surroundings and having a high level of knowledge does not necessarily make an individual resourceful. In addition, you must be able to relate what you know and are aware of to your given problem or situation. An outstanding demonstration of the inability to relate awareness and knowledge to a situation is contained in a very bad joke: "Have you ever heard the story about the man who could not roll up his car windows in the rain because his doors were locked?"

In the story about the child-proof pill bottles, the engineers decided the three-year-old girl's behavior was not normal. They felt that most children her age would not relate crushing as an option for opening pill bottles. That was an unfortunate decision on the part of the engineers, they were thinking like educated adults.

Having raised five children, three girls and two boys, and speaking from experience, I can attest that the child's behavior was not only natural, it should have been anticipated. I have seen my children go through herculean efforts to get to forbidden cookies or candy. If they knew where they were stored and decided they wanted one, their level of resourcefulness could be unbelievably high.

The ability to relate knowledge and awareness to a given situation is what keeps us from making the same mistake two or, for some of us, three times. We call it learning from experience, but, in reality, this learning is simply relating what we learned before in a similar situation to the present.

The phrase, "Necessity is the mother of invention" fits nicely here. The truth, however, is that two people faced with the same set of circumstances and in the same environment will not react the same because of differing levels of awareness, knowledge, and ability to relate.

This ability to relate does not have to be complex nor does the situation have to be a life or death one. Just about everyone in the United States knows that there are garage sales held in every city on just about every weekend, yet not everyone relates this fact to their own needs. The same is true of thrift stores, used clothing and furniture stores, and clothing rental shops.

An example of using one's ability to relate is illustrated in the following story. My son-in-law, Mike, the first year of their marriage, decided to cook the Easter meal for he and my daughter, Cindy. The meal was all planned and the meat portion of the meal was going to be glazed canned ham. When he had everything together, he thought that while the ham was cooking and the oven was on, he would surprise Cindy by baking a cake. Since it was Easter, he wanted it to be in the shape of an Easter Egg. The problem was they were newlyweds, just starting out, and didn't have any fancy shaped baking pans.

Mike searched all through the kitchen cabinets for something he could use, but it was obvious they didn't own any pan or baking dish resembling an egg that could be used to bake a cake. But, while he was checking the ham being baked, he was struck by its egg-shaped appearance. He related the shape of the ham with the shape of an egg and the fact that the ham had been packaged in a sealed metal container. In just a minute, he had his baking pan, and they enjoyed an egg shaped cake at the conclusion of their special Easter meal.

What made Mike relate the shape of the ham's container to that of an egg, when someone else might not have? No one really knows. I now find the relationship very obvious, but, before he told me this story I hadn't given it any thought. Was it his level of awareness? I don't know. He was very motivated and wanted very much to have an egg shaped cake. Maybe that is the answer. Whatever the reason, he was able to relate, and it worked.

Inability to Relate

On the negative side, every year the inability to relate what we know to a given situation costs lives. Not just a few, but many. One example is the damage to property and lives caused by people smoking in bed. Every smoker knows that a cigarette can light fires. They also know that cigarette ash burns. I have yet to meet a smoker that has never been burned or had spots burned in their clothing by ashes from a cigarette. Everyone also knows that bed linens are flammable. Yet for some strange reason, smokers continue to fall asleep while smoking in bed, killing themselves, their loved ones, and destroying millions of dollars of property each and every year.

I do not have a vendetta against smokers, I have done the same thing with my pipe, which is one of the reasons I no longer smoke. I found that I most enjoyed my pipe sitting in my favorite lounge chair, watching evening television programs. Unfortunately, I sometimes fell asleep with my pipe in my mouth, and when it fell, dumping ashes all over the place, I would be quickly awakened. When this happened, I could not be sure that some of the ash had not fallen into the bottom of the chair between the seat and the sides. I finally scared myself awake enough times and burned holes in my clothes enough times to stop smoking. But this lack of ability to relate is not just with smokers.

Every day children are poisoned by eating house plants or ingesting household cleaners or insecticides. People cut themselves by handling sharp knives while their hands are wet, and cars are driven with faulty and worn brakes. Everyone responsible knows better and is aware of the potential danger, but for some reason this knowledge and awareness is not related to their present situation.

Ability to Act

For you to use your resourcefulness, you must either be in control or be able to influence those who are in control. There will be times when the factors, knowledge, awareness and ability to relate, will be present, but you will be unable to act. These situations will usually occur while you are on the job or otherwise not in control of the situation. When they do occur, I suggest you remember the *Serenity Prayer* presented in Chapter 31 and try not to become too frustrated.

One of the reasons that the star of the *McGuyver* television series is always able to get out of the threatening situations is that his enemies always leave him some level of control.

If he were secured, spread eagle, to a wall with both hand and foot shackles tightly fastened, all the knowledge, awareness, ability to relate, and a vast store of available materials would not help him to escape. However, he still would be able to plan for action in case the situation altered in his favor.

The ability to act is not just physical, it is also mental. To be resourceful, you must be able to be decisive, you must be prepared to make the decision to act on your knowledge, awareness, and ability to relate.

Indecisiveness appears to be something we learn as we grow up and is affected by our consideration of possible consequences. The young girl, in the earlier story, when she wanted to get to the candy, was not restricted by the consequences of crushing the pill bottle. Yet the engineers did not even consider crushing as a way to open the bottle, because crushing is not an accepted "adult" or "civilized" method for opening things.

I am not suggesting that you throw caution and safety out of the problem-solving equation, only that you not let thoughts of possible consequences keep you from considering all options. If you restrict the options you feel are available to only those that are without consequence, you will not be using your full level of resourcefulness. Once you have all the options, you can use possible consequences as a screening factor.

More Examples

Doing one of the following demonstrates a "lack of resourcefulness": While looking for a job, you do not use friends and family to create a network, as recommended in Section I of this book, because you don't want it to seem that you can't find a job on your own.

On your job, you do not make suggestions for improving quality or performance, because you feel your suggestion may not be approved.

You do not shop for the best deal in banking services, because the bank's personnel may think you're strange, or you will feel embarrassed asking for the information.

You disregard carpooling as a transportation option, because you don't want to put someone out of their way or be a burden.

You don't ask your co-workers and friends for housing recommendations, because of the same reasons that you do not carpool.

You don't ask friends or family for excess furniture or utensils, because they may think you are begging.

You don't use thrift stores for furniture, kitchen, and clothing purchases, because you will be embarrassed if someone you know sees you shopping at that type of store.

You don't ask for a price reduction at a garage sale, because to do so embarrasses you.

You don't try a new recipe, because you are not sure how it will taste.

You don't seek medical or professional help when your body sends you the signals that help is needed, because you don't like doctors, or you are afraid of finding out what's wrong.

You do not tell the slob you are sharing an apartment with that you want to terminate the arrangement, because you may hurt his or her feelings.

The list of examples of not being resourceful goes on and on, and we are all guilty of some of them, because they are the "safe" solutions. Remember, the decision not to take control or act in a given situation is action in itself. It may be passive on your part, but letting a bad situation continue or not being resourceful when faced with a problem will probably result in a less than desirable solution.

As with defensive driving, all of us can learn to be more resourceful than we presently are.

The Ultimate Example

It was early morning and already hot on that Sunday in August 1982, when my daughter, Cindy, her future husband, Mike, and two of their friends decided to drive from El Paso, Texas, to Carlsbad, New Mexico. The distance was only 166 miles, but many of these miles are through some very sparsely settled, desert-like country.

About half way between El Paso and Carlsbad, the 1969 Chevelle's generator light came on, and Mike quickly pulled over to the shoulder of the road. Looking under the hood, Mike discovered that the generator (that recharges the battery) was not working (the drive shaft was frozen). Since the battery was new, the four travelers decided not to let this minor inconvenience stop them from enjoying their outing, and they continued their journey.

Within 10 miles, the fan belt broke, either from normal wear and tear or due to the friction caused by the frozen shaft on the generator.

Without a fan belt the engine would quickly overheat in the desert, and what started out as a fun trip would end a disaster. As Mike surveyed the situation, he remembered that the battery was being held in place by an old fan belt. Hoping that they would not hit any bad bumps in the road and the battery would stay in place without being secured, Mike put the old belt on the engine, and they drove toward Carlsbad. Stopping a number of times, they were able to get a few gallon jugs of water for the radiator, but our travelers were unable to find an open auto parts store or a service station that had the right size belt in stock.

Arriving at Carlsbad, only a little late, the group decided to tour the caverns and get an early start back. At this time, Mike was in the Army and needed to report back to work early Monday morning. So, after a quick tour of the caverns, they filled the jugs with water and, with a short prayer, started back to El Paso.

The return trip was not to be uneventful. As soon as they had covered enough miles to get out of the city of Carlsbad, too far to walk back, the engine started to overheat. The replacement belt had broken. While standing on the side of the deserted road, one of the group lightly commented that they had been in this identical situation just that morning, the only difference was the car was facing the other way. The big question was, what to do? Something was needed that would provide a snug closed loop around the engine pulley and the water pump.

Cindy was wearing a black elastic belt. It was a perfect fit, and the four travelers continued on their homeward journey. Unfortunately, the belt only lasted a few miles before it broke. This time, the women offered to sacrifice their bras to the effort, but they were not long enough. They considered just adding water to the radiator and hoping the engine would stay cool until they reached the next source of water, but that idea was discarded as not practical since no one knew how far it was to the next service station.

Someone hit on the idea of using shoe laces, and everyone donated their laces to the cause. They were tied together and provided some (not very many) additional miles before joining the two fan belts and the elastic belt somewhere on the highway. As they considered their remaining alternatives, our four weary travelers were now frustrated, hot, tired, and all looked like hoodlums, standing in shoes without laces, on the side of the road.

While rummaging through the trunk for the fourth time, Mike discovered some old discarded speaker wire. They decided that if they could get it tight enough, since it was wire, it might get them home. So, it was wrapped a number of times around the two pulleys and tightly secured. Mike started the engine and everyone sighed with relief as the fan and water pump turned. They hopped back into the car and were again homeward bound. The wire did well but not well enough. Approximately 100 miles north of El Paso, it too joined the rest of the junk on the highway .

By this time, our travelers had almost lost their sense of humor. This was getting a little old, and they were thinking that this could not be happening in 1982. This is a country of bounty, everything is supposed to be available when needed. Why no fan belt?

This time, they did a complete inventory. The trunk only had a spare tire and some small tools and there was nothing inside the car that could be used for a fan belt. The girls' bras were too small, and their tops and shorts would not hold up under the stress. The guys were wearing T-shirts, jeans, and jockey undershorts. Like magic, the light went on, and they all thought of the same solution. Jockey shorts have a closed loop elastic band. A closed loop equals a fan belt, and a fan belt meant getting home. Mike's friend stripped, and the jockey shorts were reduced to just a waist band. Not only did the 30-inch elastic band fit snugly but it turned the fan and water pump.

Back in the car and on the road, each of the passengers thought that it wouldn't be long before the engine would overheat again indicating that the elastic waist band had broken. The miles passed, the temperature gauge didn't move past the normal indication, and the mood in the car changed to one of good humor, and the holiday atmosphere returned. Our travelers finally returned home, a little late and a little tired, but still in good spirits.

Not only did the waist band from the jockey shorts get them home, but it was still working when the car was brought into the auto shop for a new belt on Monday. The mechanic thought someone was pulling a joke on him and wanted to know where the camera was.

The brand of the jockey shorts? Suppose I answer that question this way: the travelers in our story summed up their gratitued unanimously saying "Bless you, Inspector 12!"

SUMMARY

By reading this book, you have demonstrated that you are resourceful or at least that you are interested in gaining data and knowledge. Through practice and conscious effort, you can improve on your resourcefulness. You do this by increasing your awareness, adding to your knowledge, relating what you know to your surroundings and/or problems, and by acting on this relationship.

All four of these faculties must be present to be resourceful. Any one or two of the items, by themselves, will not only not help you but may increase your sense of frustration. Just having an awareness of your surroundings and an ability to act, without having the knowledge and relationship skills, will not help you be resourceful. Neither will knowledge and the ability to relate unless you also possess awareness and an ability to act.

You are constantly adding to your level of knowledge and should also be adding to your level of awareness, which only leaves the ability to relate and the ability to act as tools to sharpen. The ability to relate can be enhanced by playing the "What if?" game with yourself. Everyone should play this game. It works just like the defensive driving course. You make up situations, and then ask yourself "What if ...?" At home, you may ask yourself, "What if there were a fire and I could not get out the front door?" Or, "What if my car will not start tomorrow and I must get to work by ...?" And then there is, "What if the company I work for goes bankrupt and I lose my job?"

The questions you ask in the game do not even have to be this serious. You can try, "What if I do not have enough money left in my budget to pay all my bills at the end of this month?" Or, "What if I meet a friend and want to invite them for a meal at my apartment?" The objective of the "What if" game is not to worry or to be negative, but to develop your options ahead of time and increase your resourcefulness, should one of these situations, or something totally unexpected, happen.

This book has presented what I believe to be a wealth of information and thought-provoking exercises to expand your list of options. It is not the answer to your survival, only a tool. You determine your own survival success by how you develop your resourcefulness and your skill in using the tools available.

THOUGHTS

36

In December 1988, before I started writing this book, I sent our children a letter. The letter was written when I was in a thoughtful mood and expressed our (Jean and myself) love for them and contained the following list of thoughts, statements, sentences, and adages I have found to be true and/or useful in my life.

I do not take credit for any of these as original thought. Some are paraphrases of famous statements, some are statements or phrases I have heard, and others have been modified to reflect my personal beliefs and experiences.

I share these with you, not as a set of rules, or for your acceptance, but to provide some food for thought. I feel that they are a fitting conclusion for this "Survival" manual.

Treat all other persons you may come in contact with as if they are at least equal to you both mentally and physically.

Never do anything intentionally to hurt yourself or anyone else.

Do not waste your time on:
    regrets,
    grudges,
    hate.

Learn and understand your abilities and limitations.

Try to use your abilities fully.

Always try to reduce your limitations.

Try to leave this life knowing that mankind is a little better off for you having been born.

Allow everyone to die with dignity.

Work for world peace, but not at the expense of human rights or free will.

Remember that there is always someone who knows more than you on any given subject. Learn to use that person's knowledge but never the person.

Always play to win, but learn to gracefully accept loss when fairly beaten.

A day without learning something is a wasted day.

Treat your spouse and children with the same love and respect you have for yourself.

A "good marriage" may be made in Heaven, but it takes constant maintenance and hard work here on Earth to survive the test of time.

Forgiveness for yourself and others is one of the keys to good mental health.

The mind does control the body but only to a point. Know when to seek advice for your physical well-being.

An ounce of prevention is worth a ton of correction.

The greater joy and pleasure is in what you leave, never in what you take.

Look forward to tomorrow with great expectations.

If you truly have faith in your "God or Creator," unlimited strength will be yours.

"Peace of Mind" is all in how you handle disappointments and grief and your own sense of self-worth.

Money is not the root of all evil, it's what you do with it that determines its value.

Live each day as if it were your last.

Blood is thicker than water; it also has a higher specific gravity. You can lose all your friends but you will always have family.

Even the "best of friends" must be allowed to fly away.

First learn the rules of the game. If you still decide to play, play to win but always within the rules.

No one owes you anything but yourself. This debt is never paid.

Learn the difference between discipline and punishment. Apply each appropriately and in proper measure to the situation.

Sex is fun. Sex is beautiful and meaningful only when enjoyed safely with a loving partner.

Ignorance can never be a valid excuse, neither can carelessness.

Never feel guilt for something beyond your conrol.

Guilt, if allowed to get out of control, will destroy you.

Mourn the loss of a loved one, but do not let it interfere with living.

Do not grieve for the dead, they are beyond your sphere of help.

Smoking does cause cancer, so do a lot of other things.

Frogs do not cause warts.

Boredom is a self-inflicted disease.

You are usually not qualified to judge the actions of others.

You can only give your opinion until the decision is made, after that you are whining.

Never be afraid to make an informed decision.

Never be afraid to admit a mistake either to others or to yourself.

Never make the same mistake twice.

Nothing is impossible. You may not know how to do it, the world as a whole may not know how to do it, but this lack of knowledge does not make it impossible.

Know when you have said enough!!!

GOOD LUCK

Appendix

Additional Information/Recommended Readings

The books listed in this appendix are only the tip of the iceberg. With thousands of new books being printed each year, the amount of information available on almost any subject is almost beyond calculation. One of your first commitments should be to learn to seek new information. Your local library probably has more information than any other place you have access to. Use it!

SECTION I - THE JOB SEARCH

The Job Hunter's Final Exam, by Thomas M. Camden, published in 1984 by Surrey Books. *Everyone* looking for a job, whether for the first time or for career development, should read this very informative book.

The Perfect Resumé, by Tom Jackson, published in 1980 by Doubleday. The complete guide to preparing for and writing your resumé. This book goes into detail on the entire career process. It offers a number of different resume formats as well as sections dealing with college students and women reentering the job market. It contains over 50 pages of sample resumés and paragraphs. You will find over 30 books available on resumé writing, but this is one of the best.

What Color is Your Parachute, by Richard Nelson Bolles, published in 1984 by Ten Speed Press. Outstanding guide for the serious job hunter who already has set career goals and a willingness to be mobile to achieve them.

Real World 101, by James Calano and Jeff Salzman, published in 1984 by New View Press. This book is a must for the career oriented, aggressive, ladder climber. Targeted for college graduate professionals.

Smart Moves, by Sam Deep and Lyle Sussman, published in 1990 by Addison-Wesley Publishing Co., Inc. The subtitle, *14 Steps to Keep Any Boss Happy, 8 Ways to Start Meetings on Time and 1600 More Tips to Get the Best from Yourself and the People Around You*, fully describes why everyone working today should read this book. It contains much more information than you want to read in one sitting, but at least read the sections on "Managing Conflict" and "Successful Interviews" as soon as possible.

Interpersonal Communications, by Louis Savary, Mary Paolini, and George Lane, published in 1975 by Loyola University Press. A workbook for developing communication skills. Includes discussions on Self-Esteem, Acceptance, Problem Solving and the Value in Communication. Suggested reading before going to your next interview.

SECTION II - THE JOB

The Manager's Guide to Employee Benefits, by Ronald M. Foster, Jr., published in 1986 by Facts on File. Though written as a manager's guide, this book is full of information on a wide spectrum of employee benefits which every employee should read. The book contains easy to understand and complete descriptions of most benefits presently offered in the United States. It also contains a discussion of the rationale for offering, or not offering, certain benefits.

Your Rights at Work, by Darien McWhirter, published in 1989 by John Wiley & Sons, Inc. Approaches employee rights from the standpoint of fulfilling a contract. Very comprehensive text on all aspects of employees and their rights. This book contains numerous examples and cases. Though somewhat technical in spots, still worth the time to read.

Individual Rights in the Corporation, edited by Alan F. Westin & Stephen Salisbury, published in 1980 by Random House. A presentation of true situations focusing on the employee's rights.

Penalties for Misconduct on the Job, by Alfred Avins, JSD, PHD, published in 1972 by Oceana Publications, Inc. A handy guide explaining each type of misconduct, the impact on the employer and possible employee defenses. A short but very comprehensive text.

The Health Insurance Fact and Answer Book, by Geri Harrington published in 1985 by Harper and Row. Excellent book. Though somewhat technical in places, it is still an easy to read book on the various types of health insurance.

Insurance, What Do You Need? How Much Is Enough?, by David W. Kennedy, published by Knight-Rider Press. Very detailed text written for the average reader. Covers all aspects of insurance -- life, auto, health, home owner, renter and umbrella. A well researched text which includes sam-ple policies.

SECTION III - MONEY

The Kid's Complete Guide to Money, by Kathy S. Kyte, published in 1984 by Alfred A. Knopf, Inc. Though targeted to the juvenile audience, this book contains some great analysis and good ideas.

Money A to Z, by Don and Joan Gesman, published in 1984 by Facts on File, Inc. Publications. This book contains over 200 pages of Money and Financial terms and their meanings. The remaining 60 pages concentrate on practical considerations in financial planning. Excellent source book for the individual who really wants to understand money.

Financial Fitness for Singles, by Michael L. Speer, published in 1985 by J. M. Publications. Text discusses advanced money management for the career professional. It is easy to read and understand, and is packed with good advice for everyone interested in financial stability.

Everything College Didn't Teach You About Money, by Beth Brophy, published in 1985 by St. Martin's Press. Discusses money from budget to investments. Text uses scenarios to illustrate the need for money management. Very good information for *all* adults.

Make Your Paycheck Last, by Harold Moe, published in 1985 by Harsand Financial Press. Presents a very easy to follow practical approach to financial planning. This book expands on the budget concept and provides many realistic questions and answers about money. A definite must for the individual interested in going beyond financial survival.

Your Income Tax, by J. K. Lasser, published yearly by Simon & Schuster and *The Income Tax Guide*, by H & R Block, published yearly by Collier Books. Both of these books expand on *Publication 17* by providing clarifying statements and examples for filing your income tax return. They are not really needed for the single taxpayer filing the 1040A or 1040EZ forms but are good references to keep in mind as your income and family grow.

SECTION IV -- TRANSPORTATION

Used Car Prices, published yearly by Pace Publications, Inc. Contains used car prices for all American and foreign cars, trucks, and vans going back 10 years. Book includes used car checklists to assist the buyer in comparing vehicles before buying. Definitely a must for the used car buyer.

Used Car Buying Guide, published yearly by Consumer Union of United States, Inc. Published by the publishers of Consumer Reports, this book contains the details from consumer satisfaction surveys for the last six model years. Recommendations on the most maintenance free vehicles, as well as the best buys in used cars, make this a valuable tool for the serious used car buyer interested in getting the most for their money.

New Car and Used Car Buying Guides, these booklets are published by the Federal Trade Commission and are available from the Bureau of Consumer Protection, 6th & Pennsylvania Ave. N.W., Washington D.C. They contain suggestions, checklists, and work sheets for determining the best value.

Insurance, What Do You Need? How Much Is Enough?, by David W. Kennedy, published by Knight-Rider Press. Very detailed text written for the average reader. Covers all aspects of insurance -- life, auto, health, home owner, renter and umbrella. A well researched text which includes sample policies.

Auto Insurance Consumer's Guide, published by your state Insurance Commission. This guide will provide specific information on the laws and average costs of the different types of automobile insurance.

SECTION V -- SHELTER

Housemates, A Practical Guide to Living With Other People, by Teona Tone & Deanna Sclar, published in 1985 by Fawcett (Ballantine Books). The book for anyone thinking of sharing housing with another, even if you have done it already. This easy to read and informative book covers all aspects of sharing, from finding the right person, through dividing up responsibilities, to saying goodby and splitting up. Highly recommended even for those readers planning to live with parents or friends.

The Complete Roommate Handbook, by Bruce Brown, published in 1984 by Dolphin Books. Excellent fact filled guide for the selection of and living with a roommate. Concludes with a chapter on "How to Lose a Roommate." Recommended reading for *anyone* considering sharing living quarters.

How to Get Organized When You Don't Have the Time, by Stephanie Culp, published in 1986 by Writer's Digest Books. Easy to read, refreshing style containing very good ideas. Covers the problem with, and the removal of, everyday clutter.

Garage Sale Mania, by Chris Harold Stevenson, published in 1988 by Betterway Publications. An informative and fun book to read. A complete analysis of the garage sale from the perspective of both buyer and seller. For the seller, there are many suggestions on set-up, timing, and advertisement; and, for the buyer, discussions of etiquette, negotiating and even an action list are included. Good reading for even the not so serious garage sale seller or buyer.

Insurance, What Do You Need? How Much Is Enough?, by David W. Kennedy, pub-lished by Knight-Rider Press. Very detailed text written for the average reader. Covers all

aspects of insurance -- life, auto, health, home owner, renter and umbrella. A well researched text which includes sample policies.

Real Estate Law for Homeowners and Brokers, by Parnell J. T. Callahan and Louis M. Nussbaum, published in 1980 by Oceana Publications, Inc. Contains a very good chapter on "The Landlord and Tenant Relationship." Though written for the landlord, it gives the tenant a good idea of how the relationship is handled from a legal point of view.

Most states publish pamphlets on Tenant/ Landlord relationships or Leases. These are written to be easy to read and understand and can usually be found in local libraries or by contacting your state's Consumer Protection Board.

SECTION VI - FOOD

Quickies for Singles - Planning & Preparing Quick Meals for One, edited by Gwen McKee, published in 1980 by Quail Ridge Press, Inc. Lots of good menus and good ideas. Hint around, it makes an excellent gift.

Cooking for One, by Elinor Parker, published in 1984 by Harper and Row. Excellent recipes and suggestions for planning and cooking meals for one.

Betty Crocker's Cooking for One, pub-lished in 1984 by Gloden Press. Contains many recipes and helpful hints for individual dining.

Fast Food Facts, by Marion J. Franz, R.D., M.S., published by the International Diabetes Center. This is a comprehensive guide to nutritional value of fast food restaurants. The major fast food chains are listed with each of their menu items.

Great Meals in Minutes, published by Time-Life Books. This excellent, colorful book contains a wealth of menus, recipes, utensils, shopping lists and step-by-step meal preparation guides.

The Lifelong Nutrition Guide, by Brian L.G. Morgan, published in 1983 by Prentice Hall. An outstanding introduction to nutrition including how vitamins and minerals benefit good health.

Add Justice to Your Shopping List, by Marilyn Helmuth Voran, published in 1986 by Herald Press. A most thought provoking essay on the premise that the United States consumer is destroying the agriculture and economy of other countries. It makes a very strong case for limiting imports on exotic and out-of-season produce.

SECTION VII - CLOTHING

Taking Care of Clothes: An Owner's Manual for Care, Repair and Spot Removal, by Mablen Jones, published in 1982 by St. Martins Press. A complete and comprehensive guide for the proper cleaning and care of your clothes. The selection, use and care of fabrics, as well as suggestions for prolonging your clothing's life, are contained in this text. Possibly the biggest problem with clothes -- removing spots -- is addressed in easy to understand language. Plan on getting your own copy to save money on the care and upkeep of your clothes.

Clothing Care and Repair, a Singer Sewing Reference Library Book, published in 1985 by Cy Decosse. Inc. Everyone should read the first 79 pages which are devoted to labels and their meaning, and clothing care, storage and repair. This book is easy to read with lots of examples presented in color. There is even an excellent section on updating the wardrobe by making alterations. For those who know how to use a sewing machine this section will be very valuable in extending your clothing budget.

Looking Good For Guys, by Douglas Altman, published in 1989 by Rourke Publications, Inc. Excellent book on all aspects of looking fit. It starts with diet and exercise and proceeds through hygiene factors and grooming and finishes with clothing and "The Trimmings." All of this is packed into 30 colorful pages. Read it, the tips themselves are worth the time.

Clothes and Your Appearance, by Louise A. Liddell, published in 1985 by The Goodheart-Willcox Company, Inc. The first 150 pages are of interest to everyone. It opens with "What is best for you," a discussion of grooming, health and the selection of colors. The book then moves right into a discussion of wardrobe design, cleaning, recycling and repair, followed by a section on understanding labels and suggestions for getting your money's worth. If you are interested in sewing, then read on, the last 200 pages cover everything from fiber and yarn to making your own patterns and closes with a discussion of careers in the clothing industry. Many good suggestions and money saving ideas.

SECTION VIII -- HEALTH & RECREATION

Play Safe: How to Avoid Getting Sexually Transmitted Diseases, by Bea and Bryon Mandel, published in 1985 by The Center For Health Information. Easy to read guide to venereal diseases, their prevention and treatment. Should be read by everyone over the age of 13.

Campus Guide to VD: AIDS and other Sexually Transmitted Diseases, by Dr. Stephen Schleicher, published by Pamphlet Publications. Very detailed and informative book. Sober and frank discussion, focusing on the young adult. Strongly recommended reading.

Sexually Transmitted Diseases, by Galvin Hart, published in 1986 by Carolina Biological Supply Co. Dramatic and powerful visual presentations. Seeing is believing!

Dave Barry's Guide to Marriage and/or Sex, by Dave Barry with illustrations by Jerry O'Brien, published in 1987 by Rodale Press. A light and humorous approach to a very serious topic. This book is as entertaining as it is informative. It is very easy to read and the illustrations are very funny.

Who Do You Think You Are? How To Build Self-Esteem, by Joel Wells, published in 1989 by the Thomas More Association. Focuses on the understanding of self and dealing with rejection. If you have difficulty with your self inventory or with identifying yourself, be sure to read this book.

Encyclopedia of Good Health: Maintaining Good Health, by Trisha Thompson, published in 1989 by Michael Friedman Publishing Group, Inc. Though part of a Junior High School Series, this book is full of basic health information. Beginning with a look at your mind and proceeding through your body, the book addresses both mental and physical health.

Recognizing pain and the handling of minor accidents and incidents are covered, as well as the need for sleep and good diet. Very easy to read and most informative.

Getting Physical: How to Stick with Your Exercise Program, by Art Turock, published in 1988 by Doubleday. This is not an exercise book. This is a book devoted to motivation and the role motivation plays in separating people who are regular exercisers from everyone else. The message of this book and the motivational training sessions go far beyond just maintaining an exercise program. Recommended reading not just to maintain health but to strengthen the will to act in other survival areas.

The Outdoor Athlete, Total Training for Outdoor Performance, by Steve Ilg, published by Cordillera Press, Inc. An absolute must for the serious athlete, especially if you desire to stay healthy. In addition to describing a program of general health and physical fitness, Steve describes specific exercise routines for each type of outdoor activity. Even if you decide not to follow his routines, you will find the information contained is this book very beneficial.

Creative Time Management: Become More Productive & Still Have Time for Fun, by J. L. Barkas, PH.D., published in 1984 by Prentice Hall, Inc. Don't let the small size fool you. Though written primarily for students and teachers, this book is packed with examples and suggestions for managing time that can benefit everyone. The focus is on planning and resourcefulness, and the book contains charts and checklists to aid the reader perform self-evaluations.

SECTION IX -- COMPLETING YOUR SURVIVAL KIT

The Young People's Yellow Pages: A National Sourcebook for Youth, by Alvin Rosenbaum, published in 1983 by Perigee Books. A must for young adults. This book contains sources for just about anything you could possibly want. An unbelievable amount of information between its covers. Only by reading and using it can one get a full understanding of the research that was required to publish this text.

How to Avoid Getting Ripped Off, by Carol L. Clark, Ph. D., published in 1985 by Deseret Book Co. Though written as a guide to women, this book is a valuable guide to anyone trying to survive in our free enterprise society. Not only is this book packed with valuable advice, it also contains a list of resources and sources of additional information at the end of each chapter. Very straightforward and easy to read. Be sure to add this one to your library list.

S-M-A-R-T Spending, A Young Consumer's Guide, by Lois Schmitt, published in 1989, by Macmillan Publishing Co. An easy to read guide for the beginning consumer. Some of the chapters included are, Advertising, Money Management, Fraud, Warranties and Effective Complaining. Short but packed with information and cases everyone can understand.

GLOSSARY

Aggressive: Active, take charge behavior. As used, the difference between hoping a job will come along and actively seeking employment through all avenues available.

Alien Registration Form: Form required for non-citizens documenting their status in the United States and their right to work.

Apprenticeship: Working while learning a trade under an agreement with an employer. Frequently used for manual skilled, and technical jobs, such as bricklayer, carpenter, electrician, electronics technician, etc.

Assertive: Behavior that demonstrates positive action based on assurance, knowledge and confidence.

Assumption: To pick up or assume another's outstanding debt. Normally applies to home mortgages but may be encountered when purchasing a car from a private owner.

Balloon Payment: Single large final payment usually requiring refinancing. Purpose is to reduce monthly payment for the initial loan.

Bankruptcy: The voluntary declaration that an individual or company can no longer pay their outstanding debts. The court will then divide any assets of the bankrupt person or company among the creditors as payment. Once an individual or company declares bankruptcy, no reasonably affordable credit is available from any financial institution for a period of at least seven years.

Budget: An itemized written plan for allocating money to cover known or expected expenses.

Capital Gains: Profit from the sale of assets, such as bonds, stock and real estate.

Car Poor: Spending so much of available income for car and insurance that nothing is left to provide for the other necessary expenses.

Clothes Poor: Same as Car Poor, except that the initial expenditure is for clothes.

Coerce: To bring about by actual or implied force. In this book, reminding of past favors, begging and other forms of **non-violent** persuasion is implied.

Collateral: Property of value whose title is passed to a financial institution to guarantee repayment of a loan.

Condom: A sheath or tube made of rubber or similar material worn over the penis during intercourse to prevent conception and reduce the threat of infection.

Contraceptive: Any device or drug used to prevent conception (pregnancy).

Compensation: Something provided as payment for services, debts, losses, injury or suffering. Can also mean the mental mechanisms an individual uses to rationalize a real or imagined deficient personality trait or behavior.

Compensatory Time Off: Paid time off, in lieu of overtime, granted for working in excess of the normal workday.

Co-sign: To sign jointly with another. In legal terms, to guarantee jointly good faith and repayment of debts. Co-signers are sometimes called co-makers to more clearly identify responsibility.

Deductible: The amount that must be paid by the insured individual before any insurance benefits are provided.

Dependents: Individuals who rely on others for their support. When discussing taxes, if these individuals meet certain tests, the supporting individual may be entitled to some form of tax deduction.

Depreciation: A measured decrease in value of an item due to age, wear and tear, and use. When buying used items, it is the amount that the item's selling value has been reduced.

Diaphragm: A contraceptive device, usually made of latex, which is placed against the uterine cervix to block passage of sperm. Usually fitted by a doctor but applied by the woman herself prior to sexual intercourse and not worn otherwise.

Differential: As used, a set of gears in a vehicle's front or rear end that allow two shafts to move at different speeds when making turns.

Discrimination: To treat unequally because of some personal characteristic, such as race, color, age, sex, religion, national origin, or mental or physical handicap.

Dress Code: A prescribed clothing requirement, either formal or informal, set by an institution, usually an employer. For instance, everyone should wear dark suits, white shirts, dark ties and dark, well polished leather shoes.

Efficiency Apartment: An apartment consisting of one large room containing area for eating, sleeping and cooking. Most efficiencies come with private bathrooms.

Epidemic: A transmittable disease having unusually high or significantly increased incidence in a given population and period of time.

Facsimile: An exact copy.

Fad: A short lived style or interest.

Foreplay: The sexual activity which immediately precedes intercourse, including intimate kissing, touching and fondling.

Good Taste: The adherence to a given accepted list of values. As used, implies dressing in the mode or style that is currently considered acceptable by the majority.

Harassment: To annoy, disturb or torment by repeated action or attacks.

Hemophilia: An inherited disease that prevents the clotting of blood causing the constant threat of hemorrhage.

Immunity: A state of increased resistance against the harmful effects of an injurious agent, infection or toxin.

Income Averaging: The spreading of unusually large income over a period of five years to reduce the amount of income taxes.

Intercourse: See sexual intercourse.

Interview: A meeting of persons face to face. As used, a meeting where a prospective employer meets a job applicant for the purpose of determining the details of the applicants qualifications.

Invoice Price: The price stated on an invoice as the cost to the buyer. When discussing dealers of merchandise such as cars, furniture, etc., it is the price paid by the dealer.

Intrauterine Device: As used, a semi-permanent device placed inside a woman's uterus by a doctor to prevent conception. Some of these devices have recently been suspected of having dangerous side effects in some women.

IUD: See intrauterine device.

Lease: A contract specifying the terms of agreement between two parties for the paid, temporary use of one party's property.

Liability: Being legally responsible for damage to another caused by your actions or lack of action.

List Price: The stated manufacturer's recommended selling price of an item without consideration for sales, discounts or rebates.

Mutually Monogamous: Mutually means acceptable to all parties and monogamous is the practice of being married to one person at a time. As used, this term identifies two people who have promised not to have sex with anyone except each other.

Negligent: Failure in duty or performance through disregard, lack of attention or carelessness.

Net Pay: The amount of money a person has left from their salary after all the deductions for taxes, insurance and other items are removed.

Objective: A targeted goal or aim. The final planned outcome of an event.

Optimum: After considering all factors, the most favorable choice.

Phenomenon: An odd or notable thing or happening.

Ping Pong Rule: A cycle of reinfection, especially where cure takes an extended period of time. In cases of venereal disease, this rule applies when both infected parties are not treated at the same time. If only one party seeks treatment, contact with the untreated party will cause reinfection. This cycle will continue until both parties seek treatment at the same time.

Points: Measurement of driving infractions. Points are assigned by the Department of Motor Vehicles to keep track of the frequency of tickets, accidents and other traffic violations. The state uses these to determine the severity of penalties and insurance companies use them to determine the risk of insuring an applicant for insurance. Points do have an adverse impact on insurance cost.

Polygraph Test: Also called a lie detector test, this is a test using a device that records tracings of several different bodily signals, such as blood pressure, respiration, body temperature, etc. The analysis of these tracings by qualified persons are used to determine an individual's truthfulness. Our legal system considers this test to have a high degree of reliability.

Prejudices: Opinions, usually unfavorable, formed without adequate reason or justification.

Profit Sharing: The returning to the employees a share of a company's yearly profits. This may be done by giving bonuses, depositing money in an employee's retirement account, granting opportunities to purchase stock, etc.

PVC Pipe: Polyvinyl chloride pipe is a heavy duty plastic pipe that can be easily cut and permanently glued. Very easy for the novice to work with and still achieve lasting results.

Qualifications: Experience, education, skills, abilities and any other quality that meets specific job requirements.

References: Individuals, other than parents, that can provide either written or verbal recommendations that attest to the ap-plicant's character, abilities and performance.

Reimbursement: Repayment of previously paid expenses.

Repossession: To reclaim because of violation of transfer contract, such as the repossession of a car because the buyer doesn't make the agreed upon payments.

Resumé: A written summary of a person's background and qualifications.

Responsibilities: Duties or obligations placed on a person.

Rights: Those considerations that a person is entitled to under the governing laws of our society and our belief in equality.

Sabotage: A willful and intentional destruction, obstruction or hindrance.

Sexual Intercourse: Sexual union between male and female by insertion of the penis into the vagina.

Sexually Active: Participating in sexual intercourse.

Sexually Transmitted Diseases: A group of diseases that are transmitted during sexual activity but do not require actual sexual intercourse.

Smears: Specimens for microscopic study, prepared by spreading the material to be examined, usually a drop of body secretion or fluid, onto a glass slide.

Spermacide: Any substance that destroys spermatozoa (sperm).

Static Pain: As used, the normal, short lived minor aches encountered in normal daily life such as, minor headaches, sore throat, muscle and joint aches from exercise, etc.

Stereotyping: As used, a prejudice having no individual justification, such as "blondes have more fun."

Sterile: Free from living microorganisms or incapable of reproducing.

Stress: As used, a combination of mental and physical factors that threaten the well-being of an individual and that produces a defensive response, such as physical or emotional trauma or infection.

Style: The prevalent accepted mode of dress or custom.

Subsidized: Supported financially.

Take Home Pay: See net pay.

Terminal Notice: Notice given by either the employer or employee to the other indicating pending end of employment. Giving one to two weeks notice is the generally accepted practice.

True Cost: As used, the cost of an item based on all factors including alternate ways of using the money.

Unemployment Compensation: Payment made to qualifying employees when unemployed through no fault of their own. A form of insurance mandated by the federal government, administered by the state government and paid for by the employer.

Value Check List: A list identifying values of various selections used by the shopper to make an informed choice.

Venereal Diseases: A group of diseases usually transmitted as a result of sexual intercourse with an infected person.

Wholesale Price: The price that distributors of merchandise charge retailers. Usually considers quantity discounts and the retailer's need to make a profit.

Index

Did you borrow this book? Do you want a copy of your own?
Do you want a great gift for a friend or relative?

J-MART PRESS has copies of *Surviving After High School: Overcoming Life's Hurdles* and "I AM A SURVIVOR" T-shirts available for order by mail. These can be yours by just filling out the order slip and sending a check or money order to:

J-MART PRESS
P.O. BOX 8884
Va. Beach, VA 23450-8884

YES, I want to order _____ copies of Surviving After High School for $14.95 per copy, plus $1.00 for shipping and handling. Shipping is free if 2 or more copies are ordered for the same address, or if a book and T-shirt are ordered together.

sub-total _____

I already have a copy of the book, but I would like to order my "**I AM A SURVIVOR**" T-shirts for $7.00 each plus $1.00 shipping and handling. Shipping is free if 2 or more are ordered for the same address, or if ordered with a book. The T-shirts are white with a full color picture of the cover of *Surviving After High School* on the front and the words "**I AM A SURVIVOR**" in large block letters on the back.

Quantity   Size (M, L, XL)

___   ___

___   ___

sub-total _____

Virginia orders must include $0.65 per book and $0.30 for each T-shirt for sales tax.   _____

Money order or check enclosed for the total of the order.   _____

I am not ordering anything at this time, but I do have the following suggestions or comments.

Additional comments.

———————————————————— first fold ————————————————————

———————————————————— second fold ————————————————————

————————————————

————————————————

————————————————

J-MART *PRESS*
P.O. Box 8884
Va. Beach, VA 23450-8884